A MODERN HEALTHY CREDIT POLICIES OF BANKING

A MODERN HEALTHY CREDIT POLICIES OF BANKING

Anshu Rohtagi

CYBER TECH PUBLICATIONS
4264/3, Ansari Road, Daryaganj, New Delhi-110002 (India)
Ph.: 011-23244078, 011-43559448 Fax: 011-23280028
E-Mail: cyberpublicationsdelhi@yahoo.com
Website: www.cybertechpublications.com

A MODERN HEALTHY CREDIT POLICIES OF BANKING

Anshu Rohtagi

First Edition 2010

Published by :

G.S. Rawat for **Cyber Tech Publications**

4264/3, Ansari Road, Daryaganj, New Delhi-110002 (India)

Ph.: 011-23244078, 011-43559448 Fax: 011-23280028

E-Mail: cyberpublicationsdelhi@yahoo.com

Website: www.cybertechpublications.com

Printed at: Asian Offset Printers, Delhi-53

Preface

The economic analysis of juridical institutions has come to the fore in recent years and promises to become one of the most fruitful spheres of economics. Much of the work completed thus far has been strongly influenced by traditional neoclassical assumptions, namely by the concept of strict maximization in contexts of equilibrium. Still, economic analyses of law reveal the shortcomings of the traditional approach and do so perhaps better than any other branch of economics. In fact, juridical institutions are so intimately involved in daily life that it is notoriously difficult to apply the traditional assumptions of economic analysis to them. I have already attempted elsewhere to expose the dangers the neoclassical perspective brings to the analysis of juridical institutions. Economic analyses of law are certainly necessary, but they call for a less restrictive methodology than has generally been used to date, one more suited to this particular field of research. The subjectivist view is a more fitting approach.

Developed by the Austrian School, it is based on their concept of creative human action or entrepreneurial activity and implies a dynamic analysis of the general processes of social interaction. This perspective promises to make great contributions to the future development of the economic analysis of juridical institutions. In addition, most studies of juridical institutions carried out so far have had exclusively microeconomic implications because, among other reasons, theorists have simply borrowed the traditional analytical tools of neoclassical microeconomics and applied them to the analysis of law. This has been the case, for example, with respect to the economic analysis of contracts and civil liability, bankruptcy law, the family, and even criminal law and justice. Very few economic analyses of law have had mainly macroeconomic implications, and this reflects the harmful decades-long separation between these two sides of economics.

However, this need not be the case. It is necessary to recognize economics as a unified whole, where macroeconomic elements are firmly rooted in their microeconomic foundations. In addition, I will attempt to demonstrate that the economic analysis of some juridical institutions yields critical implications and conclusions that are essentially macroeconomic. Or, in other words, even when the basic analysis is microeconomic, the conclusions drawn and primary outcomes resulting from it are macroeconomic. By closing the profound artificial gap between micro and macroeconomics, we arrive at a unified theoretical treatment of legal issues in the economic analysis of law.

—*Author*

Contents

1

Introduction

This annual policy statement for 2009-10 is set in the context of exceptionally challenging circumstances in the global economy. The crisis has called into question several fundamental assumptions and beliefs governing economic resilience and financial stability. What started off as turmoil in the financial sector of the advanced economies has snowballed into the deepest and most widespread financial and economic crisis of the last 60 years. With all the advanced economies in a synchronised recession, global GDP is projected to contract for the first time since the World War II, anywhere between 0.5 and 1.0 per cent, according to the March 2009 forecast of the International Monetary Fund (IMF). The World Trade Organisation (WTO) has forecast that global trade volume will contract by 9.0 per cent in 2009.

Governments and central banks around the world have responded to the crisis through both conventional and unconventional fiscal and monetary measures. These measures have been criticised for their size, timing, sequencing and design as also, more importantly, for their economic and ideological underpinnings. The most voluble criticism has been that 'purely national responses' are inadequate to address a virulent global crisis. In recognition of a pressing need for global co-ordination and co-operation, particularly in order to inspire the trust and confidence of economic agents around the world, leaders of the G-20 group of nations met twice in the last six months. At their recent meeting in early April 2009, the G-20 leaders collectively committed to take decisive, co-ordinated and comprehensive actions to revive growth, restore stability of the financial system, restart the impaired credit markets and rebuild confidence in financial markets and institutions.

Despite some apprehensions prior to the meeting, the overall impact of the G-20 meeting in managing market perceptions has been positive. Even so, the global financial situation remains uncertain and the global economy continues to cause anxiety for several reasons. There is as yet no clear estimate of the quantum of tainted assets, and doubts persist on whether the initiatives underway are sufficient to restore the stability of the financial system. There is continued debate on the adequacy of the fiscal stimulus packages across countries, and their effectiveness in arresting the downturn, reversing job losses and reviving consumer confidence. Many major central banks have nearly or totally exhausted their conventional weaponry of calibrating policy interest rates and are now resorting to unconventional measures such as quantitative and credit easing. Given the erosion of the monetary policy transmission mechanism, there are concerns about when and to what extent monetary response, admittedly aggressive, will begin to have an impact on reviving credit flows and spurring aggregate demand.

Like all emerging economies, India too has been impacted by the crisis, and by much more than what was expected earlier. The extent of impact has caused dismay, mainly on two grounds: first, because our financial sector remains healthy, has had no direct exposure to tainted assets and its off-balance sheet activities have been limited; and second, because India's merchandise exports, at less than 15 per cent of GDP, are relatively modest. Despite these mitigating factors, the impact of the crisis on India evidences the force of globalisation as also India's growing two-way trade in goods and services and financial integration with the rest of the world.

After clocking annual growth of 8.9 per cent on an average over the last five years (2003-08), India was headed for a cyclical downturn in 2008-09. But the growth moderation has been much sharper because of the negative impact of the crisis. In fact, in the first two quarters of 2008-09, the growth slowdown was quite modest; the full impact of the crisis began to be felt post-Lehman in the third quarter, which recorded a sharp downturn in growth. The services sector, which has been our prime growth engine for the last five years, is slowing, mainly in construction, transport and communication, trade, hotels and restaurants sub-sectors. For the first time in seven years, exports have declined in absolute terms for five months in a row during October 2008-February 2009. Recent data indicate that the demand for bank credit is slackening despite comfortable liquidity in the system. Dampened demand has dented corporate margins while the uncertainty surrounding the crisis has affected business confidence. The index of industrial production (IIP) has been nearly stagnant in the last five months (October 2008 to February 2009), of which two months registered negative growth. Investment demand has also decelerated. All these indicators suggest that growth will moderate more than what had been expected earlier.

Despite the adverse impact as noted above, there are several comforting factors that have helped India weather the crisis. First, our financial markets, particularly our banks, have continued to function normally. Second, India's comfortable foreign exchange reserves provide confidence in our ability to manage our balance of payments notwithstanding lower export demand and dampened capital flows. Third, headline inflation, as measured by the wholesale price index (WPI), has declined sharply. Consumer price inflation too has begun to moderate. Fourth, because of mandated agricultural lending and social safety-net programmes, rural demand continues to be robust. Both the Government and the Reserve Bank responded to the challenge of minimising the impact of crisis on India in co-ordination and consultation. The Reserve Bank shifted its policy stance from monetary tightening in response to the elevated inflationary pressures in the first half of 2008-09 to monetary easing in response to easing inflationary pressures and moderation of growth engendered by the crisis. The Reserve Bank's policy response was aimed at containing the contagion from the global financial crisis while maintaining comfortable domestic and forex liquidity. Taking a cue from the Reserve Bank's monetary easing, most banks have reduced their deposit and lending rates.

The Central Government launched three fiscal stimulus packages during December 2008-February 2009. These stimulus packages came on top of an already announced expanded safety-net programme for the rural poor, the farm loan waiver package and payout following the Sixth Pay Commission report, all of which too added to stimulating demand.

ANNUAL POLICY STATEMENT FOR THE YEAR 2009-10

This annual policy statement for 2009-10 is set in the context of exceptionally challenging circumstances in the global economy. The crisis has called into question several fundamental assumptions and beliefs governing economic resilience and financial stability. What started off as turmoil in the financial sector of the advanced economies has snowballed into the deepest and most widespread financial and economic crisis of the last 60 years. With all the advanced economies in a synchronised recession, global GDP is projected to contract for the first time since the World War II, anywhere between 0.5 and 1.0 per cent, according to the March 2009 forecast of the International Monetary Fund (IMF). The World Trade Organisation (WTO) has forecast that global trade volume will contract by 9.0 per cent in 2009.

Governments and central banks around the world have responded to the crisis through both conventional and unconventional fiscal and monetary measures. These measures have been criticised for their size, timing, sequencing and design as also, more importantly, for their economic and ideological underpinnings. The most voluble criticism has been that 'purely national responses' are inadequate to address a virulent global crisis. In recognition of a pressing need for global co-ordination and co-operation, particularly in order to inspire the trust and confidence of economic agents around the world, leaders of the G-20 group of nations met twice in the last six months. At their recent meeting in early April 2009, the G-20 leaders collectively committed to take decisive, co-ordinated and comprehensive actions to revive growth, restore stability of the financial system, restart the impaired credit markets and rebuild confidence in financial markets and institutions.

Despite some apprehensions prior to the meeting, the overall impact of the G-20 meeting in managing market perceptions has been positive. Even so, the global financial situation remains uncertain and the global economy continues to cause anxiety for several reasons. There is as yet no clear estimate of the quantum of tainted assets, and doubts persist on whether the initiatives underway are sufficient to restore the stability of the financial system. There is continued debate on the adequacy of the fiscal stimulus packages across countries, and their effectiveness in arresting the downturn, reversing job losses and reviving consumer confidence. Many major central banks have nearly or totally exhausted their conventional weaponry of calibrating policy interest rates and are now resorting to unconventional measures such as quantitative and credit easing. Given the erosion of the monetary policy transmission mechanism, there are concerns about when and to what extent monetary response, admittedly aggressive, will begin to have an impact on reviving credit flows and spurring aggregate demand.

Like all emerging economies, India too has been impacted by the crisis, and by much more than what was expected earlier. The extent of impact has caused dismay, mainly on two grounds: first, because our financial sector remains healthy, has had no direct exposure to tainted assets and its off-balance sheet activities have been limited; and second, because India's merchandise exports, at less than 15 per cent of GDP, are relatively modest. Despite these mitigating factors, the impact of the crisis on India evidences the force of globalisation as also India's growing two-way trade in goods and services and financial integration with the rest of the world.

After clocking annual growth of 8.9 per cent on an average over the last five years (2003-08), India was headed for a cyclical downturn in 2008-09. But the growth moderation has been much sharper because of the negative impact of the crisis. In fact, in the first two quarters of 2008-09, the growth slowdown was quite modest; the full impact of the crisis began to be felt post-Lehman in the third quarter, which recorded a sharp downturn in growth. The services sector, which has been our prime growth engine for the last five years, is slowing, mainly in construction, transport and communication, trade, hotels and restaurants sub-sectors. For the first time in seven years, exports have declined in absolute terms for five months in a row during October 2008-February 2009. Recent data indicate that the demand for bank credit is slackening despite comfortable liquidity in the system. Dampened demand has dented corporate margins while the uncertainty surrounding the crisis has affected business confidence. The index of industrial production (IIP) has been nearly stagnant in the last five months (October 2008 to February 2009), of which two months registered negative growth. Investment demand has also decelerated. All these indicators suggest that growth will moderate more than what had been expected earlier.

Despite the adverse impact as noted above, there are several comforting factors that have helped India weather the crisis. First, our financial markets, particularly our banks, have continued to function normally. Second, India's comfortable foreign exchange reserves provide confidence in our ability to manage our balance of payments notwithstanding lower export demand and dampened capital flows. Third, headline inflation, as measured by the wholesale price index (WPI), has declined sharply. Consumer price inflation too has begun to moderate. Fourth, because of mandated agricultural lending and social safety-net programmes, rural demand continues to be robust. Both the Government and the Reserve Bank responded to the challenge of minimising the impact of crisis on India in co-ordination and consultation. The Reserve Bank shifted its policy stance from monetary tightening in response to the elevated inflationary pressures in the first half of 2008-09 to monetary easing in response to easing inflationary pressures and moderation of growth engendered by the crisis. The Reserve Bank's policy response was aimed at containing the contagion from the global financial crisis while maintaining comfortable domestic and forex liquidity. Taking a cue from the Reserve Bank's monetary easing, most banks have reduced their deposit and lending rates.

The Central Government launched three fiscal stimulus packages during December 2008-February 2009. These stimulus packages came on top of an already announced expanded safety-net programme for the rural poor, the farm loan waiver package and payout following the Sixth Pay Commission report, all of which too added to stimulating demand.

This annual policy statement for 2009-10 is organised in two parts. Part A covers *Monetary Policy* which provides an assessment of the *Macroeconomic and Monetary Developments* (Section I), the *Stance of Monetary Policy* (Section II) and *Monetary Measures* (Section III). Part B on *Developmental and Regulatory Policies* covers *Financial Stability* (Section I), *Interest Rate Policy* (Section II), *Financial Markets* (Section III), *Credit Delivery Mechanism and other Banking Services* (Section IV), *Prudential Measures* (Section V) *and Institutional Developments* (Section VI). This statement should be read and understood together with the analytical review of *Macroeconomic and Monetary Developments* released yesterday.

MONETARY POLICY STATEMENT 2009-10

Macroeconomic and Monetary Developments

Global Outlook

The global outlook has continued to deteriorate in the last quarter with projections for global growth in 2009 undergoing rapid downward revision. According to the IMF's March 2009 forecast, global growth is projected to shrink by 0.5 to 1.0 per cent in 2009 in contrast to an expansion of 3.2 per cent in 2008. Other projections are even more dire. The World Bank estimates global GDP to contract by 1.7 per cent and the OECD by as much as 2.7 per cent. In the US, economic activity has declined sharply, driven mainly by the decline in consumption and exports. The Euro area too is in a severe and synchronised contraction. Reflecting sharp demand contraction, consumer price inflation has reached near zero in several advanced countries, raising concerns about sustained deflation on the way forward. The unemployment rate in the US has risen to 8.5 per cent, the highest since 1983. Unemployment rates in the Euro area, the UK and Japan too increased significantly. The WTO projects that global trade will shrink by

9.0 per cent in volume terms in 2009, down from an increase of 2.0 per cent in 2008. Between 1990 and 2007, global trade grew twice as fast as global GDP; in a sharp reversal of this 'trade as the engine of growth' paradigm, in 2009 global trade is projected to shrink twice as much as global GDP.

In advanced countries, substantial injection of liquidity and successive cuts in the policy rates have resulted in the softening of short-term interest rates, particularly in the overnight segment. However, the transmission to the credit market has been impaired, suggesting that the process of deleveraging is incomplete, asset prices have yet to stabilise and that credit spreads need to narrow further. Banks and financial institutions are still in the process of recognising losses arising out of off-balance sheet exposures. This raises concerns about the extent of required recapitalisation, and this uncertainty is inhibiting fresh lending. Most importantly, the global financial system is yet to recover the forfeited trust and confidence. Under the G-20 initiative, efforts are underway to strengthen the global financial architecture and restore the global growth momentum through co-ordinated actions.

Emerging Market Economies

The IMF projects that the GDP growth of EMEs will decelerate to a range of 1.5-2.5 per cent in 2009, down from 6.1 per cent in 2008. This downturn is clear evidence that the forces of globalisation are too strong for the decoupling hypothesis to work. Even across EMEs, there are wide variations: several countries are likely to post negative growth, while significant positive contributions are expected from China and India. The crisis spread from advanced countries to EMEs, as is now clear, through both trade and finance channels. The slump in export demand and tighter trade credit caused deceleration in aggregate demand; reversal of capital flows led to equity market losses and currency depreciations; global liquidity tightening resulted in lower external credit flows to EMEs; and market rigidities and erosion of confidence led to widening of credit spreads. Like advanced countries, EMEs too responded to the challenge of managing the crisis through fiscal and monetary actions, but these measures will not have full impact until the global situation stabilises and trade and credit flows are restored. The G-20 commitment to desist from all forms of protectionism and to maintain open trade and investment regimes is a source of comfort to EMEs in an otherwise discouraging external environment.

Domestic Outlook

Economic activity in India slowed down in Q1 and Q2 of 2008-09 as compared with over 9.0 per cent growth in the previous three years. However, growth decelerated sharply in Q3 following the failure of Lehman Brothers in mid-September 2008 and knock-on effects of the global financial crisis on the Indian economy. Consequently, the growth rate during the first three quarters (April-December) of 2008-09 slowed down significantly to 6.9 per cent from 9.0 per cent in the corresponding period of the previous year (Table 1). The advance estimates of the

Central Statistical Organisation (CSO) released in February 2009 have placed the real GDP growth for 2008-09 at 7.1 per cent.

Table 1: Real GDP Growth (%)

Sector	Q1 (April-June)		Q2 (July-September)		Q3 (October-December)		April-December	
	2007-08	2008-09	2007-08	2008-09	2007-08	2008-09	2007-08	2008-09
Agriculture	4.4	3.0	4.4	2.7	6.9	-2.2	5.5	0.6
Industry	8.5	5.2	7.5	4.7	7.6	0.8	7.9	3.5
Services	10.7	10.2	10.7	9.6	10.1	9.5	10.5	9.7
Overall	9.1	7.9	9.1	7.6	8.9	5.3	9.0	6.9

Source: Central Statistical Organisation (CSO).

The last Annual Policy Statement of the Reserve Bank released in April 2008 placed real GDP growth for 2008-09 in the range of 8.0-8.5 per cent. Around that time, the IMF had projected the global growth to be at 3.7 per cent in 2008. As the year progressed and the crisis unfolded, economic prospects globally deteriorated rapidly and at home in India in Q3 2008-09. Beginning July 2008, the IMF made frequent reductions in its growth forecasts for 2008. The Reserve Bank too reflected the deteriorating outlook by revising downward its growth projection for India for 2008-09 to 7.5-8.0 per cent in the Mid-Term Review (October 2008) and further down to 7.0 per cent with a downward bias in the Third Quarter Review (January 2009). The downside risks have since materialised and the GDP growth for 2008-09 is now projected to turn out to be in the range of 6.5 to 6.7 per cent.

Agriculture

The second advance estimates of the Ministry of Agriculture released in February 2009 have placed total foodgrains production in 2008-09 at 227.9 million tonnes, lower than the production of 230.8 million tonnes in the previous year. Subsequent information on good sowing for *rabi* crops and the trend in procurement suggests that agricultural production during 2008-09 may turn out to be better than earlier anticipated.

Industry

During 2008-09 so far (April-February), industrial growth based on the index of industrial production (IIP), decelerated to 2.8 per cent, down by more than two-third from 8.8 per cent in the corresponding period of the previous year. While IIP growth was 5.0 per cent in the first half of 2008-09, the average growth in the following five months was insignificant (0.2 per cent). There, however, have been some incipient positive signs. Although the IIP contracted by 1.2 per cent in February 2009, machinery and equipment (other than transport equipment) exhibited double digit growth. In terms of use-based classification, capital goods production too registered double digit growth.

Demand Components of GDP

Private consumption and investment demand decelerated during Q3 of 2008-09. Government consumption demand, however, registered a sharp increase, reflecting the partial payout of the Sixth Pay Commission Award and other fiscal stimulus measures. As a result, the share of government consumption demand in GDP increased significantly. Deceleration in net exports growth in the successive quarters of 2008-09 had an adverse impact on the overall GDP growth (Table 2).

Table 2: Demand Components of GDP

Item	2008-09 Advance Estimates	2008-09 Q1	Q2	Q3
y-o-y Growth Rate (%)				
Private Final Consumption Expenditure	6.8	7.7	6.9	5.4
Government Final Consumption Expenditure	16.8	7.1	7.9	24.6
Gross Fixed Capital Formation	8.9	10.1	15.1	5.3
Net Exports	-60.5	-231.5	-63.8	-54.2
Share in GDP (%)				
Private Final Consumption Expenditure	57	59.8	58	59.5
Government Final Consumption Expenditure	10.6	10.3	8.7	10.0
Gross Fixed Capital Formation	32.1	32.3	35.3	31.0
Net Exports	-6.5	-2.5	-10.7	-7.5

Source: Central Statistical Organisation (CSO).

Corporate Performance

After registering robust growth during the five year period 2003-08, the performance of the private non-financial corporate sector deteriorated in the first three quarters of 2008-09. Sales growth of companies, which continued to be strong in Q1 and Q2, decelerated sharply in Q3 of 2008-09. Net profits, which recorded an average annual growth of over 40 per cent during 2003-08, recorded a significantly lower growth in the first quarter of 2008-09. In the second quarter, net profits declined, although gross profits continued to increase, *albeit* marginally. In the third quarter, even gross profits declined sharply (Table 3). Profit margins were eroded by higher input costs, increased interest outgo, significant drop in non-sales income and losses on foreign currency related transactions. While moderation in internal accruals has an adverse effect on corporate investment, decline in input prices and reduction in borrowing costs may have a favourable impact on profitability going forward.

Table 3: Private Corporate Sector - Growth Rates (%)

Item	2006-07	2007-08	2008-09		
			Q1	Q2	Q3
Sales	26.5	18.3	29.3	31.8	9.5
Expenditure	24.7	18.4	33.5	37.5	12.6
Gross Profits	44.7	22.8	11.9	8.7	-26.7
Net Profits	44.0	26.2	6.9	-2.6	-53.4

Business Confidence

The Industrial Outlook Survey of the Reserve Bank for January-March 2009 indicates a further worsening of perception for the Indian manufacturing sector. The overall business and financial sentiment, which touched a seven-year low in the preceding quarter, slid below the neutral 100 mark, for the first time since the compilation of the index began in 2002. According to the survey, the demand for working capital finance during January-March 2009 from external sources dropped due to slowdown in business, even as the availability of finance eased. The business confidence surveys conducted by other agencies are also consistent with these findings.

Lead Indicators

In terms of lead indicators of the economy, economic activity in several services sectors has been moderating. Cargo handled at major ports, passengers handled at airports, railway freight traffic and arrival of foreign tourists registered lower/negative growth. Strong rural demand, lagged impact of monetary and fiscal stimuli, softening of domestic input prices, investment demand from brown-field projects and some restructuring initiatives are expected to have a positive impact on industrial production in the months ahead.

Inflation

Headline inflation, as measured by year-on-year variations in the wholesale price index (WPI), decelerated sharply from its intra-year peak of 12.91 per cent on August 2, 2008 to 0.26 per cent by March 28, 2009. In terms of relative contribution to the fall in WPI inflation since August 2008, mineral oils and basic metals (combined weight 15.3 per cent in WPI) together accounted for over 83 per cent of the decline reflecting global trend in commodity prices. The prices of food articles, however, are still ruling high. The inflation based on various consumer price indices (CPIs) continues to be near double-digit level mainly reflecting a firm trend in prices of food articles (Table 4). WPI inflation declined further to 0.18 per cent as on April 4, 2009.

Table 4: Annual Inflation Rate (%)

Wholesale Price Index (WPI)	29-Mar-08	28-Mar-09
	(y-o-y)	(y-o-y)
WPI - All Commodities	7.75	0.26
WPI - Primary Articles	9.68	3.46
WPI - Food Articles	6.54	6.31
WPI - Fuel Group	6.78	-6.11
WPI - Manufactured Products	7.34	1.42
WPI - Manufactured Food Products	9.40	7.51
WPI - Excluding Fuel	8.01	2.01
WPI - Excluding Food Articles and Fuel	8.38	0.95
Consumer Price Index (CPI)	Feb-08	Feb-09
	(y-o-y)	(y-o-y)
CPI - Industrial Workers	5.47	9.63
CPI - Agricultural Labourers	6.38	10.79
CPl - Rural Labourers	6.11	10.79
CPI - Urban Non-manual Employees #	4.84	10.38

.# Pertains to January.

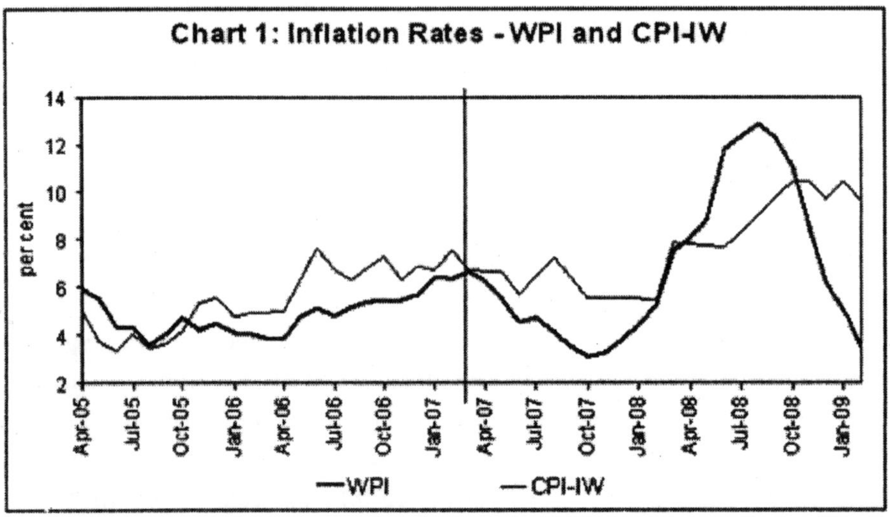

The analysis of the last four years suggests that WPI inflation and CPI inflation moved, by and large, in tandem till April 2007. Thereafter, inflation measured in WPI and CPI tended to diverge. However, the divergence in the recent period has been unusually high reflecting the volatilities in commodity prices which have a higher weight in WPI (Chart 1). With the decline in WPI inflation, CPI inflation is expected to moderate in the coming months. For its overall assessment of inflation outlook for policy purposes, the Reserve Bank continuously monitors the full array of price indicators.

Fiscal Scenario

The finances of the Central Government in 2008-09 deviated significantly from the Budget Estimates (BE). Higher revenue expenditure together with lower revenue receipts led to a sharp increase in the revenue and fiscal deficits. The deviation of deficit indicators from the targets stipulated under the Fiscal Responsibility and Budget Management (FRBM) Rules was on account of several fiscal stimulus measures undertaken by the Government to boost aggregate demand. The financing gap was met by enhancement of market borrowings (Table 5).

Table 5: Fiscal Position of the Central Government: 2008-09

Item	Amount	Difference (Rs. crore)	(per cent) Budget Estimates	Revised Estimates
1	Revenue Receipts	6,02,935	5,62,173	-6.8
2	Capital Receipts	1,47,949	3,38,780	129.0
	of which: Market Loans	1,00,571	2,61,972	160.5
3	Non-Plan Expenditure	5,07,498	6,17,996	21.8
4	Plan Expenditure	2,43,386	2,82,957	16.3
5	Revenue Expenditure	6,58,119	8,03,446	22.1
6	Capital Expenditure	92,765	97,507	5.1
7	Revenue Deficit	55,184	2,41,273	337.2
		(1.0)	(4.4)	
8	Fiscal Deficit	1,33,287	3,26,515	145.0
		(2.5)	(6.0)	

Notes : (i) The receipts are net of repayments. (ii) Figures in parentheses are percentages to GDP.

Because of the fiscal stimulus packages as also additional post-budget items of expenditure, Central Government's borrowing during 2008-09 was substantially above the initial budget estimates. In fact, the actual net borrowing was more than two and half times the initial budget estimate (Table 6).

Table 6: Central Government Borrowings: 2008-09

(Rs. crore)

	BE	RE	Actual
Item	(February 2008)	(March 2009)	
Gross Borrowing *	1,76,453	3,42,769	3,18,550
Net Borrowing	1,13,000	3,29,649	2,98,536

* Pertains to dated securities and 364-day Treasury Bills.

The net amount raised by the government by way of dated securities, additional Treasury Bills and MSS de-sequestering aggregated Rs.2,98,536 crore during 2008-09. In addition, special securities (oil and fertiliser bonds) issued by the Central Government outside the market borrowing programme amounted to Rs.95,942 crore in 2008-09.

Table 7: Net Market Borrowings of the Central and State Governments (Rs.crore)

	Item	2007-08	2008-09
A.	Central Government	1,08,998	2,98,536
i.	Dated Securities	1,10,671	2,16,972
ii.	Additional 364-day T-Bills	-1,167	13,345
iii.	Additional 182-day T-Bills	-76	10,995
iv.	Additional 91-Day T-Bills	-431	45,224
v.	MSS De-sequestering	0	12,000
B.	State Governments	56,224	1,03,766
	Total (A+B)	1,66,895	4,02,302
Memo Items:			
i.	Special Securities Issued outside the Market Borrowing Programme	38,050	95,942
ii.	Net Issuances under MSS	1,05,691	-81,781

As against the initial estimate of Rs.47,044 crore, the State Governments raised a net amount of Rs.1,03,766 crore during 2008-09 (Table 7).

The combined market borrowings of the Central and State Governments in 2008-09 were nearly two and half times their net borrowings in 2007-08. Even as the increase in borrowing was large and abrupt, it was managed in a non-disruptive manner through a combination of measures such as unwinding under the market stabilisation scheme (MSS), open market operations and easing of monetary conditions.

The weighted average yield of Central Government dated securities issued during 2008-09 was lower at 7.69 per cent as compared with 8.12 per cent in the preceding year. The weighted average maturity of these securities was 13.80 years, which was lower than 14.90 years in 2007-08.

Reflecting the continued need for fiscal stimulus in 2009-10, the borrowing requirements of both the Central and State Governments are estimated to be higher as compared with 2008-09 (Table 8).

Table 8: Borrowings of the Central and State Governments: 2009-10

(Rs. crore)

Item	Sep-08	Oct-09
Central Government		
Gross Market Borrowings	3,18,550	3,98,552
Net Market Borrowings	2,98,536	3,08,647 *
State Governments		
Net Market Borrowings	1,03,766	1,26,000 **
Total Net Market Borrowings	4,02,302	4,34,647

* Interim Budget Estimates.

** Estimated. The State Governments have been allowed an additional 0.5 per cent of Gross State Domestic Product (GSDP) as a part of the fiscal stimulus package.

According to the borrowing calendar released for the first half (April-September) of 2009-10, net market borrowings of the Central Government are likely to be of the order of Rs.2,07,364 crore. However, after adjusting for MSS unwinding and the Reserve Bank's support by way of open market operations, net supply of fresh securities is expected to be of the order of Rs.85,364 crore. Although the fresh supply of securities will be higher than the first half of the last year, it will be of much lower order as compared with the first half of 2007-08 (Table 9).

Table 9: Central Government Borrowings: First Half of the Fiscal Year (Dated Securities)

(Rs. crore)

Item	First Half (April-September) Borrowings		
	Aug-07	Sep-08	Oct-09
Gross Market Borrowings	97,000	1,06,000	2,41,000
Less: Repayments	30,554	44,028	33,636
Net Market Borrowings	66,446	61,972	2,07,364
Less: OMO Purchases	0	0	80,000
Less: MSS Unwinding*	0	0	42,000
Add: MSS Issuances (net)*	69,077	5,263	0
Net Supply of Fresh Securities	1,35,523	67,235	85,364

* Includes dated securities and Treasury Bills.

Keeping in view the large budgeted government market borrowing in 2009-10 coming on top of a substantial expansion in market borrowing in 2008-09, it was important for the Reserve Bank to provide comfort to the market so that the borrowing programme is conducted in a non-disruptive manner. Accordingly, the Reserve Bank simultaneously indicated its intention to purchase government securities under open market operations (OMO) for an indicative amount of Rs.80,000 crore during the first half of 2009-10.

To contain the growth slowdown during 2008-09, the Central Government announced three fiscal stimulus measures during December 2008-February 2009. The Government had also provided additional expenditure of Rs.1,48,093 crore (2.7 per cent of GDP) through two supplementary demands for grants during October-December 2008. The total revenue loss due to tax reductions amounted to Rs.8,700 crore (0.2 per cent of GDP) in 2008-09 and Rs.28,100 crore (0.5 per cent of GDP) in 2009-10.

The additional stimulus measures during 2008-09 work out to about 2.9 per cent of GDP. Furthermore, the revenue collection was adversely impacted by the economic slowdown. Consequently, the Interim Budget for 2009-10 revised the estimates for 2008-09 – revenue deficit to 4.4 per cent and the fiscal deficit to 6.0 per cent of GDP as against the budget estimates of 1.0 per cent and 2.5 per cent respectively. In addition, special bonds amounting to 1.8 per cent of GDP were issued to oil marketing companies and fertiliser companies during 2008-09.

As per the Interim Budget 2009-10, the revenue deficit and the fiscal deficit are projected to decline only moderately to 4.0 per cent and 5.5 per cent respectively during 2009-10. The Government in its macroeconomic framework statement, indicated that in view of the compelling need to adjust the fiscal policy to take care of exceptional circumstances through which the economy is passing, the fiscal consolidation process has to be put on hold temporarily. The process of fiscal consolidation should resume once there is an improvement in economic conditions.

Currently available information indicates that the consolidated budgeted revenue surplus of the States in 2008-09 may not materialise. Consequently, the consolidated fiscal deficit of the States is expected to rise to around 3.0 per cent of GDP. The combined fiscal deficit of the Central and State Governments during 2008-09 would be about 9.0 per cent of GDP. Accounting for special securities issued by the Central Government outside the market borrowing programme, the combined fiscal deficit works out to about 10.8 per cent of GDP.

While some of the increase in the revenue and fiscal deficits is on account of post-budget expenditure commitments such as payment of arrears resulting from the Sixth Pay Commission Award, a substantial increase is also due to the economic downturn arising from the impact of the global financial crisis. Although the fiscal stimulus packages have meant deviation from the roadmap laid out by the FRBM Act, reversing the consolidation process of the last several years, they were warranted under the prevailing circumstances. It is critically important, however, that the Centre and States re-anchor to a revised FRBM mandate once the immediacy of the crisis is behind us.

Monetary Conditions

Growth in key monetary aggregates – reserve money (RM) and money supply (M3) – in 2008-09 reflected the changing liquidity positions arising from domestic and global financial conditions and the monetary policy response. Reserve money variations during 2008-09 largely reflected the increase in the currency in circulation and reduction in the cash reserve ratio (CRR) of banks.

As indicated in the Third Quarter Review, reduction in the CRR has three inter-related effects on reserve money. First, it reduces reserve money as bankers' required cash deposits with the Reserve Bank fall. Second, the money multiplier rises. Third, with the increase in the money multiplier, M3 expands with a lag. While the initial expansionary effect is strong, the full effect is felt in 4-6 months. Reflecting these changes, the year-on-year increase in reserve money in 2008-09 was much lower than in the previous year. However, adjusted for the first round effect of CRR reduction, deceleration in reserve money growth was less pronounced. The annual M3 growth in 2008-09, though lower compared with the previous year, was also below the trajectory projected in the Third Quarter Review of January 2009 (Table 10).

Table 10: Annual Variations in Monetary Aggregates

(Per cent)

Item	Annual Variations	
	2007-08	2008-09
Reserve Money	31.0	6.4
Reserve Money (adjusted for CRR changes)	25.3	19.0
Currency in Circulation	17.2	17.0
Money Supply (M3)	21.2	18.4
M3 (Policy Projection)	17.0-17.5*	19.0**
Money Multiplier	4.33	4.82

*Policy projection for the financial year as indicated in the Annual Policy Statement 2008-09 (April 2008).

**Policy projection for the financial year as indicated in the Third Quarter Review of Monetary Policy 2008-09 (January 2009).

Monetary management during 2008-09 was dominated by the response to the spillover effects of global financial crisis and the need to address slackening of domestic demand conditions, especially during the third quarter. As the Reserve Bank had to provide foreign exchange liquidity to meet the demand from importers and contain volatility in the foreign exchange market arising out of capital outflows by foreign institutional investors (FIIs), its net foreign exchange assets (NFEA) declined. This had an overall contractionary effect on rupee liquidity. The Reserve Bank addressed this issue by providing rupee liquidity through expansion of net domestic assets (NDA) by (i) conventional open market operations; (ii) special 14-day term repo facility for banks; (iii) buy-back of securities held under the market stabilisation scheme; (iv) special market operations, including the purchase of oil bonds; (v) enlargement of export credit refinance window; (vi) special refinance facility for banks for addressing the liquidity concerns of NBFCs, mutual funds and housing finance companies; (vii) special refinance facility for financial institutions (SIDBI, NHB and Exim Bank); and (viii) funding to NBFCs through a special purpose vehicle (SPV).

Thus, a notable feature of monetary operations during the second half of 2008-09 was the substitution of foreign assets by domestic assets. Consequently, liquidity conditions have remained comfortable since mid-November 2008 as reflected in the LAF window being generally in the absorption mode and the call/notice rate remaining near or below the lower bound of the LAF corridor consistent with the stance of monetary policy.

Credit Conditions

During 2008-09, the growth in non-food bank credit (year-on-year basis) decelerated from a peak of 29.4 per cent in October 2008 to 17.5 per cent by March 2009. At this rate, non-food credit expansion was lower than that of 23.0 per cent in 2007-08 as also the indicative projection of 24.0 per cent set in the Third Quarter Review of January 2009. The intra-year changes in credit flow could be attributed to several factors. First, the demand for bank credit increased sharply during April-October 2008 as corporates found that their external sources of credit had dried up, and shifted that demand to domestic credit. Second, there was a sharp increase in credit to oil marketing companies by Rs.36,208 crore during April-October 2008 as compared with a decline of Rs.1,146 crore in the corresponding period of the previous year. In the subsequent period, however, the demand for credit moderated reflecting the slowdown of the economy in general and the industrial sector in particular. Working capital requirements had also come down because of decline in commodity prices and drawdown of inventories by the corporates. The demand for credit by oil marketing companies also moderated. In addition, substantially lower credit expansion by private and foreign banks also muted the overall flow of bank credit during the year (Table 11).

Table 11: Bank Group-wise Growth in Deposits and Credit

(Per cent)

Bank Group	**As on March 28, 2008** (y-o-y)	**As on March 27, 2009** (y-o-y)
	Deposits	
Public Sector Banks	22.9	24.1
Foreign Banks	29.1	7.8
Private Sector Banks	19.9	8.0
Scheduled Commercial Banks*	22.4	19.8
	Credit	
Public Sector Banks	22.5	20.4
Foreign Banks	28.5	4.0
Private Sector Banks	19.9	10.9
Scheduled Commercial Banks*	22.3	17.3

* Including RRBs.

Commercial banks' investment in SLR securities, adjusted for LAF, declined marginally from 28.4 per cent of NDTL in March 2008 to 26.7 per cent in March 2009.

According to the data at a disaggregated level drawn from 49 banks accounting for 95.0 per cent of total bank credit, the year-on-year growth in bank credit to industry as of February 2009 was broadly similar to that in the previous year.

While credit flow to agriculture and real estate was significantly higher, it was lower for housing. As a result, industry's share in total credit flow increased significantly in 2008-09 (Table 12).

Table 12: Annual Sectoral Flow of Credit

Sector	As on February 15, 2008 (y-o-y)			As on February 27, 2009 (y-o-y)		
	Amount (Rs. crore)	% share in total	Variations (per cent)	Amount (Rs. crore)	% share in total	Variations (per cent)
Agriculture	34,013	9.2	16.4	52,742	13.0	21.5
Industry	1,67,819	45.2	25.9	2,13,261	52.5	25.8
Real Estate	11,361	3.1	26.7	34,533	8.5	61.4
Housing	26,930	7.3	12.0	19,012	4.7	7.5
NBFCs	20,979	5.7	48.6	26,651	6.6	41.7
Overall Credit	**3,71,053**	**100.0**	22.0	**4,06,304**	**100**	**19.5**

Notes: 1. Credit growth for February 2008 is calculated with outstanding as on February 15, 2008 to obtain variation over comparable 26-week data.
2. Data are provisional.

Table 13: Sectoral Deployment of Credit: Bank Group-wise

Variation (y-o-y) (%)

	Item	Public Sector Banks		Private Sector Banks*		Foreign Banks*	
		As on Februar y 15, 2008	As on February 27, 2009	As on Februar y 15, 2008	As on February 27, 2009	As on Februar y 15, 2008	As on Februar y 27, 2009
	Non-food Gross Bank Credit (1 to 4)	**22.3**	**23.9**	**19.0**	**9.1**	**28.8**	1.6
1	**Agriculture and Allied Activities**	**19.3**	**19.2**	**-1.3**	**39.0**	**NA**	**NA**
2	**Industry**	**23.2**	**31.0**	**35.2**	**7.4**	**35.0**	**6.5**
3	**Personal Loans** *of which:*	**15.6**	**11.6**	**8.5**	**7.4**	**14.5**	**-8.1**
	Housing	13.2	10.0	13.5	4.9	-2.1	-4.4
4	**Services** *of which:*	**28.6**	**24.4**	**28.5**	**4.5**	**41.2**	**6.9**
	Real Estate Loans	47.9	79.1	6.9	13.9	-36.0	40.5
	Non-Banking Financial Companies	53.0	44.8	14.0	38.1	64.0	20.8
	Memo Item Small Enterprises**	49.0	36.7	209.5	23.2	190.4	59.5

* The share of some private sector banks and foreign banks in total bank credit to agriculture and small scale enterprises is small.
* Includes small manufacturing and service enterprises.
*
NA: Not Available.

Significant variations have also been observed in the flow of credit to different sectors by the three broad bank groups during 2008-09. Credit growth by public sector banks to industry accelerated in 2008-09.

However, credit growth to personal loans and services decelerated. Credit by all the three bank groups to real estate accelerated significantly, while that to small enterprises decelerated (Table 13).

Total Flow of Resources to the Commercial Sector

The flow of resources from non-bank sources to the commercial sector throughout 2008-09 was lower than that in the previous year, reflecting depressed domestic and international capital market conditions.

However, till mid-January 2009, higher bank credit growth compensated for the decline in resources from non-banks. Beginning from the fortnight ended January 16, 2009, non-food bank credit growth turned lower than the previous year. Reflecting moderation in both bank credit and funds from other sources, the total flow of resources to the commercial sector from banks and other sources during 2008-09 was significantly lower than that in the previous year (Table 14).

Table 14: Flow of Financial Resources to the Commercial Sector

(Rs. crore)

Item	2007-08	2008-09
From Banks	4,44,807	4,14,902
From Other Sources*	3,35,698	2,64,138
Total Resources	7,80,505	6,79,040

* Includes borrowings from financial institutions and NBFCs as well as resources mobilised from the capital market and by way of ECBs, FCCBs, ADRs/GDRs, FDI and short-term credit as per the latest available data, adjusted for double counting.

Note: Data in this table also include gross investments by LIC in corporate debt and infrastructure and social sector, which were not included in the corresponding table presented in Third Quarter Review, January 2009.

Interest Rates

Since mid-September 2008, the Reserve Bank has cut the repo rate by 400 basis points and the reverse repo rate by 250 basis points. The CRR was also reduced by 400 basis points of NDTL of banks (Table 15).

Table 15: Monetary Easing by the Reserve Bank since mid-September 2008

(Per cent)

Instrument	As at		Extent of Reduction
	Mid-September 2008	Early March 2009	(basis points)
Repo Rate	9.00	5.00	400
Reverse Repo	6.00	3.50	250
Cash Reserve Ratio @	9.00	5.00	400

@ Percentage of NDTL.

Taking cues from the reduction in the Reserve Bank's policy rates and easy liquidity conditions, all public sector banks, most private sector banks and some foreign banks have reduced their deposit and lending rates.

The reduction in the range of term deposit rates between October 2008 - April 18, 2009 has been 125-250 basis points by public sector banks, 75-200 basis points by private sector banks and 100-200 basis points by five major foreign banks.

The reduction in the range of BPLRs was 125-225 basis points by public sector banks, followed by 100-125 basis points by private sector banks and 100 basis points by five major foreign banks (Table 16).

Table 16: Reduction in Deposit and Lending Rates (October 2008 - April 2009)*

(Basis points)

Bank Group	Deposit Rates	Lending Rates (BPLR)
Public Sector Banks	125-250	125-225
Private Sector Banks	75-200	100-125
Five Major Foreign Banks	100-200	0-100

* As on April 18, 2009.

The reduction in deposit rates was more pronounced in respect of deposits of up to three year maturity.

The range of BPLRs of public sector banks, private sector and five major foreign banks declined between October 2008 and April 18, 2009 (Table 17).

Table 17: Movements in Deposit and Lending Rates

(Per cent)

	Interest Rates	October 2008	March 2009	April* 2009	Variation** (basis points)
	Term Deposit Rates				
	Public Sector Banks				
a)	Up to 1 year	2.75-10.25	2.75-8.25	2.75-8.00	0-225
b)	1 year up to 3 years	9.50-10.75	8.00-9.25	7.00-8.75	200-250
c)	Over 3 years	8.50-9.75	7.50-9.00	7.25-8.50	125-125
	Private Sector Banks				
a)	Up to 1 year	3.00-10.50	3.00-8.75	3.00-8.50	0-200
b)	1 year up to 3 years	9.00-11.00	7.50-10.25	7.50-9.50	150-150
c)	Over 3 years	8.25-11.00	7.50-9.75	7.50-9.25	75-175
	Five Major Foreign Banks				
a)	Up to 1 year	3.50-9.50	2.50-8.00	2.50-8.00	100-150
b)	1 year up to 3 years	3.60-10.00	2.50-8.00	2.50-8.00	110-200
c)	Over 3 years	3.60-10.00	2.50-8.00	2.50-8.00	110-200
	BPLR				
	Public Sector Banks	13.75-14.75	11.50-14.00	11.50-13.50	125-225
	Private Sector Banks	13.75-17.75	12.75-16.75	12.50-16.75	100-125
	Five Major Foreign Banks	14.25-16.75	14.25-15.75	14.25-15.75	0-100

* As on April 18, 2009.

** Variation of April 18, 2009 over October 2008.

Table 18: Reduction in BPLR by SCBs – Frequency Distribution (April 18, 2009 over October 2008)

(Number of banks)

Bank Group	25 bps	50 bps	75 bps	100 bps	125 bps	150 bps	175 bps	200 bps	225 bps	250 bps	Total
Public Sector Banks	–	–	1	–	8	8	2	7	–	1	27
Private Sector Banks	1	7	3	2	1	2	–	–	1	–	17
Foreign Banks	–	4	1	1	–	–	–	2	–	–	8

Note: Figures in parentheses indicate total number of banks operating in India.

Note: Figures in parentheses indicate total number of banks operating in India.

The reduction in BPLRs by most public sector banks was in the range of 125-200 basis points, followed by 50-150 basis points reduction by most private sector banks and 50 basis points reduction by foreign banks (Table 18).

The efficacy of the monetary transmission mechanism hinges on the extent and the speed with which changes in the central bank's policy rate are transmitted through the term-structure of interest rates across markets. While the response to policy changes by the Reserve Bank has been faster in the money and government securities markets, there has been concern that the large and quick changes effected in the policy rates by the Reserve Bank have not fully transmitted to banks' lending rates. During the second half of 2008-09, while the Reserve Bank has reduced its lending rate (repo rate) by 400 basis points, most banks have lowered their lending rate in the range of 50-150 basis points.

The adjustment in market interest rates in response to changes in policy rates gets reflected with some lag. However, the transmission to the credit market is somewhat slow on account of several structural rigidities. In this context, banks have brought out the following constraints in their discussions with the Reserve Bank. First, the administered interest rate structure of small savings acts as a floor to deposit interest rates. Without reduction in deposit rates, banks find it difficult to reduce lending rates exclusively on policy cues. Second, while banks are allowed to offer 'variable' interest rates on longer-term deposits, depositors have a distinct preference for fixed interest rates on such deposits which results in an asymmetric contractual relationship. In a rising interest rate scenario, while depositors retain the flexibility to prematurely withdraw their existing deposits and re-deploy the same at higher interest rates, banks have to necessarily carry these high cost deposits till their maturity in the downturn of the interest rate cycle. Third, during periods of credit boom as in 2004-07, competition among banks for wholesale deposits often hardens deposit interest rates, thereby further increasing the cost of funds. Fourth, the linkage of concessional administered lending rates, such as for agriculture and exports, to banks' BPLRs makes overall lending rates less flexible. Fifth, the persistence of large volumes of market borrowing by the government hardens interest rate expectations. From the real economy perspective, however, for monetary policy to have demand-inducing effects, lending rates will have to come down.

The changes in BPLR do not fully reflect the changes in the effective lending rates. During the pre-policy consultations with the Reserve Bank, banks pointed out that lending rates should not be assessed only in terms of reduction in BPLRs since as much as three-quarters of lending is at rates below BPLR which includes lending to agriculture, export sector, and well-rated companies, including PSUs. The weighted average lending rate, which was 11.9 per cent in 2006-07, increased to 12.3 per cent (provisional) in 2007-08. According to the information collected from select banks, the average yield on advances, a proxy measure of effective lending rate, in 2008-09 was around 10.9 per cent. As most of the commercial banks have cut their BPLRs in the second half of 2008-09, the effective lending rate towards the end of 2008-09 could be even lower than 10.9 per cent. Nevertheless, it may be noted that current deposit and lending rates are now higher than in 2004-2007, although the policy rates are now lower than in that period. This is reflective of the hysteresis in the system. Reduction in public sector banks deposit rates in 1-3 year maturity from 9.50-10.75 per cent in October 2008 to 7.00-8.75 per cent by April 2009 has not been commensurate with the moderation in inflation. Judging from the experience of 2004-07, deposit rates can be lower and should come down.

Notwithstanding the above factors, there is still a scope for banks to reduce their lending rates. Pointing to the current WPI inflation rate near zero, some have argued that real lending rates are very high. The point-to-point variations in WPI exaggerate the level of real interest rate due to divergence between various price indices as also the inflation expectations. Notwithstanding computational challenges, even when inflation is taken as 4.0-4.5 per cent based on the underlying trend, real lending rates would still appear to be high. Banks, therefore, must strive to reduce their lending rates further.

Financial Markets

Since October 2008, interest rates have declined across the term structure in the money and government securities markets (Table 19). The call/notice rates have remained near or below the lower bound of the LAF corridor from November 2008. While the secondary market yield on the 10-year government security touched an intra-year low of 5.11 per cent on December 30, 2008, it then generally increased in the wake of the large market borrowing programme of the Government, reaching 7.08 per cent on March 30, 2009. The yield has subsequently declined on account of substantial easing of liquidity and reduction in inflation.

Table 19: Interest Rates - Monthly Average

(Per cent)

Segment/Instrument	March 2008	October 2008	January 2009	March 2009	April 17, 2009
Call Money	7.37	9.90	4.18	4.17	3.47
CBLO	6.37	7.73	3.77	3.60	2.60
Market Repo	6.72	8.40	4.27	3.90	2.86
Commercial Paper	10.38	14.17	9.48	9.79	7.00
Certificates of Deposit	10.00	10.00	7.33	6.73#	4.00
91-day Treasury Bills	7.33	7.44	4.69	4.77	4.09
10-year Government Security	7.69	7.80	5.82	6.57	6.41

Pertains to mid-March 2009.

During 2008-09, the rupee, with significant intra-year variation, generally depreciated against major currencies except pound sterling on account of widening of trade and current account deficits as well as capital outflows. During the current fiscal year (up to April 17, 2009), the rupee has generally remained steady (Chart 2).

Chart 2: Exchange Rate Movements

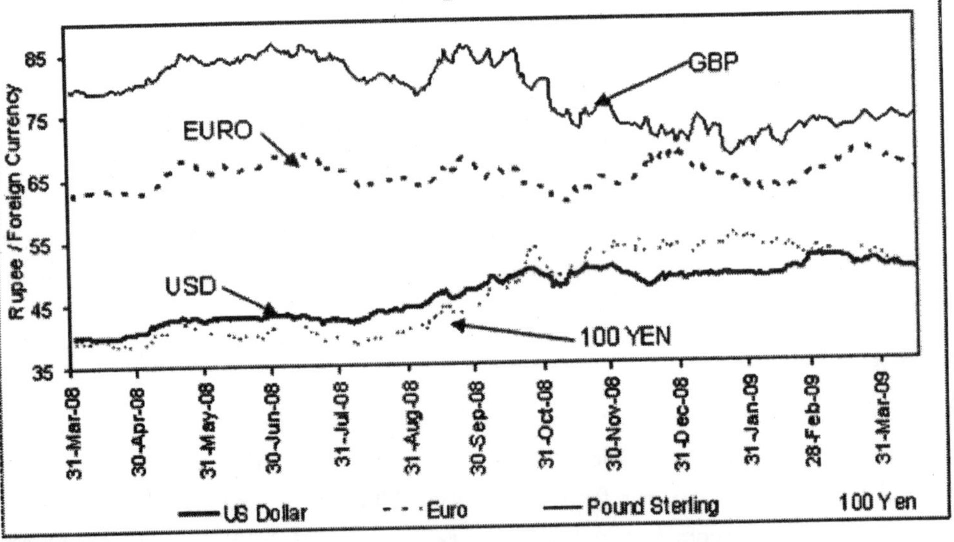

During 2008-09, equity markets weakened in tandem with global stock markets, reflecting general deterioration in sentiment, FII outflows, slowdown in industrial growth and lower corporate profits. The BSE Sensex declined to 8160 on March 9, 2009 from a peak of 20873 recorded on January 8, 2008; it closed higher at 11023 on April 17, 2009.

External Sector

India's current account deficit (CAD) widened during 2008-09 (April-December) in comparison with the corresponding period of the previous year. As net capital inflows declined sharply, the overall balance of payments (BoP) position turned negative resulting in drawdown of reserves (Table 20).

The overall approach to the management of India's foreign exchange reserves takes into account the changing composition of the balance of payments and endeavours to reflect the 'liquidity risks' associated with different types of flows and other requirements. As capital inflows during 2007-08 were far in excess of the normal absorptive capacity of the economy, there was substantial accretion to foreign exchange reserves by US$ 110.5 billion. As capital inflows reduced sharply, the foreign exchange reserves declined by US$ 53.7 billion from US$ 309.7 billion as at end-March 2008 to US$ 256.0 billion by end-December 2008, including valuation losses.

Excluding valuation effects, the decline was US$ 20.4 billion during April-December 2008. India's foreign exchange reserves were US$ 252.0 billion as at end-March 2009 which increased to US$ 253.0 billion by April 10, 2009.

Table 20: India's Balance of Payments

(US $ billion)

Item	April-December	
	Aug-07	Sep-08
Exports	113.6	133.5
Imports	182.9	238.9
Trade Balance	-69.3	-105.3
Invisibles, net	53.8	68.9
Current Account Balance	-15.5	-36.5
Capital Account*	82.7	16.1
Change in Reserves#	-67.2	20.4

* Including errors and omissions.

\# On a BoP basis (*i.e.*, excluding valuation): (-) indicates increase; (+) indicates decrease.

STANCE OF MONETARY POLICY

The policy responses in India since September 2008 have been designed largely to mitigate the adverse impact of the global financial crisis on the Indian economy. The conduct of monetary policy had to contend with the high speed and magnitude of the external shock and its spill-over effects through the real, financial and confidence channels. The evolving stance of policy has been increasingly conditioned by the need to preserve financial stability while arresting the moderation in the growth momentum.

The thrust of the various policy initiatives by the Reserve Bank has been on providing ample rupee liquidity, ensuring comfortable dollar liquidity and maintaining a market environment conducive for the continued flow of credit to productive sectors. The key policy initiatives taken by the Reserve Bank since September 2008 are set out below:

Policy Rates

- The policy repo rate under the liquidity adjustment facility (LAF) was reduced by 400 basis points from 9.0 per cent to 5.0 per cent.
- The policy reverse repo rate under the LAF was reduced by 250 basis points from 6.0 per cent to 3.5 per cent.

Rupee Liquidity

- The cash reserve ratio (CRR) was reduced by 400 basis points from 9.0 per cent of net demand and time liabilities (NDTL) of banks to 5.0 per cent.
- The statutory liquidity ratio (SLR) was reduced from 25.0 per cent of NDTL to 24.0 per cent.
- The export credit refinance limit for commercial banks was enhanced to 50.0 per cent from 15.0 per cent of outstanding export credit.
- A special 14-day term repo facility was instituted for commercial banks up to 1.5 per cent of NDTL.
- A special refinance facility was instituted for scheduled commercial banks (excluding RRBs) up to 1.0 per cent of each bank's NDTL as on October 24, 2008.
- Special refinance facilities were instituted for financial institutions (SIDBI, NHB and Exim Bank).

Forex Liquidity

- The Reserve Bank sold foreign exchange (US dollars) and made available a forex swap facility to banks.
- The interest rate ceilings on non-resident Indian (NRI) deposits were raised.
- The all-in-cost ceiling for the external commercial borrowings (ECBs) was raised. The all-in-cost ceiling for ECBs through the approval route has been dispensed with up to June 30, 2009.
- The systemically important non-deposit taking non-banking financial companies (NBFCs-ND-SI) were permitted to raise short-term foreign currency borrowings.

Regulatory Forbearance

- The risk-weights and provisioning requirements were relaxed and restructuring of stressed assets was initiated.

A detailed listing of various policy measures undertaken by the Reserve Bank since September 2008 is set out in Annex I.

Liquidity Impact

The actions of the Reserve Bank since mid-September 2008 have resulted in augmentation of actual/potential liquidity of over Rs.4,22,000 crore. In addition, the permanent reduction in the SLR by 1.0 per cent of NDTL has made available liquid funds of the order of Rs.40,000 crore for the purpose of credit expansion (Table 21).

Table 21: Actual/Potential Release of Primary Liquidity – since Mid-September 2008

	Measure/Facility	Amount (Rs. crore)
1	CRR Reduction	1,60,000
2	Unwinding/Buyback/De-sequestering of MSS Securities	97,781
3	Term Repo Facility	60,000
4	Increase in Export Credit Refinance	25,512
5	Special Refinance Facility for SCBs (Non-RRBs)	38,500
6	Refinance Facility for SIDBI/NHB/EXIM Bank	16,000
7	Liquidity Facility for NBFCs through SPV	25,000*
	Total (1 to 7)	4,22,793
	Memo: Statutory Liquidity Ratio (SLR) Reduction	40,000

* Includes an option of Rs.5,000 crore.

The liquidity situation has improved significantly following the measures taken by the Reserve Bank. The overnight money market rates, which generally hovered above the repo rate during September-October 2008, have softened considerably and have generally been close to or near the lower bound of the LAF corridor since early November 2008.

Other money market rates such as discount rates of CDs, CPs and CBLO softened in tandem with the overnight money market rates. The LAF window has been in a net absorption mode since mid-November 2008.

The liquidity problem faced by mutual funds has eased considerably. Most commercial banks have reduced their benchmark prime lending rates. The total utilisation under the recent refinance/ liquidity facilities introduced by the Reserve Bank has been low as the overall liquidity conditions remain comfortable (Table 22). However, their availability has provided comfort to the banks/ FIs, which can fall back on them in case of need.

The Reserve Bank has multiple instruments at its command such as repo and reverse repo rates, cash reserve ratio (CRR), statutory liquidity ratio (SLR), open market operations, including the market stabilisation scheme (MSS) and the LAF, special market operations, and sector-specific liquidity facilities.

In addition, the Reserve Bank also uses prudential tools to modulate flow of credit to certain sectors consistent with financial stability. The availability of multiple instruments and flexible use of these instruments in the implementation of monetary policy has enabled the Reserve Bank to modulate the liquidity and interest rate conditions amidst uncertain global macroeconomic conditions.

Table 22: Utilisation of Various Liquidity Facilities Available from the Reserve Bank– As on April 16, 2009

Refinance Facility	Availability of Facility: Terminal Dates	Limit	Outstanding	Outstanding as per centof Limit
i) Export Credit Refinance Facility	Standing Facility	36,446	590	1.6
ii) Special Refinance Facility for Scheduled Commercial Banks (excluding RRBs)	30.09.2009	38,429	1,380	3.6
iii) Special Term Repo Facility to Banks (for funding to MFs, NBFCs and HFCs)	30.09.2009	60,000	90	0.2
iv) Refinance Facility to SIDBI	31.03.2010	7,000	5,819	83.1
v) Refinance Facility to NHB	31.03.2010	4,000	3,220	80.5
vi) Refinance Facility to EXIM Bank	31.03.2010	5,000	2,800	56
vii) Liquidity Facility for NBFCs through SPV Route	30.06.2009	25,000*	750	3
Total (i to vii)	1,75,875	14,649	8.3	
Memo Item:				
Forex Swap Facility to Banks	31.03.2010	For tenor up to three months	1,030	–

* The total support from the Reserve Bank is limited to Rs.20,000 crore with an option to raise it by a further Rs.5,000 crore.

Growth Projection

The India Meteorological Department in its forecast of South-West monsoon expects a normal rainfall at 96 per cent of its long period average for the current year. The fiscal and monetary stimulus measures initiated during 2008-09 coupled with lower commodity prices could cushion the downturn in the growth momentum during 2009-10 by stabilising domestic economic activity to some extent. However, any upturn in the growth momentum is unlikely in view of the projected contraction in global demand during 2009, particularly decline in trade. While domestic financing conditions have improved, external financing conditions are expected to remain tight. Private investment demand is, therefore, expected to remain subdued. On balance, with the assumption of normal monsoon, for policy purpose, real GDP growth for 2009-10 is placed at around 6.0 per cent.

Inflation Projection

On account of slump in global demand, pressures on global commodity prices have abated markedly around the world. The sharp decline in prices of crude oil, metals, foodgrains, cotton and cement has influenced inflation expectations in most parts of the world. This is also reflected in the domestic WPI inflation reaching close to zero. Prices of manufactured products have decelerated sharply, while that of the fuel group have contracted, though inflation on account of food articles still remains high. Keeping in view the global trend in commodity prices and domestic demand-supply balance, WPI inflation is projected at around 4.0 per cent by end-March 2010.

The WPI inflation, however, is expected to be in the negative territory in the early part of 2009-10. However, this should not be interpreted as deflation for policy purposes. This expected negative inflation in India has only statistical significance and is not a reflection of demand contraction as is the case in advanced economies. This transitory WPI inflation in negative zone may not persist beyond the middle of 2009-10. The consumer price inflation as reflected in various indices is expected to moderate from its present high level but would continue to remain in positive territory through 2009-10 unlike WPI inflation. Moreover, it may also be noted that the sharp decline in WPI inflation has not been commensurately matched by a similar decline in inflation expectations.

It would be the endeavour of the Reserve Bank to ensure price stability and anchor inflation expectations. Towards this objective, the Reserve Bank will, as always, continue to take into account the behaviour of all the price indices and their components. The conduct of monetary policy would continue to condition and contain perception of inflation in the range of 4.0-4.5 per cent so that an inflation rate of around 3.0 per cent becomes the medium-term objective, consistent with India's broader integration into the global economy and with the goal of maintaining self-accelerating growth over the medium-term.

Monetary Projection

Monetary and credit aggregates have witnessed deceleration since their peak levels in October 2008. The liquidity overhang emanating from the earlier surge in capital inflows has substantially moderated in 2008-09. The Reserve Bank is committed to providing ample liquidity for all productive activities on a continuous basis. As the upside risks to inflation have declined, monetary policy has been responding to slackening economic growth in the context of significant global stress. Accordingly, for policy purposes, money supply (M3) growth for 2009-10 is placed at 17.0 per cent. Consistent with this, aggregate deposits of scheduled commercial banks are projected to grow by 18.0 per cent. The growth in adjusted non-food credit, including investment in bonds/ debentures/shares of public sector undertakings and private corporate sector and CPs, is placed at 20.0 per cent. Given the wide dispersion in credit growth noticed across bank groups during

2008-09, banks with strong deposit base should endeavour to expand credit beyond 20.0 per cent. As always, these numbers are provided as indicative projections and not as targets.

Overall Assessment

The global financial and economic outlook continues to be unsettled and uncertain. The latest assessment by major international agencies projecting sharp contraction in global trade volumes in 2009 has exacerbated the uncertainty. The current assessments project little chance of global economic recovery in 2009. Despite large scale recapitalisation, write-offs and asset substitutions, sizeable chunks of assets of systemically important banks and financial institutions remain impaired. It is also not clear if the deleveraging process is complete. In such a scenario, external financing conditions for emerging market economies may continue to remain tight and constrain their growth prospects.

Governments and central banks all over the world have responded to the ongoing global financial crisis by initiating several large, aggressive and unconventional measures. There is, however, a contentious debate on whether these measures are adequate and appropriate and when, if at all, they will start showing the desired results. There is a separate debate on whether the measures taken so far, responding as they are to short-term compulsions, are eroding long-term sustainability. Many difficult issues will need to be addressed going forward. There is unprecedented co-ordinated policy action on monetary, fiscal, regulatory and institutional reforms to address the ongoing financial and economic crisis and strengthen the international financial architecture. In this context, the initiatives by the leaders of the G-20 announced in April 2009 to:

(i) restore confidence, growth, and jobs;

(ii) repair the financial system to restore lending;

(iii) strengthen financial regulation to rebuild trust;

(iv) fund and reform the international financial institutions to overcome the crisis and prevent future ones;

(v) promote global trade and investment and reject protectionism to underpin prosperity; and

(vi) build an inclusive, green and sustainable recovery, should help overcome the uncertainty surrounding the financial and economic outlook.

Here in India, there are several immediate challenges facing the economy which would need to be addressed going forward. First, after five years of high growth, the Indian economy was headed for a moderation in the first half of 2008-09. However, the growth slowdown accentuated in the third quarter of 2008-09 on account of spillover effects of international developments. While the moderation in growth seems to have continued through the fourth quarter of 2008-09, it has been cushioned by quick and aggressive policy responses both by the Reserve Bank and the Government. Notwithstanding the contraction of global demand, growth prospects in

India continue to remain favourable compared to most other countries. While public investment can play a critical role in the short-term during a downturn, private investment has to increase as the recovery process sets in. A major macroeconomic challenge at this juncture is to support the drivers of aggregate demand to enable the economy to return to its high growth path.

The second challenge going forward is meeting the credit needs of the non-food sector. Although, for the year 2008-09 as a whole, credit by the banking sector expanded, the pace of credit flow decelerated rapidly from its peak in October 2008. This deceleration has occurred alongside a significant decline in the flow of resources from non-bank domestic and external sources. The deceleration in total resource flow partly reflects slowdown in demand, drawdown of inventories by the corporates and decline in commodity prices. The expansion in credit, however, has been uneven across sectors. There is, therefore, an urgent need to boost the flow of credit to all productive sectors of the economy, particularly to MSMEs, to aid the process of economic recovery. The Reserve Bank continues to maintain and will maintain ample liquidity in the system. It should be the endeavour of commercial banks to ensure that every creditworthy borrower is financed at a reasonable cost while, at the same time, ensuring that credit quality is maintained.

It may be noted that bank credit had accelerated during 2004-07. This, combined with significant slowdown of the economy in 2008-09, may result in some increase in NPAs. While it is not unusual for NPAs to increase during periods of high credit growth and downturn in the economy, the challenge is to maintain asset quality through early actions. This calls for a focused approach, due diligence and balanced judgment by banks.

Third, the Reserve Bank was able to manage the large borrowing programme of the Central and State Governments in 2008-09 in an orderly manner. The market borrowings of the Central and State Governments are expected to be higher in 2009-10. Thus, a major challenge is to manage the large government borrowing programme in 2009-10 in a non-disruptive manner. Large borrowings also militate against the low interest rate environment that the Reserve Bank is trying to maintain to spur investment demand in keeping with the stance of monetary policy. The Reserve Bank, therefore, would continue to use a combination of monetary and debt management tools to manage government borrowing programme to ensure successful completion of government borrowings in a smooth manner. The Reserve Bank has already announced an OMO calendar to support government market borrowing programme through secondary market purchase of government securities. During the first half of 2009-10, planned OMO purchases and MSS unwinding will add primary liquidity of about Rs.1,20,000 crore which, by way of monetary impact, is equivalent to CRR reduction of 3.0 percentage points. This should leave adequate resources with banks to expand credit.

Fourth, another challenge facing the Indian economy is to restore the fiscal consolidation process. The fiscal stimulus packages by the Government and some other measures have led to sharp increase in the revenue and fiscal deficits which, in the face of slowing private investment, have cushioned the pace of economic activity. However, it would be a challenge to unwind fiscal stimulus in an orderly manner and return to a path of credible fiscal consolidation. In this context, close monitoring of the performance of the economy and the proper sequencing of the unwinding process would have to be ensured.

Fifth, a continued challenge is to preserve our financial stability. The Reserve Bank would continue to maintain conditions which are conducive for financial stability in the face of global crisis. A sound banking sector, well-functioning financial markets and robust payment and settlement infrastructure are the pre-requisites for financial stability. The banking sector in India is sound, adequately capitalised and well-regulated. By all counts, Indian financial and economic conditions are much better than in many other countries of the world. The single factor stress tests carried out as part of the report of the Committee on Financial Sector Assessment (CFSA) (Chairman: Dr. Rakesh Mohan and Co-Chairman: Shri Ashok Chawla) have revealed that the banking system in India can withstand significant shocks arising from large potential changes in credit quality, interest rate and liquidity conditions. These stress tests for credit, market and liquidity risk show that Indian banks are generally resilient.

Sixth, the Reserve Bank has injected large liquidity in the system since mid-September 2008. It has reduced the CRR significantly and instituted some sector-specific facilities to improve the flow of credit to certain sectors. The tenure of some of these facilities has been extended to provide comfort to the market. While the Reserve Bank will continue to support all the productive requirements of the economy, it will have to ensure that as economic growth gathers momentum, the large liquidity injected in the system is withdrawn in an orderly manner. It is worth noting that even as the monetary easing by the Reserve Bank has potentially made available a large amount of liquidity to the system, at the aggregate level this has not been out of line with our monetary aggregates unlike in many advanced countries. As such, the challenge of unwinding will be less daunting for India than for other countries.

Finally, we will have to address the key challenge of ensuring an interest rate environment that supports revival of investment demand. Since October 2008, as the inflation rate has decelerated and the policy rates have been reduced, market interest rates have also come down. However, the reduction in interest rates across the term structure and across markets has not been uniform. Given the cost plus pricing structure, banks have been slow in reducing their lending rates citing high cost of deposits. In this context, it may be noted that the current deposit and lending rates are higher than in 2004-07, although the policy rates are now lower.

Reduction in deposit rates affects the cost only at the margin since existing term deposits continue at the originally contracted cost. So lending rates take longer to adjust. Judging from the experience of 2004-07, there is room for downward adjustment of deposit rates. With WPI inflation falling to near zero, possibly likely to get into a negative territory, *albeit* for a short period, and CPI inflation expected to moderate, inflationary risks have clearly abated. The Reserve Bank's current assessment is that WPI inflation could be around 4.0 per cent by end-March 2010. Banks have indicated that small savings rate acts as a floor to banks' deposit interest rate. It may, however, be noted that small savings and bank deposits are not perfect substitutes. Banks should not, therefore, be overly apprehensive about reducing deposit interest rates for fear of competition from small savings, especially as the overall systemic liquidity remains highly comfortable. There is scope for the overall interest rate structure to move down within the policy rate easing already effected by the Reserve Bank. Further action on policy rates is now being taken to reinforce this process.

Policy Stance

On the basis of the above overall assessment, the stance of monetary policy in 2009-10 will broadly be as follows:

- Ensure a policy regime that will enable credit expansion at viable rates while preserving credit quality so as to support the return of the economy to a high growth path.
- Continuously monitor the global and domestic conditions and respond swiftly and effectively through policy adjustments as warranted so as to minimise the impact of adverse developments and reinforce the impact of positive developments.
- Maintain a monetary and interest rate regime supportive of price stability and financial stability taking into account the emerging lessons of the global financial crisis.

Over the last several months, the Reserve Bank has been actively engaged in policy action to minimise the impact of the global crisis on India. The policy response of the Reserve Bank has helped in keeping our financial markets functioning in a normal manner and in arresting the growth moderation. The Reserve Bank will continue to maintain vigil, monitor domestic and global developments, and take swift and effective action to minimise the impact of the crisis and restore the economy to a high growth path consistent with price and financial stability.

MONETARY MEASURES

Bank Rate

The Bank Rate has been retained unchanged at 6.0 per cent.

Repo Rate

It is proposed:

- to reduce the repo rate under the Liquidity Adjustment Facility (LAF) by 25 basis points from 5.0 per cent to 4.75 per cent with immediate effect.

Reverse Repo Rate

It is proposed:

- to reduce the reverse repo rate under the LAF by 25 basis points from 3.5 per cent to 3.25 per cent with immediate effect.

The Reserve Bank has the flexibility to conduct repo/reverse repo auctions at a fixed rate or at variable rates as circumstances warrant. The Reserve Bank retains the option to conduct overnight or longer term repo/reverse repo under the LAF depending on market conditions and other relevant factors. The Reserve Bank will continue to use this flexibly including the right to accept or reject tender(s) under the LAF, wholly or partially, if deemed fit, so as to make efficient use of the LAF in daily liquidity management.

Cash Reserve Ratio

The cash reserve ratio (CRR) of scheduled banks has been retained unchanged at 5.0 per cent of net demand and time liabilities (NDTL).

First Quarter Review

The First Quarter Review of Monetary Policy for 2009-10 will be undertaken on July 28, 2009.

Part B. Developmental and Regulatory Policies 2009-10

The key objective of financial sector policies is to aid the process of economic growth consistent with price and financial stability. In this context, the Reserve Bank has been focusing on improving credit delivery, developing financial markets and promoting financial inclusion. Internationally, the financial intermediation process has got significantly affected by the ongoing financial crisis. Consequently, various international bodies and financial intermediaries have been contemplating changes in the financial regulatory architecture to restore normalcy in the functioning of global financial markets and strengthen financial stability. There is a great deal of thinking going on about the appropriate design of the regulatory framework that encourages credit flow while mitigating risks. Domestically, although there has been some slowdown in credit growth, particularly in the second half of 2008-09, the banking system remains inherently sound and the financial markets including inter-bank markets are functioning normally. Nevertheless, the unfolding of the global financial crisis underscores the need for further strengthening of regulation and supervision even as India remains outside the epicentre of the global crisis.

Box: International Co-operation - Recent Initiatives

- Several international initiatives have been taken in the recent period for formulating proposals for strengthening the financial system. The major initiatives in this regard include the following:

- Several reports have been released recently such as the Financial Stability Forum's (now Financial Stability Board) Report on 'Enhancing Market and Institutional Resilience', the Geneva Report on 'The Fundamental Principles of Financial Regulation', Larosiere Report on 'The High Level Group on Financial Supervision in the EU' and the Turner Review on 'Regulatory Response to the Global Banking Crisis'.
- The G-20 countries have also taken several initiatives. In the summit held in Washington in November 2008, the G-20 countries laid down an action plan and constituted four Working Groups, *viz.*,

  (i) Enhancing Sound Regulation and Strengthening Transparency;

  (ii) Reinforcing International Co-operation and Promoting Integrity in Financial Markets;

  (iii) Reform of the IMF; and

  (iv) The World Bank and other Multilateral Development Banks (MDBs).

  The first group on Enhancing Sound Regulation and Strengthening Transparency was co-chaired by Dr. Rakesh Mohan, Deputy Governor, Reserve Bank of India along with Mr. Tiff Macklem of Canada.
- The leaders of the G-20 again met in London on April 2, 2009 and laid down the 'Global Plan for Recovery and Reform'.
- Drawing mainly from the recommendations of the group on Enhancing Sound Regulation and Strengthening Transparency, the G-20 also made a declaration for strengthening the financial system. The declaration agreed to make far reaching reforms in the areas of expanding the membership of international bodies, international co-operation, prudential regulations, scope of regulations, compensation, tax havens and non-co-operative jurisdictions, accounting standards and credit rating agencies.
- With a view to increasing international co-operation, the Financial Stability Forum (FSF), rechristened as Financial Stability Board (FSB), has been expanded to include more emerging market economies and its mandate has been broadened. India has been invited to join the FSB as a member. Alongside the current mandate of the FSF – to assess vulnerabilities affecting the financial system and identify and oversee action needed to address them – the FSB will advise on market developments and monitor best practices in meeting regulatory standards, among others.
- The Basel Committee on Banking Supervision (BCBS) has also been expanded and India has been invited to nominate a member to the Committee. Accordingly, Smt. Usha Thorat, Deputy Governor, Reserve Bank of India has been nominated as a member of the BCBS.

  * A Group of 30 (G-30) released the report on 'Financial Reform – A Framework for Financial Stability' on January 15, 2009 to strengthen prudential regulations and supervision.

FINANCIAL STABILITY

The current crisis has triggered several initiatives in an unprecedented co-ordinated manner at the global level with a view to resolving the crisis and strengthening the international financial architecture (Box).

While India has been a part of the global initiative, recently a comprehensive assessment of the Indian financial sector has been conducted by the Committee on Financial Sector Assessment (CFSA) (Chairman: Dr. Rakesh Mohan and Co-Chairman: Shri Ashok Chawla) constituted by the Government of India, in consultation with the Reserve Bank. The Committee submitted its report to the Finance Minister on March 25, 2009 at New Delhi. The Report was also released to the public on March 30, 2009 and placed on the Reserve Bank's website. While the Committee found India's financial sector to be broadly sound and resilient, it also identified specific concerns. The Committee has made several recommendations towards furthering financial sector development over the medium term. Keeping in view both international and domestic initiatives in the financial sector, it is proposed:

- to constitute a Task Force to look into all the issues that have arisen with regard to the G-20 Working Groups and the report of the CFSA and suggest follow-up actions relevant for the Reserve Bank in the domestic context on an on-going basis, for every quarter;
- in consultation with all regulators and the Government to consider the setting up of a Working Group to implement the recommendations of the CFSA;
- to set up a Financial Stability Unit in the Reserve Bank drawing upon inter-disciplinary expertise from supervisory, regulatory, statistics, economics and financial markets departments for carrying out periodic stress testing and for preparing financial stability reports.

Interest Rate Policy

(a) BPLR System: Review

Consequent to the Mid-Term Review of October 2005, the Indian Banks' Association (IBA) issued guidelines for determination of benchmark prime lending rate (BPLR) by banks for appropriate pricing of credit. Over time, however, the system of BPLR has evolved in such a manner that it has lost its relevance as a meaningful reference rate as bulk of loans is advanced below BPLR. Furthermore, this impedes the smooth transmission of monetary signals and makes the loan pricing system non-transparent. It has, therefore, become necessary to review the current procedures and processes of pricing of credit. Accordingly, it is proposed:

- to constitute a Working Group to review the present BPLR system and suggest changes to make credit pricing more transparent. The Working Group would consult all the stakeholders and submit its report by end-August 2009.

(b) Payment of Interest on Savings Bank Account on a Daily Product Basis

At present, interest on savings bank accounts is calculated on the minimum balances held in the accounts during the period from the 10th day to the last day of each calendar month. Several banks have suggested that interest on savings bank accounts may be calculated either on the minimum balances in the deposit accounts during the period from the first to the last day of each calendar month or on a daily product basis.

The matter was referred to the IBA, which was of the view that payment of interest on a daily product basis would be feasible only when computerisation in banks is completed. In view of the present satisfactory level of computerisation in commercial bank branches, it is proposed that:

- payment of interest on savings bank accounts by scheduled commercial banks (SCBs) would be calculated on a daily product basis with effect from April 1, 2010.
- Modalities in this regard will be worked out in consultation with banks.

FINANCIAL MARKETS

Money Market

(a) Special Refinance Facility: Extension

A special refinance facility was introduced on November 1, 2008 under Section 17(3B) of the Reserve Bank of India Act, 1934 to provide funding to scheduled commercial banks (excluding regional rural banks) up to 1.0 per cent of their net demand and time liabilities (NDTL) as on October 24, 2008 at the repo rate. It is proposed:

- to extend this special refinance facility up to March 31, 2010.

(b) Special Term Repo Facility: Extension

The Reserve Bank introduced a special 14-day term repo facility for banks in September 2008 through relaxation in the maintenance of SLR up to 1.5 per cent of their NDTL, to enable them to meet the liquidity requirements of mutual funds (MFs), non-banking financial companies (NBFCs) and housing finance companies (HFCs). The auctions for the special 14-day term repo are conducted on a daily basis. On a review, it is proposed:

- to extend the time for availability of this special term repo facility to banks up to March 31, 2010;
- to conduct these 14-day term repo auctions on a weekly basis.

(c) Export Credit Refinance: Review

With a view to providing flexibility in the liquidity management of banks, the limit of the standing liquidity facility to banks in terms of export credit refinance (ECR) under Section 17(3A) of the RBI Act was raised from 15.0 per cent of the eligible outstanding rupee export credit as on the preceding fortnight to 50.0 per cent in November 2008. It is proposed:

- to review the ECR limit in March 2010.

(d) Money Market Mutual Funds

The liquidity stress recently faced by mutual funds, particularly the money market mutual funds (MMMFs), was caused primarily on account of mobilisation of significant resources from large corporates and banks with redemption facilities on par with current accounts of banks. In this regard, the Securities and Exchange Board of India (SEBI) has taken several measures to mitigate the liquidity risks. In view of the systemic implications of the activities of such funds, it is proposed:

- to identify and address the macro-prudential concerns arising from the current framework in consultation with SEBI.

(e) Interest Rate Futures

The Technical Advisory Committee (TAC) for Money, Foreign Exchange and Government Securities Markets had released the report of the Working Group on Interest Rate Futures (Chairman: Shri V. K. Sharma) in August 2008. The Working Group had recommended, ***inter alia,*** the introduction of a physically settled contract based on a 10-year notional coupon bearing government bond. The Reserve Bank has already permitted banks to take trading positions in interest rate futures (IRFs). The RBI-SEBI Standing Technical Committee has completed the preparatory work and an exchange traded IRFs contract on the 10-year notional coupon bearing government bond is expected to be launched shortly.

Government Securities Market

(a) Central Government Securities

(i) Floating Rate Bonds

The floating rate bonds (FRBs) issued by the Government of India till September 2004 were linked to the cut-off yields of the 364-day Treasury Bills (TBs), which led to certain issues relating to the pricing of FRBs in the secondary market. Reflecting this experience and in consultation with market participants and the Technical Advisory Committee on Money, Foreign Exchange and Government Securities Markets, the structure has been revised. The revised structure contemplates that: (i) the auction will be conducted through the 'price based' process as against the 'spread based' process earlier; and (ii) the base yield for FRBs will be linked to the primary market cut-off yield of the 182-day TBs. The revised structure is expected to simplify the methodology for pricing of FRBs in the secondary market. The revised issuance structure for FRBs has been built into the negotiated dealing system (NDS) auction format being developed by the Clearing Corporation of India Limited (CCIL). The indicative calendar for the issuance of Central Government securities provides for the issuance of FRBs. Accordingly:

- any new issuance of floating rate bonds would be in terms of the revised issuance structure.

(ii) Auction Process of Government of India Securities

As indicated in the Mid-Term Review of October 2008, the recommendations of the Internal Working Group (Chairman: H.R. Khan) involving the Reserve Bank such as reduction of the time gap between bid submission and declaration of auction results have already been implemented. The other recommendations of the Working Group such as: (i) withdrawal of the facility of bidding in physical form and submission of competitive bids only through the NDS; and (ii) submission of a single consolidated bid on behalf of all its constituents by the bank/primary dealer (PD) in respect of non-competitive bids will be implemented after the amendments in the specific notification and in the scheme for non-competitive bidding facility by the Government of India.

(iii) Ways and Means Advances to the Government of India: Status

The Reserve Bank, in consultation with the Government of India, has revised the extant limits for the Ways and Means Advances (WMA) for the financial year 2009-10. As per the revised arrangements, the WMA limits will continue to be fixed on a half-yearly basis, and are placed at Rs.20,000 crore for the first half and Rs.10,000 crore for the second half of 2009-10. The applicable interest rate on WMAs and overdrafts will, as it is the practice now, continue to be linked to the repo rate. The Reserve Bank of India, however, retains the flexibility to revise the limits in consultation with the Government of India, taking into consideration the prevailing circumstances.

(b) Debt Management for State Governments

(i) Non-Competitive Bidding in the Auction of State Development Loans (SDLs): Status

In order to widen the investor base and enhance the liquidity for SDLs, a scheme for non-competitive bidding in the auction of SDLs was notified by all the State Governments on July 20, 2007. Subsequent to the announcement in the Mid-Term Review of October 2008, the necessary system changes required to handle non-competitive bidding in the auction of SDLs have been carried out in the NDS auction platform developed by the CCIL.

The scheme for non-competitive bidding in SDLs will be operationalised during the current financial year.

(ii) Ways and Means Advances Limits for the State Governments: Status

The State-wise limits of normal WMA for the year 2009-10 have been kept unchanged at the limits set for the year 2008-09. Accordingly, the aggregate normal WMA limit for State

Governments is placed at Rs.9,925 crore, including the WMA limit of Rs.50 crore for the Government of the Union Territory of Puducherry. All other terms and conditions of the scheme remain unchanged.

(c) Development of Market Infrastructure

(i) Separate Trading for Registered Interest and Principal of Securities (STRIPS)

Stripping is the process of converting periodic coupon payments and the principal of an existing Government security into tradable zero-coupon securities, *i.e.,* separate trading for registered interest and principal of securities (STRIPS). The availability of STRIPS across the term structure will aid the development of a sovereign zero-coupon yield curve. As indicated in the Annual Policy Statement of April 2008, all operational arrangements for the introduction of STRIPS are ready. The required software development, critical for the introduction of STRIPS, has been carried out as part of the public debt office – NDS (PDO-NDS) platform maintained by the Reserve Bank. Furthermore, in order to ensure sufficient volume/liquidity in STRIPS and considering the fungibility of coupon STRIPS, securities have been identified that will be eligible for stripping/reconstitution by the market participants. Accordingly:

- draft guidelines prepared in consultation with the market participants are being placed on the Reserve Bank's website for comments and feedback by end-May 2009. With the finalisation of the guidelines, STRIPS will be launched during the current financial year.

(ii) Revision of Repo Accounting

The accounting norms on repo transactions prescribed by the Reserve Bank in 2003, treated repo as a set of two independent outright transactions. Consequent upon the amendment in 2006 to the Reserve Bank of India Act, 1934, repo has been defined as an instrument for borrowing funds by selling securities. Accordingly, it was proposed to revise the accounting guidelines to capture the economic essence of repo as a collateralised lending and borrowing instrument and not as outright sale and purchase. Accordingly, it is proposed:

- to issue revised guidelines on repo accounting, taking into account comments on the draft guidelines earlier placed on the Reserve Bank's website, by end-June 2009 for implementation from April 1, 2010.

(iii) Multi-modal Settlements in Government Securities: Status

As indicated in the Annual Policy Statement of April 2008, a new settlement mechanism (Multi-modal Settlement) through commercial banks has been put in place to facilitate entities such as mutual funds (MFs), which do not hold a current account with the Reserve Bank, to directly participate in the government securities market. Under the new mechanism, while settlement of the securities leg continues to take place in the SGL account maintained with the Reserve Bank, the funds leg will settle through the 'designated settlement banks' (DSBs) appointed by the CCIL. The guidelines in the matter were issued on June 2, 2008. From June 30, 2008 onwards, secondary market transactions in government securities undertaken by MFs are being settled only through this mechanism.

The facility of multi-modal settlements can also be availed of by other non-bank entities such as insurance companies, pension funds and co-operative banks which do not maintain a current account with the Reserve Bank.

(iv) Clearing and Settlement of OTC Rupee Interest Rate Derivatives: Status

As indicated in the Mid-Term Review of October 2008, the CCIL has operationalised a clearing and settlement arrangement for over-the-counter (OTC) rupee interest rate derivatives on a non-guaranteed basis since November 27, 2008. As at end-March 2009, 13 members have decided to participate in the non-guaranteed settlement of OTC rupee interest rate derivatives. The trade reporting platform for OTC rupee interest rate derivatives is already functional.

(v) Settlement of OTC Trades in Corporate Bonds

For facilitating settlement of OTC corporate bond transactions in real-time gross settlement (RTGS) system on a DvP-I basis (*i.e.*, on a trade-by-trade basis), it has been decided, in consultation with the SEBI, to allow the clearing houses of the exchanges to have a transitory pooling account facility with the Reserve Bank. Under the proposed settlement mechanism, the buyer of securities will transfer the funds through his bank to this transitory account through RTGS. The clearing house will thereafter transfer the securities from the seller's account to the buyer's account and effect the release of funds from the transitory account to the seller's account.

Foreign Exchange Market

(a) ECBs: Extension of Relaxation of all-in-cost Ceilings

As per extant ECB policy, the all-in-cost ceilings for ECBs are: LIBOR plus 300 bps for ECBs with average maturity period of three years and up to five years; and LIBOR plus 500 bps for ECBs with average maturity of more than five years. However, these all-in-cost ceilings have been dispensed with up to June 30, 2009 subject to the condition that ECB proposals above the prescribed all-in-cost ceilings, irrespective of the amount of the borrowing, will come under the approval route. Considering the continuing tightness of credit spreads in the international markets, it is proposed:

- to extend the relaxation in all-in-cost ceilings until December 31, 2009.

(b) Liberalisation of the Policy on Buyback of FCCBs

Recognising the benefits accruing to the Indian companies as well as to the economy, the policy on the premature buyback of FCCBs was liberalised in December 2008. The proposals for buyback of FCCBs by Indian companies are being considered both under the approval and automatic routes, provided buyback is financed out of their foreign currency resources held in India or abroad and/or out of fresh ECBs raised in conformity with the current ECB norms and out of internal accruals up to US $ 50 million of the redemption value per company. The entire procedure for buyback of FCCBs is required to be completed by December 31, 2009 and details of the buyback are also required to be reported to the Reserve Bank.

In terms of the extant norms, the Reserve Bank has been considering, under the approval route, proposals from Indian companies for buyback of FCCBs, out of internal accruals, up to US $ 50 million redemption value per company, at a minimum discount of 25 per cent on the book value. Up to April 15, 2009, the Reserve Bank has approved 18 proposals for buyback of FCCBs involving US $ 765 million with the discount ranging from 25 per cent to 50 per cent.

The current policy has been reviewed. Keeping in view the benefits accruing to Indian companies, it is proposed to increase the total amount of permissible buyback, out of internal accruals, from US$ 50 million of the redemption value per company to US $ 100 million, by linking the higher amount of buyback to larger discounts. Accordingly:

- Indian companies may, henceforth, be permitted, under the approval route, to buy back FCCBs out of internal accruals with a minimum discount of 25 per cent of book value for redemption amount of up to US $ 50 million, 35 per cent of book value for redemption amount more than US $ 50 million and up to 75 million; and 50 per cent of book value for redemption amount more than US $ 75 million and up to US $ 100 million.

(c) Loans against Non-resident Deposits

As per the extant norms, Authorised Dealer Category–I and authorised banks are permitted to grant loans up to Rs.20 lakh against the security of funds held in NR(E)RA and FCNR(B) deposits. On a review, it is proposed:

- to enhance the cap of Rs.20 lakh to Rs.1 crore with immediate effect.

(d) Currency Futures

Since the launch of the first currency futures exchange in September 2008, currency futures contracts are being traded in three recognised exchanges. The average daily volume of currency futures contracts traded on all the exchanges increased from Rs.260 crore in September 2008 to Rs.2,181 crore in December 2008 and further to Rs.5,235 crore in March 2009. The functioning of the exchanges continues to be reviewed by the RBI-SEBI Standing Technical Committee. On the recommendation of the Committee, the position limits on the clients and trading members have been doubled from US $ 5 million and US $ 25 million respectively to US $ 10 million and US $ 50 million. However, the upper limits of 6 per cent and 15 per cent of the total open interest on the clients and trading members remain unchanged. The position limit for banks continues at 15 per cent of total open interest or US $ 100 million, whichever is higher.

CREDIT DELIVERY MECHANISM AND OTHER BANKING SERVICES

(a) Credit Flow to the MSE Sector

As indicated in the Mid-Term Review of October 2008, the Reserve Bank appointed a Working Group on Rehabilitation of Sick SMEs (Chairman: Dr. K.C. Chakrabarty). The Working Group made several significant recommendations pertaining not only to the issue of rehabilitation of sick SMEs but also to the larger issues of credit flow to the SME sector and other developmental issues. While the recommendations on which action is to be initiated by the Government of India, State Governments and SIDBI are being forwarded to them, it is proposed:

- to issue guidelines to banks based on the recommendations of the Group, by April 30, 2009.

Having regard to the need to accelerate the credit flow to the micro and small enterprises (MSEs) sector so critical for employment, output and exports, it is proposed:

- to ask the Standing Advisory Committee on MSEs to review the Credit Guarantee Scheme so as to make it more effective.

(b) Rural Co-operative Banks

(i) Licensing of Co-operatives

The Committee on Financial Sector Assessment (Chairman: Dr. Rakesh Mohan and Co-Chairman: Shri Ashok Chawla) has observed that there is a need to draw up a roadmap for ensuring that only licensed banks operate in the co-operative space. The Committee further suggested the need for a roadmap to ensure that banks which fail to obtain a licence by 2012 should not be allowed to operate. This will expedite the process of consolidation and weeding out of non-viable entities from the co-operative space. Accordingly, it is proposed:

- to work out a roadmap for achieving this objective in a non-disruptive manner in consultation with NABARD.

(ii) Revival of Rural Co-operative Credit Structure: Status

As indicated in the Annual Policy Statement of April 2008, the Government of India approved a package for revival of the short term rural co-operative credit structure based on the recommendations of the Task Force on Revival of Rural Co-operative Credit Institutions (Chairman: Prof. A. Vaidyanathan). So far, 25 States have executed Memoranda of Understanding (MoUs) with the Government of India and the NABARD, as envisaged in the package. Eight States have made necessary amendments in their Co-operative Societies Acts. An aggregate amount of Rs. 4,740 crore has been released by the NABARD as the Government of India's share for recapitalisation of primary agricultural credit societies (PACS) in eight States as on February 28, 2009. Eight State Governments have released their shares of Rs.459 crore for recapitalisation of PACS. The National Implementing and Monitoring Committee (NIMC), set up by the Government of India, is guiding and monitoring the implementation of the revival package on an all-India basis.

(c) Regional Rural Banks

(i) Capital to Risk-weighted Assets Ratio for RRBs

The Committee on Financial Sector Assessment (Chairman: Dr. Rakesh Mohan and Co-Chairman: Shri Ashok Chawla) has suggested a phased introduction of capital to risk-weighted assets ratio (CRAR) in the case of RRBs, along with the recapitalisation of RRBs after consolidation of these entities. It is, therefore, proposed:

- to introduce CRAR for RRBs in a phased manner, taking into account the status of recapitalisation and amalgamation. A time-table for this purpose would be announced in consultation with NABARD.

(ii) Assistance to RRBs for Adoption of ICT Solutions for Financial Inclusion: Status

The Report of the Working Group on Defraying Costs of ICT Solutions for Regional Rural Banks (Chairman: Shri G. Padmanabhan) was placed on the Reserve Bank's website in August 2008 for comments from public. The Group has, *inter alia,* noted that apart from the North-Eastern region and Jammu and Kashmir, there are 204 districts in several States which have been identified by the Committee on Financial Inclusion (Chairman: Dr. C. Rangarajan) as areas where there is a high level of financial exclusion. It is, therefore, suggested that these areas could also be considered for special treatment. With a view to enabling RRBs to adopt IT based solutions for financial inclusion, it is proposed:

- to work out, in consultation with NABARD, the manner of providing assistance to RRBs adopting ICT solutions for financial inclusion in districts identified as having high level of exclusion by the Committee on Financial Inclusion.

(iii) Amalgamation of RRBs

Consequent upon the amalgamation of 156 RRBs into 45 new RRBs sponsored by 20 banks in 17 States, the total number of RRBs declined from 196 to 86 as at end-March 2009 (which includes a new RRB set up in the Union Territory of Puducherry). The amalgamation process is almost complete.

(iv) Recapitalisation of RRBs

The Union Budget 2007-08 announced that RRBs, which have a negative net worth, would be recapitalised in a phased manner. As on March 31, 2009, 26 RRBs have been fully recapitalised with an amount of Rs. 1,783 crore and one RRB has been partially recapitalised with an amount of Rs.13 crore. The process of recapitalisation has been completed except in respect of one RRB in the State of Uttar Pradesh.

(v) Scheduling of Amalgamated RRBs

Out of 45 amalgamated RRBs, 25 RRBs have been included in the Second Schedule to the RBI Act, 1934 while 76 erstwhile RRBs have been excluded from the Second Schedule in terms of the notification dated September 22, 2008 published in the Gazette of India dated November 15, 2008.

(vi) Branch Licensing: Further Liberalisation

The Mid-Term Review of October 2008 proposed to allow RRBs greater flexibility in opening new branches as long as they made profits and their financials improved. The RRBs have obtained 345 licenses for opening branches in the financial year 2008-09 and have opened 316 branches in the same period.

(vii) Technology Upgradation of RRBs

As indicated in the Mid-Term Review of October 2008, the recommendation of the Working Group (Chairman: Shri G. Srinivasan) to prepare a roadmap for migration to core banking solutions (CBS) by RRBs, was forwarded to all sponsor banks in October 2008 for implementation. The Report has, among others, set September 2011 as the target date for all RRBs to move towards CBS. Also, all RRB branches opened after September 2009 are required to be CBS compliant from day one. In March 2009, sponsor banks were advised to give their feedback/status on implementation of the recommendations of the report in respect of RRBs sponsored by them.

(d) Delivery of Credit to Agriculture and other Segments of the Priority Sector

(i) Kisan Credit Card Scheme

The Kisan Credit Card (KCC) scheme, introduced in 1998-99 to enable farmers to purchase agricultural inputs and draw cash for their production needs, was revised to provide adequate and timely finance for meeting the comprehensive credit requirements of farmers under a single window, with flexible and simplified procedure, adopting a whole farm approach. During 2008-09 (up to December 2008), public sector banks (PSBs) issued 3.9 million KCCs with sanctioned limits aggregating Rs.23,366 crore. Since the inception of the scheme, PSBs have issued 35.08 million KCCs with sanctioned limits aggregating Rs.1,77,607 crore.

(ii) Rural Infrastructure Development Fund

The Interim Budget 2009-10 announced the continuation of financing of rural infrastructure projects for 2009-10 by way of RIDF XV which would be set up with NABARD with a corpus of Rs.14,000 crore, and a separate window under RIDF XV for rural roads component of Bharat Nirman Programme with a corpus of Rs.4,000 crore.

Consequent upon the announcement made in the Union Budget 2008-09, several funds were set up such as: (i) Short-Term Co-operative Rural Credit (STCRC) (Refinance) Fund with the

NABARD with a corpus of Rs.5,000 crore; (ii) MSME (Refinance) Fund and MSME (Risk Capital) Fund with the Small Industries Development Bank of India (SIDBI) with corpus of Rs.1,600 crore and Rs.1,000 crore; and (iii) Rural Housing Fund with the National Housing Bank (NHB) with corpus of Rs.1,000 crore. The Annual Policy Statement of April 2008 announced that the shortfall in achievement of 10 per cent sub-target for lending to weaker sections by domestic scheduled commercial banks will also be taken into account for the purpose of allocating amounts for contribution to the Rural Infrastructure Development Fund (RIDF) maintained with the NABARD or funds with other financial institutions, as specified by the Reserve Bank, with effect from April 2009.

Consequent upon the announcement of measures by the Reserve Bank on November 15, 2008 to sustain the growth momentum in the employment-intensive sectors of micro and small enterprises and housing, the corpus of MSME (Refinance) Fund and Rural Housing Fund was enhanced by Rs.2,000 crore (to Rs.3,600 crore) and by Rs.1,000 crore (to Rs.2,000 crore) respectively. As on March 31, 2009 various scheduled commercial banks have placed deposits of Rs.4,622 crore in STCRC (Refinance) Fund, Rs.3,326 crore in MSME (Refinance) Fund, Rs.250 crore in MSME (Risk Capital) Fund and Rs.1,760 crore in Rural Housing Fund.

(e) Interest Subvention Relief to Farmers

The Union Budget 2008-09 announced continuation of the interest subvention scheme for short-term crop loans, introduced in 2006-07. The rate of subvention was increased from 2 per cent to 3 per cent for 2008-09. The Interim Budget 2009-10 announced that the Government of India would also continue to provide interest subvention in 2009-10 to ensure that farmers get short-term crop loans up to Rs.3 lakh at 7.0 per cent per annum.

(f) Micro-finance

The self-help group (SHG)-bank linkage programme has emerged as the major micro-finance programme in the country and is being implemented by commercial banks, RRBs and co-operative banks. As on March 31, 2008 3.6 million SHGs had outstanding bank loans of Rs.17,000 crore, an increase of 25 per cent over March 31, 2007 in respect of number of SHGs credit linked. During 2007-08, banks financed 1.2 million SHGs for Rs.8,849 crore. As at end-March 2008, SHGs had 5 million savings accounts with banks for Rs.3,785 crore.

(g) Financial Inclusion

(i) Pilot Project of State Level Bankers' Committee (SLBCs) for 100 per cent Financial Inclusion

So far, 344 districts have been identified by SLBCs for 100 per cent financial inclusion. Of these, 175 districts in 21 States and 7 Union Territories have reported having achieved the target. All districts of Haryana, Himachal Pradesh, Karnataka, Kerala, Uttarakhand, Goa, Chandigarh, Puducherry, Daman & Diu, Dadra & Nagar Haveli and Lakshadweep have reported having achieved the target of 100 per cent financial inclusion. As indicated in the Mid-Term Review of October 2008, the findings of the external agencies entrusted with conducting evaluation studies in achieving the target of 100 per cent financial inclusion in 26 districts were placed on the Reserve Bank's website for wider dissemination. Based on the findings, banks were advised in January 2009, among other things, to (i) ensure provision of banking services nearer to the location of the no-frills account holders through a variety of channels; (ii) provide General Credit Card (GCC)/small overdrafts along with no-frills accounts to encourage the account holders to actively operate the accounts; (iii) conduct awareness drives so that the no-frills account holders were made aware of the facilities offered; (iv) review the extent of coverage in districts declared as 100 per cent financially included; and (v) efficiently leverage on the technology enabled financial inclusion solutions currently available.

(ii) Special Task Force in North-Eastern Region

As indicated in the Mid-Term Review of October 2008, a scheme of providing financial support to banks by the Reserve Bank for setting up banking facilities (currency chests, extension of foreign exchange and Government business facilities) at centres, in the North-Eastern region (NER), which are not found to be commercially viable by banks, was formulated, provided the State Governments made available necessary premises and other infrastructural support. The Government of Meghalaya has agreed to the proposal of providing premises and security, and bids have been received by PSBs and RRBs for setting up branches at centres identified by the State Government and are being processed. Action is being intitiated in respect of other States in NER where requests have been received.

(iii) Setting up of Credit Counselling Centres on a Pilot Basis

So far, banks have reported setting up or proposing to set up 123 credit counselling centres in various States of the country. The feedback received in this regard indicated that most of these centres were in effect set up as extensions of the bank branches and engaged in promotion of bank specific products. Accordingly, a model scheme on financial literacy and credit counselling centres (FLCCs) was formulated and communicated to all scheduled commercial banks and RRBs with the advice to set up the centres as distinct entities maintaining an arm's length from the bank so that the FLCC's services are available to even other banks' customers in the district.

(iv) Setting up of Rural Self Employment Training Institutes

The Reserve Bank has issued guidelines, framed by the Government of India, to the SLBC convenor banks to set up at least one Rural Self Employment Training Institute (RSETI) in each district by 2010. These institutions will train at least one youth in a family below poverty line (BPL) in various fields and enhance capacity building. In all, 134 RSETIs have been set up as on December 31, 2008. A target for opening of 100 RSETIs by banks was set for the year 2008-09 and a grant of Rs. one crore per RSETI has been earmarked by the Planning Commission for setting up the institutes. The Regional Offices of the Reserve Bank have been advised to monitor the progress of setting up of RSETIs under their jurisdiction on a quarterly basis.

(h) High Level Committee on Lead Bank Scheme

As announced in the Mid-Term Review of the Annual Policy Statement for the year 2007-08, a High Level Committee (Chairperson: Smt. Usha Thorat) with members drawn from various financial institutions, banks and Chief Secretaries of select States was constituted to review the Lead Bank Scheme. The Committee had several rounds of discussions with different State Governments, banks and other stakeholders, including academicians, micro-finance institutions (MFIs) and non-governmental organisations (NGOs). The Committee's draft report will be placed on the Reserve Bank's website by May 15, 2009.

(i) Amendment to Banking Ombudsman Scheme 2006

The scope of the Banking Ombudsman Scheme, 2006 was widened to include, *inter alia*, deficiencies arising out of internet banking. Under the amended Scheme, customers can lodge complaints against banks for non-adherence to the provisions of the fair practices code for lenders or the code of bank's commitment to customers issued by the Banking Codes and Standards Board of India (BCSBI).

PRUDENTIAL MEASURES

(a) Further Relaxations in the Branch Authorisation Policy

The current branch authorisation policy requires banks to have a medium term plan in respect of branch expansion. The request for opening of off-site ATMs was also required to be a part of such plans. On a review, it is proposed:

- to allow scheduled commercial banks (SCBs) to set up offsite ATMs without prior approval subject to reporting.

With respect to branch authorisation policy, it is proposed:

- to constitute a Group to review the extant framework of branch authorisation policy with a view to providing greater flexibility, enhanced penetration and competitive efficiency consistent with financial stability.

(b) Presence of Foreign Banks in India: Review

In February 2005, the Government of India and the Reserve Bank released the 'Roadmap for Presence of Foreign Banks in India' laying out a two-track and gradualist approach aimed at increasing the efficiency and stability of the banking sector in India. One track was the consolidation of the domestic banking system, both in private and public sectors, and the second track was the gradual enhancement of the presence of foreign banks in a synchronised manner.

The roadmap was divided into two phases, the first phase spanning the period March 2005 - March 2009, and the second phase beginning April 2009 after a review of the experience gained in the first phase. In view of the current global financial market turmoil, there are uncertainties surrounding the financial strength of banks around the world. Further, the regulatory and supervisory policies at national and international levels are under review. In view of this, it is considered advisable, for the time being, to continue with the current policy and procedures governing the presence of foreign banks in India. The proposed review will be taken up after due consultation with the stakeholders once there is greater clarity regarding stability, recovery of the global financial system, and a shared understanding on the regulatory and supervisory architecture around the world.

(c) Mitigating Procyclicality: Use of Floating Provisions

The G-20 Working Group on Enhancing Sound Regulation and Strengthening Transparency has recommended, as a part of measures to mitigate procyclicality, that capital buffers above minimum requirements and loan loss provisions should be built up in good times in order to enhance the ability of the regulated financial institutions to withstand large shocks. This would require modification in the Reserve Bank's circular of June 22, 2006. The Reserve Bank has been encouraging banks to build floating provisions as a buffer for the possible stress on asset quality later. It is proposed:

- to issue further detailed guidelines on mitigating procyclicality later this year after FSB, BCBS and Committee on Global Financial System (CGFS) finalise their recommendations in this regard.

(d) Credit Rating Agencies

In India, all credit rating agencies are registered with the SEBI. The Reserve Bank has accorded accreditation to four SEBI registered credit rating agencies for the limited purpose of using their ratings for assigning risk weights within the framework of the Basel II Accord. Since the Indian banking system has migrated to the Basel II framework, there is a need to review the performance of the credit rating agencies for continuation of the accreditation, especially by looking at the latest data relating to cumulative default rate and transition matrix of the rating agencies. Accordingly:

- the Reserve Bank will liaise with SEBI on the issue of rating agencies' adherence to Code of Conduct Fundamentals of the International Organisation Securities Commissions (IOSCO).

(e) Liquidity Risk

In terms of the asset liability management, liquidity of banks in India is tracked through traditional maturity or cash flow mismatches. The Reserve Bank has examined the issue of banks establishing a more robust liquidity risk management framework that is well integrated into the bank-wide risk management process by adopting global liquidity planning. In this context, banks will be required to integrate their various foreign currency assets and liabilities positions from their branch operations in India with the rupee asset liability position. Accordingly, it is proposed:

- to prepare a draft circular detailing the modalities for adopting the integrated liquidity risk management system as also the guidance note on 'Liquidity Risk Management' based on Basel Committee's 'Principles for Sound Liquidity Risk Management and Supervision' brought out in September 2008 as well as other international best practices which would be placed on the Reserve Bank's website by June 15, 2009.

(f) Financial Inclusion: Relaxing Eligibility Criteria for Banking Correspondents

With the objective of achieving greater financial inclusion and increasing the outreach of the banking sector, banks were permitted, to use the services of NGOs/MFIs set up as societies, trusts, Section 25 companies, post offices, co-operative societies and more recently retired bank employees, ex-servicemen and retired government employees as banking correspondents (BCs). Scaling up the BC model is a challenge. It is, therefore, proposed:

- to constitute a Working Group to examine the experience to date of the business correspondent (BC) model and suggest measures, to enlarge the category of persons that can act as BCs, keeping in view the regulatory and supervisory framework and consumer protection issues.
- to increase the maximum distance criterion for the operation of the BC for rural, semi-urban and urban areas from the existing 15 kms. to 30 kms.

(g) Risk Weights for Exposure to Central Counterparties

A central counterparty (CCP) is an entity that interposes itself between counterparties to contracts traded within one or more financial markets, becoming the legal counterparty such that it is the buyer to every seller and the seller to every buyer. The CCIL has been acting as a CCP for banks in various segments of the financial market. Similarly, contracts like interest rate futures and currency futures, which are traded on the stock exchanges, are also settled through the clearing houses attached to these exchanges.

Banks settling trades through CCIL/stock exchanges have two types of exposures to these CCPs. First, on account of the on-balance sheet and off-balance sheet transactions undertaken through the CCP; and second, the exposure on account of deposits/collateral kept with the CCPs to meet the margin requirements. It has been decided to lay down the norms for capital adequacy treatment of such exposures. Accordingly:

- the exposures on account of derivatives/securities financing transactions trades outstanding against all the CCPs, will be assigned zero exposure value, as it is presumed that the CCPs' exposures to their counterparties are fully collateralised on a daily basis, thereby providing protection for the central counterparty's credit risk exposures;

- the margin amounts/collaterals maintained with the CCPs will attract risk weights appropriate to the nature of the CCP. For CCIL, the risk weight will be 20 per cent and for other CCPs, it will be according to the ratings assigned to these entities as per the New Capital Adequacy Framework.

- the above prescription will be subject to review on an on-going basis by the Reserve Bank about the adequacy of margin, quality of collateral and risk management systems of the clearing house/CCP.

(h) Private Pool of Capital

It has been observed that Indian banks have recently been engaged in sponsoring and managing private pools of capital such as venture capital funds and infrastructure funds. The G-30 Report on 'Financial Reform – A Framework for Financial Stability' released on January 15, 2009, observed that large, systemically important banking institutions should be restricted in undertaking proprietary activities that present particularly high risks and serious conflicts of interest. Sponsorship and management of commingled private pools of capital (that is, hedge and private equity funds in which the banking institutions own capital is commingled with client funds) should ordinarily be prohibited and large proprietary trading should be limited by strict capital and liquidity requirements. Therefore, there is need for banks to have greater awareness of the risks inherent in such activities and limit such exposures commensurate with their risk management and available capital. Keeping in view the reputational risk involved in such activities, the Reserve Bank had mandated maintenance of certain level of economic capital in some of the cases approved in the recent past. It is now proposed:

- to issue a paper on prudential issues in banks' floating and managing private pools of capital for eliciting public comments which will form the basis for finalising regulatory guidelines by September 30, 2009.

(i) Stress Testing

In the Mid-Term Review of October 2008, it was indicated that the Reserve Bank would be upgrading the stress testing guidelines. Subsequently, the BCBS has issued a paper on 'Principles for Sound Stress Testing Practices and Supervision' in January 2009 for comments. The paper draws lessons for banks and supervisors emerging from the financial crisis and addresses weaknesses in stress testing, including the specific areas of risk mitigation and risk transfer. In this context, the CFSA has recommended that there is a need for the banks themselves to carry out such periodic stress testing. It is proposed to upgrade the stress testing guidelines once BCBS finalises the paper based on comments received.

(j) Securitisation of Bank Loans

The securitisation framework in India is considered to be reasonably prudent and has been able to minimise the incentives that have led to the problems which surfaced in the current crisis.

It has come to the Reserve Bank's notice that some banks have securitised loans immediately after originating or purchasing these from other banks. Banks are also dividing the total loan for one project into different tranches and securitising a few tranches even before the total disbursement is complete, thus passing on the project implementation risk also to the investors. It is, therefore, proposed:

- to prescribe a minimum lock-in-period and minimum retention criteria for securitising the loans originated and purchased by banks.

(k) Certificate of Registration to Credit Information Companies

In response to the Reserve Bank's press release of April 18, 2007 inviting applications for grant of Certificate of Registration from companies desirous of entering into the business of credit information under the Credit Information Companies (Regulation) Act, 2005, 13 applications were received. A High Level Advisory Committee (Chairman: Dr. R.H. Patil) set up by the Reserve Bank screened the applications and recommended the names of four applicants for issue of Certificate of Registration. Accordingly, 'in principle' approvals have been issued to these four applicants.

INSTITUTIONAL DEVELOPMENTS

Payment and Settlement Systems

(a) Final Guidelines for Prepaid Payment Instruments in India

The enactment of the Payment and Settlement Systems Act, 2007 has brought the payment systems involved in the issuance of prepaid payment instruments under the regulatory jurisdiction of the Reserve Bank. The Reserve Bank had earlier placed the draft guidelines for issuance/ operation of such instruments in public domain for wider dissemination and feedback. Taking into account the comments received from various entities within and outside the country, it is now proposed:

- to permit SCBs which comply with the eligibility criteria to issue all categories of prepaid payment instruments;
- eligible non-bank entities, including NBFCs, will be permitted to issue semi-closed instruments, which can be used to purchase all types of goods and services at an identified network of establishments.

The operating guidelines in this regard are being issued separately.

(b) Consolidation of Information Technology Systems: Data Centres

The Reserve Bank has set up data centres which were made operational in the second half of 2008. The state-of-the-art data centres provide for a high level of availability of information technology (IT) systems and ensure optimum business continuity management. The critical payment and settlement systems of the Reserve Bank are now operated using the systems at the data centres. Adequate disaster recovery drills are conducted at periodic intervals. While all participating member banks have been able to ensure full participation in these drills by operating from their disaster recovery (DR) sites, there are a few banks which have not been able to meet this objective. In view of the critical importance of such drills and in order to achieve overall systemic efficiency:

- banks are urged to ensure full compliance of these requirements.

(c) Adequacy of the Fallback Arrangements for Managed IT Systems

Currently, a number of banks have resorted to the retention of service providers to manage their IT-based operational requirements. It has, therefore, become imperative that banks have adequate plans/systems in place so as to manage risks arising out of such outsourcing arrangements. These risks arise on account of excessive dependence by the system on a single entity (concentration risk), inadequate systems (operational risks) as also on account of failure of these service providers. The Reserve Bank has already issued comprehensive outsourcing guidelines in November 2006. The risk management aspects detailed therein are of particular relevance to a technology service provider. Hence, it is proposed that:

- banks should undertake a comprehensive review of all such outsourced arrangements including on-site inspections of critical service providers and ensure that adequate fallback arrangements are put in place.

(d) Network Based Operations: RBI Supported Systems"

The Reserve Bank has taken steps to make the application systems [NDS, real time gross settlement (RTGS), centralised funds management system (CFMS) and structured financial messaging solution (SFMS)] provided by it to operate in an network based environment using the Multi Protocol Label Switching (MPLS). The MPLS approach by using a meshed network topology provides increased redundancies *vis-a-vis* a point to point connectivity at cheaper costs without impacting the security aspects. Accordingly:

- banks are advised to migrate to the MPLS system on a time bound basis.

(e) Recent Developments

(i) Electronic Payment Systems

The coverage of bank branches under the electronic payment network, *viz.*, the RTGS and the National Electronic Funds Transfer (NEFT) has increased significantly. While the NEFT network has increased to 54,200 branches at end-March 2009, the RTGS network has increased to 55,000 branches. The RTGS handles, on an average, 80,000 transactions per day, with a peak of 1,28,295 transactions processed as on March 30, 2009.

(ii) National Electronic Clearing Service

The volume of transactions through national electronic clearing service (NECS), introduced in September 2008, is also increasing. With a view to moving towards the centralised NECS system, the electronic clearing service (ECS) (credit) in Mumbai has been merged with the NECS. As such no separate local ECS clearing is operative in Mumbai.

(iii) National Financial Switch

The national financial switch (NFS) membership/volume is steadily on the increase. As on March 31, 2009 the NFS network covered a total of 38,714 automated teller machines (ATMs) of 34 banks. On an average, a daily volume of 8,90,180 transactions (of which 2,56,156 transactions pertained to balance enquiry and 6,34,024 pertained to cash withdrawal) were routed through the NFS in March 2009 as against a daily volume of 2,67,598 transactions in March 2008. Furthermore, on an average, the daily value settled through the NFS was around Rs.45 crore in March 2009 as against Rs.26 crore in March 2008. Since April 1, 2009 customers have the facility of using ATM of any bank for cash withdrawal, free of cost, thereby making ATMs national payment outlets rather than bank-specific outlets. This measure has seen a surge in transactions in the NFS network with a peak of 1.1 million transactions on a single day on April 11, 2009.

(iv) Mobile Payments

As indicated in the Mid-Term Review of October 2008, the operative guidelines for mobile payments were issued on October 8, 2008. So far, 19 banks have obtained permission from the Reserve Bank to provide mobile payment facilities to their customers.

(v) Rationalisation of Charges for Payment Systems

The Reserve Bank has rationalised various charges for payment systems. Accordingly, service charges levied for transfer of funds under outward RTGS transactions shall not exceed Rs.25 for transactions of Rs.1 lakh and up to Rs.5 lakh, and Rs.50 for transactions of Rs.5 lakh and above. Similarly, for outward NEFT transactions, service charges levied shall not exceed Rs.5 for transfer of funds up to Rs.1 lakh and Rs.25 for transactions of Rs.1 lakh and above.

The Reserve Bank has also prescribed maximum charges which could be levied for collection of outstation cheques under which the service charges would not exceed Rs.50 for cheque value up to Rs.10,000. A maximum charge of Rs.100 would be levied for cheque value of Rs.10,000 – Rs.100,000. The service charge would not exceed Rs.150 of cheque value Rs.100,001 and above.

(vi) Cheque Truncation System

The cheque truncation system (CTS) pilot project was operationalised in Delhi in February 2008 and more than 90 per cent of the cheque volume of Delhi clearing house is now processed through the CTS. The Reserve Bank continues to take steps towards extending the CTS across the country and accordingly, it has been decided to set up the CTS in Chennai.

(f) The Payment and Settlement Systems Act, 2007

As indicated in the Mid-Term Review of October 2008, the process of issuing authorisation to persons to operate various payment systems has commenced following the notification of the Payment and Settlement Systems Act, 2007 in August 2008. In terms of the Act, all payment system providers/operators including credit card issuing companies and entities engaged in money transfer activity would require authorisation.

Urban Co-operative Banks

(a) Area of Operations of UCBs

In order to facilitate the growth of well-functioning urban co-operative banks (UCBs) in States, which enter into Memorandum of Understanding (MoU), it is proposed:

- to permit extension of area of operation of Tier II UCBs in Grade I to the entire State of registration with the prior approval of the Reserve Bank.

(b) Review of Regulatory and Supervisory Framework: UCBs

UCBs are presently on Basel I capital framework with surrogate (additional risk-weight) capital charge on market risks. The Advisory Panel on Financial Regulation and Supervision to the Committee on Financial Sector Assessment (Chairman: Dr. Rakesh Mohan and Co-Chairman: Shri Ashok Chawla), which looked into the present regulatory and supervisory framework for UCBs, has observed that it would be premature for full migration of UCBs to Basel II at this juncture.

However, it recommended assigning duration based capital charge for market risk for scheduled UCBs that are systemically important and comparable in size to medium-sized commercial banks. Furthermore, the Panelrecommended: (i) a review of the existing internal control systems, risk management systems, asset liability management (ALM) and disclosure norms for UCBs; and (ii) the issue of appropriate guidelines. Accordingly, it is proposed:

- to review the existing instructions and issue appropriate guidelines to UCBs on internal controls, risk management systems, ALM and disclosure norms;
- to apply capital charge for market risks in respect of large-sized and systemically important UCBs with effect from April 1, 2010.

(c) Vision Document for UCBs

The Vision Document for UCBs envisaged signing of MoU with the State and Central Governments for harmonisation of dual regulation and supervision of UCBs and setting up of Task Force on Urban Co-operative Banks (TAFCUB) for identification of viable UCBs for their rehabilitation and non-viable UCBs for their non-disruptive exit.

Subsequent to the release of the Vision Document in public domain in March 2005, the Reserve Bank has entered into MoUs with 25 State Governments (nine entered during April 2008 to March 2009). As of date, 99 per cent of UCBs and 99 per cent of deposits of the UCB sector are covered under MoU arrangements.

The number of UCBs in Grade III and IV, signifying various degrees of sickness, has since declined to 496 as on March 31, 2008 from 725 as on March 31, 2005. Till March 31, 2009 licences had been cancelled or rejected in respect of 85 banks and 31 unlicensed banks in MoU States have been issued banking licences. Since the recommencement of new branch authorisation, 232 licences have been issued for opening of branches by UCBs in MoU States. The initiatives for voluntary mergers and amalgamations of weak UCBs for bringing consolidation in the sector were also carried forward and new policy guidelines on mergers were announced. Sixty-eight mergers between healthy and weak banks have been effected so far. In view of the improved financial condition and enhanced regulatory and supervisory jurisdiction of the Reserve Bank, additional business opportunities were opened up for well-functioning multi-state UCBs and UCBs in MoU States.

(d) Information Technology Support to UCBs

Based on the recommendations of the Working Group which looked into ways of supporting IT initiatives of the UCBs, IDRBT is being asked to facilitate UCBs availing of Core Banking Platform on an Application Service Provider (ASP) model. With this, the UCBs will be able to put in place cost-effective, modern technology so as to render better customer service and sound regulatory compliance.

Non-Banking Financial Companies

(a) CRAR for NBFCs-ND-SI

The Mid-Term Review of October 2008 had indicated that the CRAR for NBFCs-ND-SI would be raised from 10 per cent to 12 per cent by March 31, 2009 and further to 15 per cent by March 31, 2010. Taking into account the difficulty in raising equity capital in the current economic environment, it has been decided:

- to defer the implementation of CRAR of 12 per cent to March 31, 2010 and of 15 per cent to March 31, 2011.

(b) Time-frame for Realisation of Assets by Securitisation Companies/Reconstruction Companies

In terms of the extant guidelines, securitisation companies (SCs)/ reconstruction companies (RCs) are required to realise the financial assets within a specified time-frame, which shall not in any case exceed five years from the date of acquisition of financial assets. Requests for extending the time frame in this regard are being examined. As an *interim* measure, it is proposed:

- to give an extension of two more years for realisation of the assets in respect of the security receipts (SRs) issued by SCs/RCs which have completed five years.

(c) Repossession of Vehicles by NBFCs

The issue of repossession of vehicles in the event of non-payment of interest and/or principal of loans given by NBFCs has recently come into focus, and some courts have also ruled in this regard. The Reserve Bank has already advised NBFCs to put in place a Fair Practices Code with the approval of their boards which, *inter alia,* covers recovery of loans. The issue has been discussed with the industry participants and in view of certain queries raised, it is further clarified that:

- NBFCs must have a built-in re-possession clause in the contract/loan agreement with the borrower which must be legally enforceable. To ensure transparency, the terms and conditions of the contract/loan agreement should contain detailed provisions in this regard.

A circular to NBFCs to this effect is being issued separately.

(d) Special Liquidity Facility for Eligible NBFCs-ND-SI

The Central Government had announced an arrangement for providing liquidity support to eligible NBFCs-ND-SI for meeting the temporary liquidity mismatches through the Industrial Development Bank of India Stressed Asset Stabilisation Fund (IDBI SASF) Trust, which has been notified as special purpose vehicle for undertaking this operation. The facility is meant exclusively for meeting the temporary liquidity mismatches of the NBFCs and not for asset growth. The facility was available for eligible paper issued by NBFCs up to March 31, 2009 with an overall ceiling of Rs.20,000 crore, which was subsequently extended for eligible paper for a further period of three months till June 30, 2009. The facility has been availed to the extent of Rs.750 crore till date.

Policy Measures by the Reserve Bank of India: September 2008 Onwards

September 2008

- A firm assurance to meet any demand-supply gaps of foreign exchange in the domestic foreign exchange market.

- A second LAF was re-introduced on a daily basis.
- Interest rate ceilings on FCNR(B) and NR(E)RA deposits were increased by 50 basis points each to LIBOR/swap rates minus 25 basis points and LIBOR/swap rates plus 50 basis points respectively.
- As a temporary measure, scheduled banks were allowed to avail of additional liquidity support under the LAF to the extent of up to one per cent of their net demand and time liabilities from their SLR portfolio and seek waiver of penal interest.

October 2008

- The CRR was reduced by 250 basis points from 9.0 per cent to 6.5 per cent effective from the fortnight beginning October 11, 2008.
- A 14-day special repo facility for a notified amount of Rs.20,000 crore was instituted to alleviate liquidity stress faced by mutual funds, and banks were allowed temporary use of SLR securities for collateral purposes by an additional 0.5 per cent of NDTL exclusively for this purpose.
- Commercial banks and all-India term lending and refinancing institutions were allowed to lend against and buy back certificates of deposit (CDs) held by mutual funds.
- The Reserve Bank temporarily provided a sum of Rs.25,000 crore as the first instalment under the Agricultural Debt Waiver and Debt Relief Scheme to scheduled banks and NABARD immediately, pending Parliamentary sanction and consequent release of funds by the Central Government.
- Interest rate ceilings on FCNR(B) and NR(E)RA deposits were increased further by 50 basis points each to LIBOR/swap rates plus 25 basis points and LIBOR/swap rates plus 100 basis points respectively.
- Banks were permitted to borrow funds from their overseas branches and correspondent banks to the extent of 50 per cent of their unimpaired Tier-I capital or US $ 10 million, whichever is higher.
- The Reserve Bank announced that it would institute special market operations to meet the foreign exchange requirements of public sector oil marketing companies against oil bonds when they become available.
- On October 20, 2008 the repo rate under the LAF was reduced by 100 basis points to 8.0 per cent.
- The systemically important non-deposit taking non-banking financial companies (NBFCs-ND-SI) were permitted to raise short-term foreign currency borrowings.
- External commercial borrowings (ECBs) up to US $ 500 million per borrower per financial year were permitted for rupee expenditure and/or foreign currency expenditure for

permissible end-uses under the automatic route. Further, the all-in-cost ceiling for ECBs of average maturity period of three years and up to five years was raised to 300 basis points, and over five years, to 500 basis points above 6-month LIBOR.

November 2008

- The repo rate under the LAF was reduced by 50 basis points to 7.5 per cent with effect from November 3, 2008.
- The CRR was reduced by 100 basis points from 6.5 per cent to 5.5 per cent of NDTL.
- The statutory liquidity ratio (SLR), which was relaxed on a temporary basis earlier, was made permanent and reduced to 24 per cent of NDTL effective November 8, 2008.
- In order to provide further liquidity comfort, a special refinance facility for scheduled commercial banks (excluding RRBs) up to 1.0 per cent of each bank's NDTL as on October 24, 2008 was introduced under Section 17(3B) of the Reserve Bank of India Act, 1934 up to a maximum period of 90 days.
- On October 15, 2008 the Reserve Bank introduced a 14-day special repo facility allowing banks to avail additional liquidity support exclusively for the purpose of meeting the liquidity requirements of mutual funds to the extent of 0.5 per cent of their NDTL. Subsequently, this facility was extended for NBFCs and the relaxation in the maintenance of the SLR was enhanced to the extent of up to 1.5 per cent of their NDTL.
- Buy-back of MSS dated securities was announced to provide another avenue for injecting liquidity to be calibrated with the market borrowing programme of the Government of India.
- The special term repo facility introduced for the purpose of meeting the liquidity requirements of MFs and NBFCs, was extended till end-March 2009. Banks can avail of this facility either on an incremental basis or on a rollover basis within the entitlement of up to 1.5 per cent of their NDTL.
- Interest rate ceilings on FCNR(B) and NR(E)RA deposits were further raised by 75 basis points each to LIBOR/swap rates plus 100 basis points and LIBOR/swap rates plus 175 basis points respectively.
- Housing finance companies (HFCs) registered with the National Housing Bank (NHB) were permitted to raise short-term foreign currency borrowings under the approval route.
- The Reserve Bank permitted Indian corporates to prematurely buy back their FCCBs at prevailing discounted rates.
- The period of entitlement of the first slab of pre-shipment rupee export credit was extended from 180 days to 270 days.

- The aggregate limit of export credit refinance (ECR) facility for scheduled banks (excluding RRBs) was enhanced from 15 per cent to 50 per cent of the outstanding export credit eligible for refinance.
- SIDBI and the NHB were allocated Rs. 2000 crore and Rs.1000 crore respectively against banks' estimated shortfall in priority sector lending in March 2009.
- Banks were encouraged to use the special refinance facility under Section 17(3B) of the Reserve Bank of India Act, 1934 for the purpose of lending to micro and small enterprises.
- The provisioning requirements for all types of standard assets were reduced to a uniform level of 0.40 per cent, except in the case of direct advances to the agricultural and SME sectors which continue to attract provisioning of 0.25 per cent, as hitherto.
- Risk weights on banks' exposures to all unrated claims on corporates, claims secured by commercial real estate and claims on NBFCs-ND-SI were reduced to 100 per cent from 150 per cent.
- The special refinance facility under Section 17(3B) of the Reserve Bank of India Act, 1934 introduced on November 1, 2008 was extended up to June 30, 2009.
- The special term repo facility was expanded to enable banks to accommodate the funding needs of HFCs. The facility was extended up to June 30, 2009.
- On November 7, 2008 Indian public and private sector banks that have foreign branches or subsidiaries were provided a forex swap facility of tenor up to three months with the Reserve Bank. Further, for funding the swap, banks were allowed to borrow under the LAF for the corresponding tenor at the prevailing repo rate. This facility was subsequently extended up to June 30, 2009.
- The period of entitlement of the first slab of post-shipment rupee export credit was extended from 90 days to 180 days.

December 2008

- The repo rate under the LAF was reduced by 100 basis points from 7.5 per cent to 6.5 per cent and the reverse repo rate by 100 basis points from 6.0 per cent to 5.0 per cent, effective December 8, 2008.
- A refinance facility was introduced for SIDBI, NHB and EXIM Bank for Rs. 7,000 crore, Rs.4,000 crore and Rs.5,000 crore respectively. This facility will be available up to March 31, 2010.
- Authorised Dealers Category-I banks were permitted to consider applications for premature buy-back of FCCBs from their customers.
- Loans granted by banks to HFCs for on-lending for housing up to Rs.20 lakh per dwelling unit were classified under priority sector.

- Commercial real estate exposures restructured up to June 30, 2009 were allowed to be treated as standard assets. As a one-time measure, the second restructuring done by banks of exposures (other than exposures to commercial real estate, capital market exposures and personal/consumer loans) up to June 30, 2009 was also made eligible for concessional regulatory treatment.
- The prescribed interest rate as applicable to post-shipment rupee export credit (not exceeding BPLR minus 2.5 percentage points) was extended to overdue bills up to 180 days.

January 2009

- The repo rate under the LAF was reduced by 100 basis points from 6.5 per cent to 5.5 per cent with effect from January 5, 2009.
- The reverse repo rate under the LAF was reduced by 100 basis points from 5.0 per cent to 4.0 per cent with effect from January 5, 2009.
- The CRR was reduced from 5.5 per cent to 5.0 per cent of NDTL effective from the fortnight beginning January 17, 2009.
- In order to address the temporary liquidity constraints of systemically important non-deposit taking non-banking financial companies (NBFCs-ND-SI), the Government announced the setting up of a special purpose vehicle (SPV). According to the scheme announced, the SPV was allowed to mobilise resources through issuance of government guaranteed securities for investment in CPs and NCDs of NBFCs-ND-SI. Government guaranteed securities were required to be purchased by the Reserve Bank. The SPV was to ensure that the NBFCs used the money only for addressing liquidity constraints and not for business expansion. The total support from the Reserve Bank was limited to Rs.20,000 crore with an option to raise it by a further Rs.5,000 crore.
- The special term repo facility under LAF for the purpose of meeting the funding requirements of MFs, NBFCs and HFCs was extended up to September 30, 2009.
- The special refinance facility for scheduled commercial banks under Section 17 (3B) of the RBI Act, 1934 was extended up to September 30, 2009.
- The all-in-cost ceiling for ECBs through the approval route has been dispensed with up to June 30, 2009.

February 2009

- The Forex Swap facility was extended till March 31, 2010.
- Banks were allowed to apply special regulatory treatment for accounts which were standard on September 1, 2008 and taken up for restructuring up to January 31, 2009

even if these had turned non-performing along this period. Subsequently, the time schedule for taking up restructuring was extended up to March 31, 2009.

- The ceiling rate on export credit in foreign currency was raised from LIBOR + 100 basis points to LIBOR + 350 basis points on February 5, 2009 subject to the condition that the banks would not levy any other charges.
- Correspondingly, the ceiling interest rate on the lines of credit with overseas banks was also increased from 6 months LIBOR/ EURO LIBOR/ EURIBOR + 75 basis points to six months LIBOR/ EURO LIBOR/ EURIBOR + 150 basis points.

March 2009

- The repo rate under the LAF was reduced by 50 basis points from 5.5 per cent to 5.0 per cent with effect from March 5, 2009.
- The reverse repo rate under the LAF was reduced by 50 basis points from 4.0 per cent to 3.5 per cent with effect from March 5, 2009.
- The MoU signed by the RBI with the Government on March 25, 2004 on the MSS was amended on February 26, 2009 to enable the transfer of a part of the amount in the MSS cash account to the normal cash account as part of the Government's market borrowing programme for meeting Government's approved expenditure. An amount of Rs.12,000 crore was transferred from the MSS account to the normal cash account of the Government of India on March 4, 2009 and an equivalent amount of Government securities issued under the MSS formed a part of the normal market borrowing of the Government of India. Based on the emerging fund requirements of the Government, Rs.33,000 crore of MSS would be de-sequestered against the approved market borrowing programme or bought back in the fiscal year 2009-10.
- The Reserve Bank announced OMO purchase of government securities of the order of Rs.80,000 crore in the first half of 2009-10, of which Rs.40,000 crore is envisaged for the first quarter of 2009-10.
- The facility of providing liquidity support to meet the temporary liquidity mismatches for eligible non-banking non-deposit taking systematically important financial companies (NBFCs-ND-SI), which was initially available for any paper issued up to March 31, 2009 was extended for any paper issued up to June 30, 2009. Accordingly, the SPV would cease to make fresh purchases after September 30, 2009 and would recover all dues by December 31, 2009.

G-20 Working Group on Enhancing Sound Regulation and Strengthening Transparency: Current Status of the Reserve Bank on the Recommendations

Measures for strengthening the regulation of the financial system were considered by the G-20 Working Group on Enhancing Sound Regulation and Strengthening Transparency. The recommendations of the Group and the status with regard to the relevant items for India are set out below.

System-wide Approach to Financial Regulation

Recommendation 1

As a supplement to their core mandate, the mandates of all national financial regulators, central banks, and oversight authorities, and of all international financial bodies and standard setters (IASB, BCBS, IAIS and IOSCO) should take account of financial system stability.

- Over the last few years, financial stability has emerged as a key objective of the Reserve Bank's policy. Accordingly, several measures have been taken in recent years to promote financial stability. As recommended by the Committee on Financial Sector Assessment (CFSA), a Financial Stability Unit is being set up.

Recommendation 2

Within each country, there should be an effective mechanism for appropriate domestic financial sector authorities to jointly assess the systemic risks across the financial system and to co-ordinate the domestic policy response to limit the build-up in systemic risk. The structure of this coordinating mechanism should be transparent, with clear assignments of roles, responsibilities and accountability for each authority.

- In India, the High Level Co-ordination Committee on Financial Markets (HLCCFM) provides a co-ordination mechanism among financial sector regulators, *viz.*, Reserve Bank of India (RBI), Securities and Exchange Board of India (SEBI), Insurance Regulatory and Development Authority (IRDA) and Provident Fund Regulatory and Development Authority (PFRDA). It is supported by other technical committees/sub-committees, which examine issues relating to entities under various regulators that have cross-sector implications.
- There are separate technical committees for RBI regulated entities, SEBI regulated entities and IRDA regulated entities. These committees review capital market related developments and based on an early warning system attempt to identify any unusual developments that may require co-ordinated action. Exchange-traded currency futures and interest rate futures, financial conglomerate monitoring framework, crisis management group and a corporate bond and securitisation advisory committee have been introduced through co-ordination of inter-regulatory agencies.

Recommendation 3

Financial sector authorities should have suitable macroprudential tools to address systemic vulnerabilities.

- The Reserve Bank has been using various macro-prudential tools to address banking system risks. For instance, during the expansionary phase of 2004-07, the Reserve Bank took various measures to restrict unbridled growth of credit. These included increased provisioning for standard advances and increased risk weights in respect of certain asset classes. However, subsequently, during slow credit growth phase beginning November 2008, those counter-cyclical measures were reversed. The Reserve Bank will continue to make efforts to develop and use further macro-prudential tools and would also consider using any tools that may be developed or recommended by international standard setting bodies.

Recommendation 4

The expanded FSF, together with the IMF, should create an effective mechanism for key financial authorities in each country to regularly come together around an international table to jointly assess the systemic risks across the global financial system and to coordinate policy responses.

- The G-20 has redesignated the Financial Stability Forum (FSF) to Financial Stability Board (FSB) and its membership has, *inter alia,* been enlarged to include, all G-20 member countries, including India. The Reserve Bank, the Government of India and the SEBI look forward to contributing actively and effectively to the work and initiatives of the FSB and the BCBS.

Scope of Regulation

Recommendation 5

All systemically important financial institutions, markets and instruments should be subject to an appropriate degree of regulation and oversight, consistently applied and proportionate to their local and global systemic importance. Non-systemically important financial institutions, markets and instruments could also be subject to some form of registration requirement or oversight, depending on the type and degree of risk posed, for example for the integrity or efficiency of markets.

National authorities should have the authority to expand the perimeter of regulation in a timely way, recognizing that it may vary across countries and through time.

- Banks, which form the largest segment of the Indian financial system, are closely regulated by the Reserve Bank. In recent years, the Reserve Bank has extended its detailed prudential regulation to systemically important non-deposit taking NBFCs (NBFCs-ND-SI) also. The Reserve Bank oversees the payment and settlement systems, regulates money markets, foreign exchange market and government securities market.
- Issues relating to expansion of the perimeter of regulation to those institutions which are not prudentially regulated and are systemically important could be deliberated in the HLCCFM.

Recommendation 6

The systemic importance of financial institutions, markets and instruments depends on a wide range of factors, including their size, leverage, interconnectedness, as well as funding mismatches. The IMF, in consultation with the BIS and the expanded FSF and other bodies, should jointly develop a common international framework and guidelines to help national authorities assess whether a financial institution, market or an instrument is systemically important as consistently as possible across jurisdictions.

- The Reserve Bank is committed to follow sound international practices and standards. When a common international framework is available to help national authorities to assess whether a financial institution, market or an instrument is systemically important, the Reserve Bank will use the framework to further sharpen its focus with regard to the supervision of those institutions considered systemically important in consultation with the Government and other regulatory authorities, as necessary, consistent with the legal framework.

Recommendation 7

Large complex financial institutions require particularly robust oversight given their systemic importance, which arises in part from their size and interconnectedness (or correlation) with other institutions, and from their influence on markets.

- Following the report on financial conglomerates (FCs), a monitoring mechanism for the identified FCs has been in place since 2004 in co-operation with other regulators. Since April 2005, the FC monitoring mechanism has been further strengthened with the introduction of half-yearly discussion with the CEOs of the major group entities within the FC.
- As indicated in the Mid-term Review of October 2008, an 'approach paper' on the supervision of financial conglomerates has since been prepared by an Internal Group. The recommendations of the Group are being examined from the regulatory and supervisory perspectives for initiating appropriate action.
- As part of its endeavour to strengthen the supervision of banking groups, the Reserve Bank extended the major elements of prudential regulations, *viz.,* capital adequacy and exposure norms to all the subsidiaries of commercial banks in 2003.

Recommendation 8

The boundaries of the regulatory framework should be reviewed periodically within national jurisdictions, in light of financial innovation and broader trends in the financial system. International bodies will promote good practice and consistent approaches in this area.

- The Reserve Bank regularly interacts with other regulators of the financial system within the national jurisdiction, *viz.,* SEBI, the securities regulator, IRDA, the insurance regulator and PFRDA, the regulator of pension funds. The Reserve Bank has also been associated with various international bodies such as G-20 and the BIS, and now also with the FSB and the BCBS.

- The issue of review of the boundaries of the regulatory framework will be kept in focus, both in the interaction with sectoral regulators within the national jurisdiction and with international bodies.

Oversight of Credit Rating Agencies

Recommendation 9

All credit rating agencies whose ratings are used for regulatory purposes should be subject to a regulatory oversight regime that includes registration and that requires compliance with the substance of the IOSCO Code of Conduct Fundamentals. National authorities should obtain the authority to enforce compliance and require changes to a rating agency's practices and procedures for managing conflicts of interest and for assuring the transparency and quality of the rating process.

- In India, all credit rating agencies are registered with the SEBI. The Reserve Bank has accorded accreditation to four credit rating agencies registered with the SEBI for the limited purpose of using their ratings for assigning risk weights within the framework of the Basel II Accord which has been implemented by all banks as at the end of March 2009. Prior to the accreditation, the Reserve Bank had undertaken a review of the rating agencies' practices and procedures to ensure that they comply with the criteria prescribed for accreditation in the Basel II framework.
- Since the Indian banking system has migrated to the Basel II framework, there is a need to review the performance of the credit rating agencies for continuation of the accreditation, especially by looking at the latest data relating to cumulative default rate and transition matrix of the rating agencies. The Reserve Bank will liaise with the SEBI on the issue of rating agencies' adherence to the IOSCO Code of Conduct Fundamentals.

Private Pools of Capital

Recommendation 10

Private pools of capital, including hedge funds, can be a source of risk owing to their combined size in the market, their use of leverage and maturity mismatches, and their connectedness with other parts of the financial system. They or their managers should therefore be required to register with financial authorities and disclose appropriate information to assess the risks they pose.

- In India, venture capital funds and mutual funds are registered and regulated by the SEBI. Hedge funds do not operate in India at present. The Reserve Bank proposes to issue a paper on prudential issues in banks' floating and managing private pools of capital to finalise the regulatory guidelines.

Transparent Assessment of Regulatory Regimes

Recommendation 11

All G-20 members should commit to undertake a Financial Sector Assessment Program (FSAP) report and to publish its conclusions. National authorities may also periodically undertake a self-assessment of their regulatory frameworks based on internationally agreed methodologies and tools.

- India first participated in an FSAP in 2001 conducted by the IMF and the World Bank and also associated with the independent assessment of standards and codes by the Fund/ Bank. It also conducted a self-assessment of compliance with international standards and codes in 2002 and its review in 2004 and put these reports in public domain. Since the last FSAP in 2001, India has undertaken a series of ongoing reforms in the financial sector aimed at improving its soundness, resilience and depth. India has completed a comprehensive self-assessment of the financial sector in 2009 under a Committee on Financial Sector Assessment (Chairman: Dr. Rakesh Mohan and Co-Chairman: Shri Ashok Chawla) based on the IMF-WB methodology. The assessment, comprising six volumes, has been published and put in the public domain along with the comments of the internationally acclaimed Peer Reviewers on March 30, 2009. The Reserve Bank will set up a Task Force to take steps for implementation of the recommendations of the two G-20 Working Groups *viz.*, Enhancing Sound Regulations and Strengthening Transparency, and Reinforcing International Co-operation and Promoting Integrity in Financial Markets and will also continuously monitor the implementation. The Task Force will also look into all the issues that have arisen and what follow-up actions relevant to the Reserve Bank need to be taken regarding the recently released report of the Committee on Financial Sector Assessment. The Task Force would suggest an implementation schedule for every quarter on a rolling basis.

Procyclicality

Recommendation 12

The FSF and other bodies, particularly the BCBS, should develop and implement supervisory and regulatory approaches to mitigate procyclicality in the financial system by promoting the build-up of capital buffers during the economic expansion and by dampening the adverse interaction between fair valuation, leverage and maturity mismatches in times of stress.

- As against the Basel norm for minimum CRAR of 8 per cent, in India, banks are required to maintain a minimum CRAR of 9 per cent. The overall CRAR of all scheduled commercial banks continued to be strong and it was at 13 per cent at the end-March 2008 and 13.1 per cent at end-December 2008. The Reserve Bank recognises the need for mitigating the element of procyclicality embedded in the regulatory norms as it may exacerbate cyclical trends. With this objective in view, the Reserve Bank has been employing a menu of macroprudential tools to mitigate the impact of procyclicality.

- FSB and member bodies, BCBS and CGFS have been entrusted with the work of developing regulatory and supervisory approaches to mitigate procyclicality. They are expected to develop a strategic plan by Fall 2009. India will take further action in this regard as per global consensus emerging from the work of international bodies.

Recommendation 13

Accounting standard setters should strengthen accounting recognition of loan loss provisions by considering alternative approaches for recognizing and measuring loan losses that incorporate a broader range of available credit information. They should also examine changes to relevant standards to dampen adverse dynamics associated with fair value accounting, including improvements to valuations when data or modelling is weak. Accounting standards setters and prudential supervisors should work together to identify solutions that are consistent with the complementary objectives of promoting the stability of the financial sector and of providing transparency of economic results in financial reports.

- The Reserve Bank introduced the asset classification and loan provisioning norms in the year 1991-92 which prescribe the minimum provisioning based on classification of assets. Certain areas of difference exist between the requirements of accounting standards in respect of loan loss provisioning (accounting perspective) and the Reserve Bank's present regulatory approach and the Basel II approach of calculating expected loan losses (regulatory perspective). Internationally, there are attempts for a convergence in this regard between the Accounting Task Force (ATF) of the BCBS and the IASB. The Reserve Bank will fine tune its policies in tandem with developments at international level in this regard.
- The Reserve Bank has, over the years, issued guidelines on valuation of various instruments/ assets in conformity with the international best practices while keeping India-specific conditions in view. In order to encourage market discipline, the Reserve Bank has developed a set of disclosure requirements which allow the market participants to assess key pieces of information on capital adequacy, risk exposure, risk assessment processes and key business parameters which provide a consistent and understandable disclosure framework that enhances comparability. Banks are also required to comply with the Accounting Standard (AS) on disclosure of accounting policies issued by the Institute of Chartered Accountants of India (ICAI).

Capital

Recommendation 14

Capital should serve as an effective buffer to absorb losses over the cycle, so as to protect both the solvency of financial institutions in the event of losses, and their ability to lend.

In the near term, capital buffers above required minimums should be allowed to decline in response to deteriorating economic conditions and credit quality, and urgent consideration should be given to measures that would facilitate access to additional private sector capital in the downturn.

Once conditions in the financial system have recovered, the adequacy of the international standard for the minimum level of capital for banks should be reviewed and the quality and global consistency of capital should be enhanced. In addition, capital buffers above minimum requirements and loan-loss provisions should be built up in good times in order to enhance the ability of regulated financial institutions to withstand large shocks.

- Once conditions in the global financial system recover, the Reserve Bank would consider enhancing the minimum capital standards in tandem with the proposals at the international level. The build-up of capital and provisioning buffers in good times will be encouraged by the Reserve Bank so that capital can absorb unexpected losses and be drawn down during difficult times.

Recommendation 15

G-20 leaders should support the progressive adoption of the Basel II capital framework, which will continue to be improved on an ongoing basis, across the G-20.

- All commercial banks in India were Basel II compliant as on March 31, 2009. Initially the base approach of the Basel II framework have been adopted. The Reserve Bank has placed on its website a draft circular giving an indicative timeframe for implementation of the advanced approach of the Basel II framework. The enhancement to current Basel II framework by the international standard setting bodies will be considered for implementation as appropriate.

Liquidity

Recommendation 16

Prudential supervisors and central banks should deliver a global framework for promoting stronger liquidity buffers at banks, including cross-border institutions, to ensure that they can withstand prolonged periods of market and funding liquidity stress.

- Indian banks have a significant holding of liquid instruments as they are required to maintain cash reserve ratio and statutory liquidity ratio (5 per cent and 24 per cent of their net demand and time liabilities, as at present). The substantial CRR/SLR holding offers, in effect, a good liquidity buffer. There are prudential norms governing unsecured overnight borrowings by banks and inter-bank liabilities.
- The Reserve Bank has examined the issue of banks establishing a more robust liquidity risk management framework that is well integrated into the bank-wide risk management process by adopting global liquidity planning. In this context, banks will be required to

integrate their various foreign currency assets and liabilities positions from their branch operations in India with the rupee asset liability position.

Infrastructure for OTC Derivatives

Recommendation 17

Financial institutions should continue to strengthen the infrastructure supporting OTC derivatives markets. In the case of credit derivatives, this includes standardizing contracts to facilitate their clearing through a central counterparty. National authorities should enhance incentives as needed for the use of central counterparties to clear OTC credit derivatives.

Recommendation 18

Central counterparties should be subject to transparent and effective oversight by prudential supervisors and other relevant authorities, including central banks, and meet high standards in terms of risk management, operational arrangements, default procedures, fair access and transparency. The CPSS and IOSCO should review their experiences in applying their recommendations for central counterparties to derivatives.

- The CCIL provides an institutional structure for the clearing and settlement of transactions undertaken in government securities, money market instruments and foreign exchange products and has adopted the core principles set by the CPSS and IOSCO. In October 2007, CCIL has joined as a member of the CCP 12, an international organisation of central counterparty (CCP) clearing organisations.
- CCIL's role is being gradually extended to the OTC derivatives segment, initially as a reporting platform and thereafter, covering the settlement aspect.
- The Payment and Settlement Systems Act, 2007 has designated the Reserve Bank as the authority to regulate and supervise the payment and settlement systems in the country.
- The netting procedure and settlement finality, earlier governed by contractual agreement/s, have been accorded legal recognition under the Act. The Reserve Bank is empowered to issue directions and guidelines to the system providers, prescribe the duties to be performed by them and audit and inspect their systems/premises.
- The recommendations of the CPSS and the IOSCO when available will be applied as appropriate to the CCIL.

Compensation Schemes and Risk Management

Recommendation 19

Large financial institutions should ensure that their compensation frameworks are consistent with their long-term goals and with prudent risk-taking. As such, the Boards of Directors of financial institutions should set clear lines of responsibility and accountability throughout their organizations to ensure that the design and operation of its remuneration system supports the firm's goals, including its overall risk tolerance. Shareholders may have a role in this process. Boards should also ensure there are appropriate mechanisms for monitoring remuneration schemes.

Recommendation 20

In order to promote incentives for prudent risk taking, each financial institution must review its compensation framework to ensure it follows sound practice principles developed by the FSF. These include the need for remuneration systems to provide incentives consistent with the firm's long-term goals, to be adjusted for the risk taken by employees, and for the variable components of compensation to vary symmetrically according to performance.

Recommendation 21

Prudential supervisors should enhance their oversight of compensation schemes by taking the design of remuneration systems into account when assessing risk management practices. The BCBS should more explicitly integrate this dimension in its guidance for the assessment of risk management practices by national prudential supervisors.

- In terms of Section 35 B of the Banking Regulation Act, 1949 banks in the private sector and foreign banks in India are required to obtain the approval of the Reserve Bank for remuneration payable to their CEOs (the remuneration of public sector bank CEOs is fixed by the Government of India).
- While devising the total remuneration package (including all perquisites and bonus) of CEOs and whole-time directors, Boards of private banks are required to ensure that the total package is reasonable in the light of industry norms including size of the business in India. The Compensation Committee which looks into the remuneration issue is required to have adequate representation of independent directors and directors, if any, representing major institutional shareholders in India. Remuneration of foreign banks' CEOs is mainly driven by the policies of their head offices.
- The Reserve Bank would recommend the implementation of the sound procedures/ principles developed by the FSB for financial institutions regarding the compensation packages.

Transparency

Recommendation 22

Accounting standard setters should accelerate efforts to reduce the complexity of accounting standards for financial instruments and enhance presentation standards to allow the users of financial statements to better assess the uncertainty surrounding the valuation of financial instruments.

- International Accounting Standards/International Financial Reporting Standards (IAS/ IFRS) are adopted as a basis for formulation of Indian standards and due consideration is given to local customs, usage, practices, legal and regulatory environment. The Reserve Bank has taken a proactive role in the area of adherence by banks to the Accounting Standards. The Reserve Bank also actually participates in the standard setting process through its nominees in the Accounting Standards Board and the National Advisory Committee on Accounting Standards.

- IASB is in the process of issuing a new globally accepted standard in place of the existing financial instruments standard (IAS 39 *Financial Instruments: Recognition and Measurement)* that would address issues arising from the financial crisis in a comprehensive manner. Implementation of the standard in the Indian context will arise after it is finalised by IASB and adopted by ICAI as a part of its convergence programme.
- The Reserve Bank has, over the years, issued guidelines on valuation of various instruments/ assets in conformity with the international best practices while keeping India-specific conditions in view.
- The securitisation framework in India is considered to be reasonably prudent and has been able to minimise the incentives that have led to the problems which surfaced in the current crisis.

Recommendation 23

The IASB should enhance its efforts to facilitate the global convergence towards a single set of high-quality accounting standards by sharing the experience of countries that have completed this process and by providing technical assistance.

- The recently published report of the CFSA on India's financial sector assessment has stated that the Indian accounting standards are generally in alignment with international accounting standards, except for some modifications to suit local customs, usages and level of development in the country. There has been significant progress in the area of convergence of accounting standards. The Indian accounting standards are expected to be fully convergent with IFRSs with effect from April 1, 2011 when IFRSs are likely to be adopted in India for listed and other public interest entities.

Enforcement

Recommendation 24

The effective enforcement of regulation should be a priority of all financial regulators. As such, national financial regulators and oversight authorities should ensure the effectiveness of their enforcement activities and that appropriate resources are available for monitoring the application of regulation and for prosecuting offenders. The enforcement function should be independent from other activities or from external influences.

- Regulations issued by the Reserve Bank are monitored by its supervisory department. The Banking Regulation Act, 1949 has prescribed extensive penalties for non submission or willful omission of information, for making false statements, and for not following directions issued by the Reserve Bank. Apart from this, the Reserve Bank can impose penalties under specific powers granted to it under the Act. Similar provisions exist in the Credit Information Companies (Regulation) Act, 2005 and the Payment and Settlement Systems Act, 2007. The penalties imposed by the Reserve Bank under the BR Act are placed in public domain.

Technical Assistance and Capacity Building in Emerging Market Economies

Recommendation 25

Recognizing that the degree of development of financial systems varies considerably across the G20, national authorities should commit to assist each other in enhancing their capacity to strengthen regulatory frameworks. In addition, IOSCO, the IAIS and the BCBS should have the appropriate capacity to provide technical assistance. The needs of emerging market economies deserve particular consideration.

- India has been striving for adopting the international best practices, tailored to country-specific conditions. Accordingly, the capacity building of all stakeholders has been progressively upgraded. The Reserve Bank has also conducted several international seminars often in collaboration with international bodies, to upgrade the skill levels in various developing economies. The Reserve Bank will continue such efforts.

G-20 Leaders' Declaration

The other important elements for strengthening the financial system as contained in the G-20 Leaders' declaration are:

International Cooperation

To establish the remaining supervisory colleges for significant cross border firms by June 2009 building on 28 already in place.

- India has been actively participating in supervisory colleges conducted by overseas home regulators of foreign banks operating in India. No Indian bank has significant presence in foreign jurisdictions so as to render them systemically important there. As and when Indian banks attain critical level of operations, the Reserve Bank will consider convening supervisory colleges.

To implement the FSF principles for cross-border crisis management immediately, and that home authorities of each major international financial institutions should ensure that the group of authorities with a common interest in that financial institution meet at least annually;

To support continued efforts by the IMF, FSB, World Bank, and BCBS to develop an international framework for cross-border bank resolution arrangements;

- An Internal Working Group constituted to lay down the road map for adoption of a suitable framework for cross-border supervision and supervisory co-operation with overseas regulators has submitted its report in January 2009. The recommendations of the Group are being examined for initiating further action.
- Further, an Inter-departmental Group is examining additional areas/issues which need to be brought under supervisory focus, including modalities for on-site supervision of overseas branches and subsidiaries of Indian banks. The group is expected to submit its report by end May, 2009.
- As and when international framework is developed by international agencies/standard setters, India will adopt the same in line with country specific needs.

Tax havens and non-cooperative jurisdictions

Increased disclosure requirements on the part of taxpayers and financial institutions to report transactions involving non-cooperative jurisdictions.

- In India, banks have been advised to be extremely cautious while continuing relationships with respondent banks located in countries with poor know-your-customer (KYC) standards and countries identified as 'non-co-operative' in the fight against money laundering and terrorist financing.
- The AML/CFT guidelines issued by the Reserve Bank are in consonance with the FATF recommendations and the Reserve Bank would continue to incorporate in its regulations latest international best practices.

2

Macroeconomic and Monetary Developments in 2008-09

The Reserve Bank of India has released the document "Macroeconomic and Monetary Developments in 2008-09" to serve as a backdrop to the Annual Policy Statement for 2009-10 being announced on April 21, 2009.

The highlights of macroeconomic and monetary developments during 2008-09 are:

OVERVIEW

The global economic conditions deteriorated sharply during the year 2008 with several advanced economies experiencing their sharpest declines. The associated adverse shocks spread across emerging market economies (EMEs) particularly by the fourth quarter of the year and accentuated the synchronised global slowdown.

Inflation conditions witnessed sharp volatility during the year as headline inflation in major advanced economies firmed up considerably up to July 2008, but declined sharply thereafter. The global financial environment entered a crisis phase in mid-September 2008, following the growing distress among large international financial institutions.

The knock-on effect of these unprecedented adverse global developments became evident in the macroeconomic performance of the Indian economy, as it experienced some loss of growth momentum with major drivers witnessing moderation. While private consumption and investment are witnessing moderation, the fiscal stimulus along with other committed expenditures of the Government could, however, arrest the moderation in growth.

An important challenge in the macroeconomic and monetary policy making during 2008-09 has been to manage the volatility emerging in respect of several key economic indicators of the Indian economy. Notwithstanding several challenges, particularly from the global economy, the Indian economy remained relatively resilient, its financial institutions and private corporate sector remained sound and solvent. Furthermore, the macroeconomic management helped in maintaining lower volatility in both the financial and the real sectors in India relative to several other advanced and emerging market economies.

Output

The global financial crisis interrupted the growth momentum of India, despite the strong dominance of domestic sources of growth. There was clear moderation in growth by the third quarter of 2008-09. In relation to the agricultural sector, industry and services sectors have been affected more by the adverse external shocks, with some contribution to their growth deceleration arising from cyclical slowdown in certain sectors after a prolonged phase of high growth.

The Central Statistical Organisation (CSO)'s estimates (February 2009) of real GDP growth was placed at 5.3 per cent during the third quarter of 2008-09 as compared with 8.9 per cent during the corresponding quarter of the previous year, reflecting deceleration in growth of all its constituent sectors. During 2008-09, the area covered under sowing of various crops declined marginally during the kharif season on account of moderate shortfall in rainfall. On the other hand, the prospects for rabi production remain favourable with area sown under rabi crops being higher than a year ago. Total foodgrains production during 2008-09 was placed at 227.9 million tonnes (Second Advance Estimates) as compared with 230.8 million tonnes during 2007-08.

In the wake of a near normal long range monsoon forecast of the India Meteorological Department (April 17, 2009) during the South-West monsoon season 2009, the prospects for agricultural production remain satisfactory.

The loss of growth momentum in the industrial sector was evident as the year-on-year expansion in the Index of Industrial Production was of 2.8 per cent during 2008-09 (April-February) as against 8.8 per cent in the corresponding period of the previous year. The manufacturing sector and the electricity sector registered growth of 2.8 per cent and 2.4 per cent as compared with 9.3 per cent and 6.6 per cent, respectively, during the above period.

The infrastructure sector recorded growth of 3.0 per cent during 2008-09 (April-February), down from 5.8 per cent during the corresponding period of the previous year, reflecting deceleration in all the sectors except coal. In the context of the severity of the impact of the crisis on the real economy of countries around the world, the growth outcome reflects the resilience of the Indian economy.

Aggregate Demand

The role of aggregate demand in a phase of weakening growth impulses came to the forefront of public policy in 2008-09. The sharp contraction in external demand - as evident in falling global output, employment and global trade – clearly affected India's export performance. Domestic demand, in the form of both private consumption and investment expenditure moderated, particularly in the third quarter of 2008-09. However, Government final consumption, however, rose on account of discretionary fiscal stimulus measures and committed expenditures of the Central Government.

During 2008-09, the combined finances of the Central and State Governments were adversely impacted due to the economic slowdown. The Central Government finances came under stress during 2008-09, both on the revenue and the expenditure sides, on account of fiscal measures taken to reduce inflationary pressures during the first half and to arrest the moderation of economic growth in the second half of the year. As a result, the key deficit indicators viz., revenue deficit and fiscal deficit widened to 4.4 per cent and 6.0 per cent, respectively, in the revised estimates for 2008-09 from 1.0 per cent and 2.5 per cent, respectively, in the budget estimates.

The Union Interim Budget for 2009-10 has indicated the relaxation in the FRBM targets for 2008-09 and 2009-10, in order to ensure expansion in aggregate demand through fiscal stimulus measures. However, as a medium-term objective, it has recognised the need to revert to fiscal consolidation process at the earliest.

Corporate performance remained subdued during 2008-09 with the impact on profitability being particularly adverse during the third quarter.

The rate of Gross Domestic Saving (GDS) peaked at 37.7 per cent GDP in 2007-08, mainly due to improved saving performance of the private corporate and public sectors. The rate of Gross Domestic Capital Formation (GDCF) also peaked to 39.1 per cent of GDP in 2007-08. The saving-investment balance widened during 2007-08 reflecting continuous surge in investment activity ahead of the saving rate. The slowing of economic activity in 2008-09 may, however, affect both saving and investment rates for the year.

The External Economy

In the face of deteriorating external environment, the adverse effects of the contagion transmitting through different components of India's balance of payments (BoP) could largely be contained through policy actions. A noteworthy feature during 2008-09 was that the effect of external shocks transmitting to India through the BoP could be contained with loss of reserves mainly in the third quarter of the year, when the global crisis deepened and spread significantly with more visible real effects.

India's BoP position in 2008-09 (April-December) was characterised by a widened trade deficit leading to a higher current account and lower net capital inflows. In the face of deteriorating external environment, the adverse effects of the contagion transmitting through different components of India's balance of payments (BoP) remained largely contained.

The rapid contraction in the global trade was reflected in negative growth experienced during the third quarter, which was last observed in 2001-02. The growth in imports also decelerated to single digit level during the third quarter, led by lower crude oil prices and weakening domestic demand. The merchandise trade deficit further widened to US$ 113.8 billion during April-February 2008-09 (US $ 82.2 billion a year ago).

Net surpluses under invisibles increased in April-December 2008, primarily led by private transfers and software services, though a moderation in such inflows set in the third quarter. Thus, the current account deficit widened to a level of US$ 36.5 billion (US$ 15.5 billion in April-December 2007)

The adverse impact of the global financial market turmoil was also felt in terms of reduced inflow of the long and short-term debt and reversal of portfolio inflows. A positive development was, however, relative resilience of FDI inflows (US $ 31.7 billion in April-February 2008-09) in the face of reversal of capital flows, reflecting the attractiveness of India as a long term investment destination.

As on April 10, 2009, the foreign exchange reserves stood at US $ 253 billion, showing a decline of US$ 56.7 billion (including valuation) over the level at end-March 2008.

India's external debt, debt sustainability indicators and the level of foreign exchange reserves continue to remain at comfortable levels and would ensure external stability.

Monetary Conditions

The global crisis, which created intense uncertainties for funding liquidity in the face of tight market liquidity for financial instruments trading in almost all financial markets, brought to the fore the strong interactions between funding liquidity and market liquidity. As the global liquidity crisis started to affect the domestic money and foreign exchange markets in the last quarter of 2008, the Reserve Bank ensured adequate provision of both domestic and foreign exchange liquidity to the market through banks, with the aim of restoring normal functioning of the market, and thereby facilitating adequate flow of credit to the productive sectors of the economy.

The monetary policy stance of the Reserve Bank shifted from concerns related to inflation in the first half of 2008-09 to maintaining financial stability and arresting the moderation of growth in the second half. While money supply evolved consistent with indicative projections, credit to private sector reflected the conditions evolving in the real sector of the economy.

Growth in broad money (M3), year-on-year (y-o-y), was 18.4 per cent at end-March, 2009 as compared with 21.2 per cent a year ago, reflecting deceleration in the expansion of bank credit and capital inflows.

Aggregate deposits of banks, y-o-y, was 18.8 per cent at end-March 2009 as compared with 21.7 per cent a year ago.

Non-food credit growth (y-o-y) of SCBs to the commercial sector remained strong up to October 2008 on the backdrop of drying up of other sources of funds to industry but witnessed sustained deceleration thereafter. Non-food credit by SCBs was moderated to 17.5 per cent, y-o-y, at end-March 2009 as compared with 23.0 per cent a year ago.

The contractionary impact of decline in net foreign exchange assets on reserve money and domestic liquidity was offset by expansion through open market operations (OMOs), unwinding of MSS and other measures to augment rupee liquidity. Adjusted for the first round effect of the changes in CRR, reserve money growth (y-o-y) as on March 31, 2009 was lower at 19.0 per cent as compared with 25.3 per cent a year ago.

Financial Markets

The process of deleveraging and dysfunctional financial markets in the advanced economies, which accentuated into a global financial crisis, has highlighted the importance of orderly functioning of markets for achieving macroeconomic objectives.

In the third quarter of 2008-09, when liquidity dried down in the global economy markets and credit markets almost froze, there were knock-on effects on domestic money and foreign exchange markets, which prompted the Reserve Bank to initiate measures to ensure adequate provision of rupee and foreign exchange liquidity.

An important distinction between the actions taken by the Reserve Bank and the other central banks is that the interaction is still largely through the banking channel. Another noticeable distinction is that there has not been any dilution of the collateral taken by the Reserve Bank. The array of instruments available allow for flexibility in Reserve Bank's operations.

While orderly conditions could be restored in the money market by November 2008, the pressure on the exchange rate continued, alongside pressure on the country's balance of payments and draw down of foreign exchange reserves. The equity markets followed the general global sentiments and market trends and after a phase of sharp downward movement, the market has shown some recovery since March 2009.

In the government securities market, reflecting the economy's need for large fiscal stimulus, the gross market borrowings of the Government in 2008-09 were substantially higher than those for 2007-08, and the entire market borrowing programme was managed smoothly by the Reserve Bank.

In the credit market following significant reduction in policy rates by the Reserve Bank, the lending rates of banks have begun to exhibit some moderation.

In the context of the high volatility that was witnessed in global financial markets in 2008-09, one notable aspect of the Indian markets was that all markets functioned normally, with occasional volatility for short periods.

Price Situation

The large order of volatility in the inflation outcome witnessed in India during 2008-09 is unprecedented. The sharp volatility in international commodity prices largely contributed to the spiralling inflation in the first half, and then to the subsequent decline from a higher base at fast pace in the second half of 2008-09. In India, inflation, as measured by year-on-year variations in the Wholesale Price Index (WPI), reached an intra-year peak of 12.91 per cent on August 02, 2008. Subsequently, it fell sharply to 0.26 per cent as at end-March 2009 and further to 0.18 per cent as on April 4, 2009.

As external and supply side factors along with demand pressures conditioned the inflation trend during 2008-09, demand management policy measures had to be employed in a calibrated manner. While the first half of 2008-09 warranted for adjustment of aggregate demand on an economy wide basis, the sharp fall in inflation in the second half facilitated aggressive monetary easing, which aim at arresting the economic slowdown. Unlike the WPI based inflation, CPI based inflation in India, however, remains high, with recent evidence of very modest moderation, and the transmission process of lower inflation at the wholesale level to inflation at the retail level has emerged as an important issue in the conduct of Reserve Bank's monetary policy.

Various measures of consumer price inflation, though started declining, still remained high in the range of 9.6-10.8 per cent during January/February 2009 as compared with 5.2-6.4 per cent in February 2008.

Macroeconomic Outlook

An assessment of the economic conditions at the current juncture indicates that the global economic conditions have deteriorated sharply during 2008 and the forecasts of the various international agencies point to deepening of recessionary conditions during 2009 as well.

Reflecting global developments and their impact on the Indian economy, as well as domestic cyclical factors, the various surveys of economic activity point towards prevalence of less than optimistic sentiment for the outlook of the Indian economy in the coming months. The Professional Forecasters' Survey conducted by the Reserve Bank in December 2008 suggested moderation in economic activity in 2008-09 and 2009-10. The Reserve Bank's Industrial Outlook Survey of Manufacturing Companies in the Private Sector indicates that the business expectations indices based on the assessment for January-March 2009 and expectations for April-June 2009 declined sharply by 20.7 per cent and 13.9 per cent, respectively, over the previous quarters.

Stance of Monetary Policy 2008-09

The policy responses in India since September 2008 have been designed largely to mitigate the adverse impact of the global financial crisis on the Indian economy. The conduct of monetary policy had to contend with the high speed and magnitude of the external shock and its spill-over effects through the real, financial and confidence channels. The evolving stance of policy has been increasingly conditioned by the need to preserve financial stability while arresting the moderation in the growth momentum.

The thrust of the various policy initiatives by the Reserve Bank has been on providing ample rupee liquidity, ensuring comfortable dollar liquidity and maintaining a market environment conducive for the continued flow of credit to productive sectors. The key policy initiatives taken by the Reserve Bank since September 2008 are set out below:

Policy Rates

- The policy repo rate under the liquidity adjustment facility (LAF) was reduced by 400 basis points from 9.0 per cent to 5.0 per cent.
- The policy reverse repo rate under the LAF was reduced by 250 basis points from 6.0 per cent to 3.5 per cent.

Rupee Liquidity

- The cash reserve ratio (CRR) was reduced by 400 basis points from 9.0 per cent of net demand and time liabilities (NDTL) of banks to 5.0 per cent.
- The statutory liquidity ratio (SLR) was reduced from 25.0 per cent of NDTL to 24.0 per cent.
- The export credit refinance limit for commercial banks was enhanced to 50.0 per cent from 15.0 per cent of outstanding export credit.
- A special 14-day term repo facility was instituted for commercial banks up to 1.5 per cent of NDTL.
- A special refinance facility was instituted for scheduled commercial banks (excluding RRBs) up to 1.0 per cent of each bank's NDTL as on October 24, 2008.
- Special refinance facilities were instituted for financial institutions (SIDBI, NHB and Exim Bank).

Forex Liquidity

- The Reserve Bank sold foreign exchange (US dollars) and made available a forex swap facility to banks.
- The interest rate ceilings on non-resident Indian (NRI) deposits were raised.
- The all-in-cost ceiling for the external commercial borrowings (ECBs) was raised. The all-in-cost ceiling for ECBs through the approval route has been dispensed with up to June 30, 2009.

- The systemically important non-deposit taking non-banking financial companies (NBFCs-ND-SI) were permitted to raise short-term foreign currency borrowings.

Regulatory Forbearance

- The risk-weights and provisioning requirements were relaxed and restructuring of stressed assets was initiated.

Liquidity Impact

The actions of the Reserve Bank since mid-September 2008 have resulted in augmentation of actual/potential liquidity of over Rs.4,22,000 crore. In addition, the permanent reduction in the SLR by 1.0 per cent of NDTL has made available liquid funds of the order of Rs.40,000 crore for the purpose of credit expansion

The liquidity situation has improved significantly following the measures taken by the Reserve Bank. The overnight money market rates, which generally hovered above the repo rate during September-October 2008, have softened considerably and have generally been close to or near the lower bound of the LAF corridor since early November 2008. Other money market rates such as discount rates of CDs, CPs and CBLO softened in tandem with the overnight money market rates. The LAF window has been in a net absorption mode since mid-November 2008. The liquidity problem faced by mutual funds has eased considerably. Most commercial banks have reduced their benchmark prime lending rates. The total utilisation under the recent refinance/ liquidity facilities introduced by the Reserve Bank has been low as the overall liquidity conditions remain comfortable. However, their availability has provided comfort to the banks/FIs, which can fall back on them in case of need

3

Adjusting Housing Credit Policies by Banks

Question: What is the background for this adjustment of policies?

Answer: As of 2003, the Government has put forward a series of macro-control policies on both the supply and demand of the real estate market, comprehensively utilizing means such as land, credit, tax and administration, so as to rationally steer housing consumption, rein in investment in the real estate industry, promote structural adjustment and curb the excessive increase of housing prices.

These macro-control polices and measures are of great significance in contributing to a long-term and healthy development of the real estate market. Some achievements have already been made so far. However, due to different policy enforcement in various regions and the change of market demands, irrational increase of housing prices have occurred in some cities in spite of the comparative decrease of the growth rate of investment in the real estate industry recently. The burden on housing purchasers for self-residing purposes have therefore gone up, which have attracted the attention of both the Central Party Committee and the State Council to a great extent.

The *Notice on Adjusting Housing Credit Policies and Deposit Rates for Excess Reserves* published by the PBC on March 16, 2005 stipulates that the minimum down payment ratio of housing loans would be heightened from 20% to 30% for cities or regions seeing excessive increases of real estate prices, and that the cities and regions subject to down payment adjustment in particular would be decided by commercial banks on their own based on the increases of real estate prices for various regions published by related government departments. The present *Notice of Opinions of the Ministry of Construction and other Ministries on Adjusting the Demand-supply Structure of Housing and Stabilizing the Growth Rate of Housing Prices Forwarded by the General Office of the State Council* clearly stipulates that the minimum down payment ratio of housing loans shall be increased on a discriminative basis as of June 1, 2006.

Question: What is the main content of this adjustment of policies?

Answer: The main content of this adjustment of polices is as follows: firstly, the minimum down payment ratio of housing loans (excluding housing provident fund loans) extended by commercial banks (including rural cooperative banks, urban and rural credit cooperatives, the same hereinafter) should be no less than 30%; secondly, the minimum down payment ratio of housing loans for purchasing houses for self-residing purpose and with a construction size below 90 M^2 will be maintained at 20% as previously stipulated.

Question: Why the minimum down payment ratio on borrowers for purchasing houses less than 90 M^2 and for self-residing purpose is not heightened?

Answer: According to the basic principle regarding the government's macro-control targeted at the real estate market, housing consumption loans should be treated differently, guided for different categories and no "one-size-fits-all" policy should be applied. Firstly, we should support medium and low income households to solve their housing problems via purchasing medium and small sized houses for self-residing purposes; secondly, we should actively foster an energy-saving housing consumption concept; thirdly, we will steer real estate developers to adjust their product structure and build houses not only in compliance with China's energy restraints but also satisfying the basic housing demands of the public.

Question: Why "houses for self-residing purposes" is emphasized?

Answer: The *Regulations on Individual Housing Loans* published by the PBC in 1998 definitely stipulates that housing loans refer to loans extended toward borrowers for purchasing ordinary homes for self-residing purposes. Ever since commercial banks' housing loan services were originated, the objective is to support residents to purchase ordinary housing for self-residing purposes. With the increase of residents' income and the rapid development of the real estate market, housing loans have also become financing resources for real estate investment in the mean time of satisfying a magnitude of demand for purchasing homes for self-residing purposes.

To rein in speculation in the real estate market, control irrational increase of demand and housing prices, credit policies of commercial banks must adhere to the principle of "mainly supporting housing purchase for self-residing purposes". This will not only prevent conducts of purchasing multiple houses less than 90 M^2 via bank loans, but also encourage commercial banks to enhance risk management capability and conscientiously prevent loan risks by means of categorizing the demands into self-residing purposes and for investing purposes. It is worthy emphasizing that borrowers should truthfully declare the usage of the homes to be purchased when applying for housing loans, and should not declare homes bought not for self-residing purpose as for self-residing purpose. Commercial banks should timely record related information in "PBC's Individual Credit Information Basic Database" as required. Borrowers should heighten their awareness of creditworthiness. Any information misreporting shall have a negative effect on the borrower's credit record so that borrowers are expected to treat this issue earnestly and declare truthfully.

Commercial banks can acquire not only borrowers' credit information via the PBC's "Individual Credit Information Basic Database" but also information regarding housing trading and registration through local real estate authorities in order to make a judgment on whether the homes are bought for "self-residing purposes" to the greatest extent.

Question: What will be the effect of this adjustment of policies?

Answer: Housing credit policy adjustment this time was made on a discriminative basis aimed at reining in irrational increase of housing demands and housing prices as well as at satisfying the housing demands of the medium and lower income households by supporting the structural adjustment of housing supply. Heightening the minimum down payment ratio is conducive to curbing the irrational housing demand. To take a home priced at 1 million yuan as an example, 1 million yuan is enough to make down payment for the purchase of 5 homes when the minimum down payment ratio is set at 20%, while it can only make down payment for the purchase of 3.3 housing units when the minimum down payment ratio is raised to 30%, so that the purchasing demand could be reduced somewhat. In the process of adjusting supply structure, the decrease of demand is conducive to alleviating the increase pressure on housing prices.

Notice of the General Office of the State Council on Forwarding the Opinions of the Ministry of Construction and other Ministries on Adjusting the Demand-supply Structure of Housing and Stabilizing Housing Prices

People's governments of all provinces, autonomous regions, municipalities directly under the central government, all ministries, commissions and institutions directly managed by the State Council:

The State Council has approved the *Opinions on Adjusting the Demand-supply Structure of Housing and Stabilizing Housing Prices* formulated by Ministry of Construction, National Development and Reform Commission, Ministry of Supervision, Ministry of Finance, Ministry of Land and Resources, People's Bank of China, State Administration of Taxation, National Bureau of Statistics and China Banking Regulatory Commission and hereby forwards to you for implementation.

The real estate industry is an important new pillar industry in our country. Guiding and promoting a continuous, stable and healthy development of the real estate industry is conducive to maintaining a steady and relatively fast growth of national economy, satisfying the basic housing consumption demand of the general public and achieving the objective of building a well-off society on a comprehensive basis. At present, we should further strengthen guiding and controlling the market by mainly targeting the inherent problems in the development of the real estate industry. In accordance with the requirement of the scientific development perspective, we should insist on applying and improving related policies, adjusting housing structure and fostering rational consumption; we should insist on deepening reform, seeking both temporary solution and permanent cure, strengthening the rule of law and standardizing orders; we should set priorities and categorize guidance on a differential basis. People's governments in all regions, esp. in the cities, should conscientiously take charge and make it part of your responsibilities to adjust housing supply structure and restrain excessive increase of housing prices so as to promote the healthy development of the real estate industry. Related departments of the State Council shall form a joint examination group to conduct a collective examination on whether the central government's policies on controlling the real estate market have been put into effect in all regions since 2005. Those cities which exhibit an unsatisfactory implementation of these policies, fail to effectively control housing prices or come up with strained problems in terms of housing restructuring or displacing the residents shall be criticized and ordered to correct within a time limit.

Opinions on Adjusting the Demand-supply Structure of Housing and Stabilizing Housing Prices

Since last year, various regions and departments have enforced Central Party Committee's decisions and measures on strengthening control of the real estate market, which has primarily curbed the momentum of housing investment and price increases. However, problems in the real estate industry have not been solved fundamentally, as reflected in that housing prices in a few cities have gone up too quickly, housing supply structure is rather unreasonable and the real estate market is relatively chaotic. In order to conscientiously solve the present problems in the real estate market, all policies and measures put forward in the *Notice of the General Office of the State Council on Conscientiously Stabilizing Housing Prices* (General Office of the State Council Cable [2005]No.26) and *Opinions of the Ministry of Construction and other Ministries on Stabilizing Housing Prices forwarded by the State Council* (General Office of the State Council Document [2005] No. 8) should be implemented earnestly and continuously and adjusted properly in accordance with the new situation in the real estate market. Opinions regarding adjusting housing supply structure and stabilizing housing price are hereby put forward as follows:

Conscientiously Adjusting the Housing Supply Structure

Stipulating and implementing the housing construction plan. Ordinary commercial homes of medium and low prices and of medium and small sizes for local residents' self-residing purposes should be developed on priority. People's governments of cities at all levels (including counties) should formulate housing construction plans and include the construction objectives for ordinary commercial houses, economically affordable houses and low rent houses in the 11th 5-year program, esp. this year and next year, as well as local development plans of the near term. The housing construction plans of cities at all levels should be published no later than the end of September 2006. People's governments of municipalities directly under central government, cities with independent budget and provincial capital cities should file their housing construction plans with the Ministry of Construction, while other cities should file their housing construction plans with construction authorities at provincial levels. Construction (Planning) authorities should strengthen supervision on planning functions together with supervisory authorities and urge the implementation nationwide.

Specifying the housing structure ratio. In the 11th 5-year program, ordinary commercial houses shall be developed on priority. Since June 1, 2006, newly approved and newly developed ordinary housing construction projects must consist of units with construction size below 90 M^2 (including economically affordable houses) accounting for more than 70% of the total construction areas. In case of special circumstances, municipalities directly under the central government, cities with independent budget and provincial capital cities need to secure approval from the Ministry of Construction if they want to change the above ratio. Projects approved already but not yet granted construction licenses should be adjusted accordingly if they do not meet the above requirements.

Further Applying the Roles of Taxation, Credit and Land Policies to Make Adjustments

Adjusting business tax in the home transferring process. In order to restrain the purchasing demand out of speculation or investment purposes, selling of houses within 5 years since their purchases are subject to full business taxation on the revenue gained as of June 1, 2006. Individual selling of ordinary houses exceeding 5 years (inclusive) since their purchases are exempt from business taxes. Individual selling of non-ordinary houses exceeding 5 years (inclusive) since their purchases are subject to business taxes levied on the difference between the sales revenue and cost of purchase. Tax authorities should be strict with tax enforcement and prevent from levy loopholes and discretionary reduction or exemption.

Hardening conditionality on credit extension to real estate enterprises. In order to restrain real estate development enterprises stockpiling land and houses with the support of bank loans, commercial banks are not allowed to extend loans to real estate enterprises if they can not satisfy conditions such as the project equity requirement of at least 35% of the total funds needed. For development enterprises with relatively large unused land or vacant commercial houses, commercial banks should be strict with loan extension or any other form of rollover credit extension in accordance with the principle of prudential operation. Commercial banks are not allowed to accept commercial houses vacant for more than 3 years as collateral of their loans. Appropriately adjusting housing consumption policies on a discriminative basis. In order to control the excessive increase of housing prices, the minimum down payment ratio of individual housing mortgage loans must not be less than 30% as of June 1, 2006. Considering the housing demand of medium and low income people, the minimum payment ratio for purchasing houses for self-residing purposes and with sizes less than 90 M^2 will remain at 20%.

Ensuring land supply for low priced as well as medium and small sized ordinary commercial houses. People's governments at all levels should formulate annual land-using plan and scientifically ascertain land supply for real estate development. Priority should be given to land supply of medium and low priced as well as medium and small sized ordinary commercial houses (including economically affordable houses) and low rent houses. The annual land supply for such houses must be at least 70% of the total land supply for residential purposes. Construction enterprises should be selected through tendering and bidding for land prices and housing prices on the basis that housing unit structure and housing prices are subject to restriction. Suspension of land supply for developing villa-like real estates shall be continued and land supply for low-density as well as big-sized houses will be strictly controlled.

Strengthening disposal of land left unused. Departments such as Land and Planning should strengthen supervision on land for developing real estates. For land left unused for more 1 year since its contracted construction date, high fees shall be levied according to laws and construction enterprises shall be ordered to start and complete projects within a time limit. For land left unused for more than 2 years since its contracted construction date, the land use right shall be revoked free of charge. Land with construction initiated on the contracted date but failing to reach 1/3 of the total construction area or with investment failing to reach 1/4 of the total amount and with an unauthorized suspension of constructing for over 1 year shall be considered as land left unused.

Rationally Controlling the Scale and Speed of Urban Residence Dismantling and Removal

Strictly controlling passive housing demand. All regions should, in accordance with the *Notice of the General Office of the State Council on Controlling the Scale of Urban Residence Dismantling and Removal* (State Council General Office Document [2004] 46), strengthen the planning management of residence dismantling and removal, rationally controlling the scale and speed of urban residence dismantling and removal so as to slow down the excessive increase of passive housing demand. Residence dismantling and removal scale in all regions should be controlled within the level of that in 2005.

All regions should proceed with residence dismantling and removal according to their abilities and refrain from engaging in massive residence dismantling and construction. In the case that relocation and compensation policies are not in place, residence dismantling should not be conducted and legitimate rights of the masses should be by no means damaged.

Further adjusting and standardizing the order of the real estate market

Strengthening supervision in the whole course of real estate construction. Projects approved but yet to be constructed must be planned and reviewed again. Projects failing to meet the planning requirements, with house unit structure exceeding the stipulations in particular, shall not be granted the planning license, construction license and commercial house pre-sale license. In case that the designs or the projects are altered without approval or houses are constructed violating stipulations, such house shall be dealt with according to laws or even confiscated.

Conscientiously correcting irregularities in the real estate market. The real estate as well as the industrial and commercial administration authorities should investigate into and penalize conducts against laws and regulations such as contract frauds in the trading process, and should strengthen investigation and penalty on enterprises which grudge the sale of available houses, viciously speculate or bid up housing prices. In case that the misconducts are extremely grave and serious, economic fines shall be imposed on these enterprises according to laws and regulations till having their business licenses revoked and responsible officers held accountable for the consequence.

Gradually solving the housing difficulty of low income households

Speeding up the establishment of urban low rent housing system. Low rent houses is the main channel to solve the housing difficulty of low income households so the coverage of low rent house system should be widened gradually and stably. Cities still without a low rent housing system must establish it before the end of 2006 and rationally ascertain as well as publish the construction scale of such low rent houses for this year and next year. The financing sources for low rent houses must be in place. People's governments in cities must use a proportion of the net profit from the sale of land for the construction of low rent houses, while finance departments at all levels should reinforce their support in this regard as well. By the end of 2006, all regions must arrange the construction of low rent houses to some extent.

Standardizing the development of economically affordable houses. All regions should continue their efforts in constructing economically affordable houses so as to solve the problems in the course of construction and sales as well as truly satisfy the housing demand of low income households. Various policies regarding the economically affordable houses should be strictly implemented and supervision should be strengthened in order to stop misconducts by some regulatory departments such as purchasing houses in disguised forms to seek unjustified gains. Cooperative housing construction using funds collectively raised shall be strictly controlled, while unjustified allocation of material benefits in the form of such housing construction based on administrative powers of some units must be prohibited.

Actively developing the house secondary market and house leasing market. We should encourage residents to appropriately improve their housing conditions by means of exchange or rental. In the mean time, we should increase the supply of medium and low priced as well as medium and small sized houses from more sources.

Improving the statistics and information disclosure system of real estates

Establishing and improving information system and information release system for the real estate market. People's governments in the cities should expedite the survey of housing conditions, fully command information regarding local housing aggregates, structure, conditions and consumption characters, establish and improve the information system and information release system for the real estate market and increase information transparency in the real estate market. Market surveillance and analysis system should be improved while statistics and real estate authorities should periodically publicize situation regarding market supply and demand and housing prices so as to release information of market supply and demand fully, timely and accurately.

Insisting on correctly guiding orientation of public opinion. Publicity regarding the real estate market policies should be strengthened to ensure objective and fair report of the situation in the real estate market and lead the public to establish a correct understanding of housing consumption. Misconducts such as providing false information, viciously speculating and misleading the consumers' expectation will be dealt with seriously.

Ministry of Construction, National Development and Reform Commission, Ministry of Supervision, Ministry of Finance, Ministry of Land and Resources, People's Bank of China, State Administration of Taxation, National Bureau of Statistics and China Banking Regulatory Commission

4

Money, Banking and Credit

Monetary and credit management aspects have their own peculiar significance in the macro-economic management. In monetary management system , on the one hand, there is a need to orient the quantity of money supply in accordance with the actual demand of the economy on regular basis. On the other hand, the flow of financial resources in credit management system cannot be left to the discretion of commercial banks and financial institutions, it is also necessary to direct the flow of these resources in greater quantities to the socially debilitated but productive and priority-accorded sectors.

In the context of Nepal having adopted an open economy, an excessive level of liquidity will initially exert pressure on the balance of payments and foreign exchange reserve and subsequently cause adverse effects on the domestic price situation. Thus, it will be necessary to maintain a balanced monetary position to attain the economic growth rate envisaged in the plan. The sustainable economic growth can only be achieved if the monetary balance is maintained.

Another important objective of monetary management is to achieve maximum mobilisation of internal resources. The monetary policy needs to be oriented towards encouraging the people to save through the creation of a competitive environment among banks and financial institutions and motivating the desirous entrepreneurs to mobilise the available resources through the collection of' the scattered savings in production and employment generating programme in the country. In this perspective, it is necessary along with a planned process of economic development to initiate programmes that can create new financial bases for the economy, consolidate the existing ones and encourage healthy competition. A review of the requirements and availability of resources reveals that there is a tremendous resource gap between resource requirements arid its availability in the country; this is indeed indicative of the fact that a large share of private savings is still lying outside the domain of institutional systems, In this context, an efficient mobilisation of internal resources can further enhance the participation of the private sector in the economic development of the nation.

CURRENT CHALLENGES IN THE MONETARY SECTOR

It is necessary to Control the rate of monetary expansion in harmony with the development of' the real sector in order to maintain internal and external balance in the economy but. this has not, been achieved as yet The main factors contributing to the Prevalence Of this Situation are (a) failure to minimize the role of' the government, (b) continued increase in net, foreign assets leading to increase in liquidity, (c) failure to enhance resource mobilization by banks and institution it) a warranyed manner, (d) the position of the money market and the scarcity of alternative monetary tools, (e) lack of dynamism in the capital market, and (f) the absence of a competitive environment.

Over the recent years, there were some efforts made to prevent the government sector from becoming a cause for monetary expansion by gradually limiting its role but there has not been any significant decline in the government role except in a very few instances. The present government has adopted the policy of limiting the role of the government gradually to prevent it from causing monetary expansion and developing the private sector as the backbone of the economy. In this context, it is incumbent upon HMG to observe strict monetary discipline. The continued growth in net foreign exchange assets and the subsequent liquidity generated by this have become the main factors causing monetary expansion. There have not developed any effective measures to counteract the adverse impact of the above mentioned growth on monetary liquidity. The central bank can issue or sell government treasury bills or Nepal Rastra Bank bonds under its ownership in order to control the monetary expansion created by the increased foreign exchange reserve. However, this measure also does not seem to be easily attainable in the context of the extent of security and the limited demand for the securities. It is the repayment of long term external loans and the adoption of a flexible import policy that can possibly remedy this adverse effect of increased reserve. However, this requires the identification of an appropriate level of foreign exchange reserve.

One of the main reasons behind the failure to achieve monetary stability is the lack of warranted increase in mobilisation of internal resources by banks and financial institutions. With the objective of enhancing the efficiency of capital through healthy competition among financial institutions and thus achieving maximum utilization of internal resources, the Nepal Rastra Bank gradually liberalised the bank's interest rates and allowed full autonomy in this respect in August, 1989. This policy of independent interest rates was expected to reduce the disparity between deposits and credit through an increased rate of interest on the deposits but this, too, did not materialise. Consequently, the Nepal Rastra Bank adopted an increment of 2 percentage points in the bank rate for the commercial banks to adopt an expensive monetary policy. The implementation of this policy also could not raise the interest rates as expected. The existing banks and financial institutions in the country have not been able to undertake the functions of mobilising the deposits, increasing the flow of credit disbursement by identifying potential sectors for investments, developing new saving schemes, and creating a favourable environment to win the confidence of the general public in the banking system. Consequently, the banking sector has not been able to develop a profound financial intensity. A greater proportion of financial assets in Gross National Income alone can ensure the efficacy of monetary policies, and in this context, it is essential for the banks and financial institutions to create an atmosphere conducive to financial development. Other factors preventing the monetary development and stability are the preliminary stage of the money market and the lack of proper monetary tools. The money market even after having traversed through a long stretch of planned economic development has remained in its rudimentary stage. There exist severely limited alternative monetary instruments in the money market to facilitate the investors to make use of their savings. The government treasury bills and the central bank securities are only short term investment expedients to the institutional investors. The market for call money has not shown a favourable development either. In this situation it has become imperative to make appropriate arrangements to develop new alternative instruments to infuse dynamism into the money market.

It requires a dynamic capital market to mobilise the internal resources and attain a favourable economic growth rate. Our capital market, however, is still in a preliminary stage. The Security Exchange Centre has not been able to arrange any institutional brokers, nor has it been able to manage swiftly the issuance and sale of' shares and bonds of' industrial units. It is primarily concentrated in operating a second market for especially government securities. Consequently, the capital market has not been able to mobilise the internal resources in expected quantities.

The absence of requisite financial development even after a long period of planned economic development efforts can be attributed to the lack of a competitive spirit among banks and financial institutions. It is necessary to develop new financial institutions, leasing companies, banks in the private sector or with joint foreign investment and other specialized agencies for the creation of a competitive environment. These arrangements can develop the prerequisite infrastructure for the creation of a healthy competitive atmosphere and only then can a systematic utlisation of the savings scattered among the general public be assured.

The rural branches of commercial banks opened in the rural areas of Nepal do not seem to have activated their role effectively in deposit mobilisation and loan distribution. In view of the contradictory situation where the ratio of a banking office and population points towards the lack of adequate number of branches of commercial banks on one hand, and the existing branches have failed to deliver results, on the other, the banking sector and credit system of ours appear to be fraught with challenges. The unorganised market appears to be playing a role greater than that of the institutional market in meeting the credit needs; this situation seems to have minimised the contextual importance of interest rates and credit policies. The great disparities between the interest rates of institutional and unorganised market have evidently created the existence of a dual credit system. As long as this dual system continues, the efficacy of the credit system and monetary policy naturally becomes reduced.

To solve the above problems, it is necessary to further extend the banking system. Along with establishing new branches of banks and financial institutions, the existing branches need to be properly developed and expanded. This requires promoting a habit among the people to deposit their savings in banks and making it more attractive. By developing new monetary and fiscal tools and providing returns to these savings the financial saving should , thus, be made more attractive in comparison to investment in other unproductive assets.

This also requires arrangements for appropriate interest rate structure and grades, otherwise the financial savings may not grow as expected. Increased financial savings alone will not be sufficient, it will be necessary to channel them to productive employment oriented sectors. This again calls for proper identification of viable projects and fulfillment of an adequate loan demand of the entrepreneurs. The entrepreneurs will be obliged to resort to borrowings from the unorganised market to fulfil their needs, if they have to encounter various cumbersome procedures and hindrances in obtaining loans and also if the loans are not available in time in sufficient amounts.

To solve this problem, it is necessary to simplify and upgrade the quality of loan distribution procedures. As regards credit utilisation, the commercial banks have not been able to make available credit facilities in the priorities sectors as targeted. The commercial banks have failed, in particular, to identify viable agricultural, cottage and small scale projects and attract entrepreneurs towards them. However, without the promotion of such activities, the development of one of the poorest agricultural nations like Nepal does not seem to be an eventual possibility at all. A healthy development of the financial sector and an additional increase in the income of the common people can create a stronger base for additional investment in development activities through the enhanced financial savings accumulated in the banks. This is also one of the reasons why the commercial banks should be stronger and more capable of directing the flow of credit extension to the priority-accorded sectors. It is necessary to further motivate the commercial banks towards this end.

The disparity between the rate of interest offered on deposits and the one charged on loans reflects the efficiency of the financial sector. This disparity is of a higher degree in Nepal. This has given rise to a situation where on the one hand, the deposit mobilisation has not occurred as expected and, on the other, there looms in the horizon the fear of credit facilities becoming more expensive. To remedy this situation, the banks need to control their overhead costs, lighten the burden of redundant staff and render the banking activities more efficient and cost effective through the utilization of new, innovative tools and technologies. It is equally important in this context to observe strict financial discipline and avoid red-tapism and procrastination in making policy decisions and in working procedures.

MONETARY AND CREDIT PROGRAMME IN THE EIGHTH PLAN

In view of the significant role of the banks and financial institutions in resource mobilisation, it is absolutely a prerequisite condition to enhance the efficiency and Soundness of the banking and financial sectors. The banking promotion and credit programmes of the Eighth Plan have been formulated with a view to increasing the employment opportunities the productive base of the economy- through the mobilisation of resources and consolidation of their proper utifisation.

Utilisation of Indirect Monetary Instruments

Nepal has now adopted a liberal economic system. The banking and monetary policies also have been so trained that they reconcile with this liberal policy. Accordingly the desirable standards of monetary and banking resources will be determined wit h the help of indirect instruments without, any direct interference. With the objective of assisting ill the refinement of excessive liquidity observed in the economy, a liquidity proportion of 36 percent was fixed with arrangements for cash balance to be compulsorily available to the tune of 12 percent of the deposits and 24 percent of total deposits to be invested in government treasury bills or bonds issued by the central bank. The provision of maintaining additional liquidity of 24 percent of deposit will be done away within the very initial Years of the Eighth Plan.

The monetary sector will instead accord preference to open market techniques in order to assist in the macro economic management. In the event of an excessive demand for financial resources in the economy, the Nepal Rastra Bank will reduce the liquidity through the sale of treasury bills or bonds issued by His Majesty's Government or the bank itself. The Nepal Rastra bank when bringing about changes in the bank rates as an indirect monetary instruments will inform the banks, financial institution and the general public about the nature of' the monetary policy, whether it is expansionary or concretionary.

Credit Extension to Priority-Sectors

The present provision for a bank to extend a specified proportion of total credit outlay to priority sectors calls for a review in the present context of the liberal economic and monetary policies. The banks are allowed to use their own discretion whether to extend credit facility to such sectors to the tune of' 12 percent of the total credit in the present system. However, in spite of adopting the liberal policy, the concept of priority sectors and a directed flow of financial resources to them cannot be totally forsaken in view of the great need of capital among the skilled and enthusiastic entrepreneurs with meager income and, above all, the government's commitment to development of the rural sector. Therefore, it is targeted to establish separate rural development banks on a regional basis solely for the development of the rural sector. These banks will function as specialized agencies to channelize the flow of credit to the priority sectors. A detailed programme in this regard will be put forth for inplementation within the initial years of the Eighth Plan.

Formulation of Monetary Programme

An efficient utilisation of resources is equally as important as the arrangement of resources for economic management. Therefore, internal and external stability in using financial resources needs to be specially emphasized. In the Nepalese context, if there is a monetary or credit expansion beyond a sustainable limit, there will be an increase in the prices of goods and services on the domestic front, which will lead to increased import to meet the growing demand. This will adversely affect the balance of payments situation, deplete foreign exchange reserves and on the whole create imbalances in the external sector as a whole. To avoid the emergence of such situation in the economy, a monetary programme will be formulated on the basis of an extensive analysis of the economy at the beginning of every fiscal year by reconciling the physical sector and monetary or credit sector with each other for maintaining a balanced situation. Therefore, the growth rate of mo ney supply and credit structure will be determined in a manner compatible with the changes in different variables such as sustainable economic growth rate, inflation, and external situation etc. As stated above in the same context, monetary and credit management will be conducted by utilising indirect instruments.

Policy of Positive Rates of Interest

In the event of the real rates of interest acquiring a negative trend, there may appear hindrances to the mobilisation of financial resources. Similarly, if the interest rates are not maintained at an appropriate level, the resources may be utilised in less productive sectors and the economy may not obtain reasonable returns from the investment. Therefore, it is necessary for a policy on interest rates to be able to solve this problem, and efforts will be made to the fullest possible extent to make positive interest rates. Hence, the monetary and financial policies will be put into use in keeping with the same objective.

Government Role and Interference in Credit Management

In one of the poorest nations like Nepal where there live a large section of population below the absolute poverty line it is necessary to enhance their productivity and increase employment opportunities for them. And, in the context of the changed economic policies, it becomes a national duty to make available some returns of development efforts to these people, too. The credit extension under various programmes to be conducted in the priority sector, in particular, needs to be directed mainly to these people alone. Our past experiences have demonstrated that a simple and convenient procurement of a loan is of greater significance than its rate of interest.

The banks and financial institutions should mobilise credit extension to these groups in such a manner that they make some profit over and above the realisation of the actual cost. This section of the population also should not be treated as an exception in the application of the technique of determining an interest rate on the basis of demand and supply situation. However, the creation of an environment in which there is an assurance of the credit facility is a prerequisite condition. The confidence of being able to obtain loans can infuse dynamism into the economic activities of these people, too.

At the very initial stage of the implementation of the credit programmes in the Eighth Plan, special attention will be paid to the needs of the targeted groups and the utility of credit. Similarly short term expedient measures such as granting subsidy or waiving interest or even the loan amount on political or personal grounds, although they may look attractive initially, will be highly discouraged as they may deplete or debilitate the allocation of the resources of the economy in the long run.

Total Bank Credit Structure

In the past, a considerable share of the limited bank credit outlay was procured by the government. Furthermore, the public enterprises also obtained huge sums of money on government guarantee. In consequence, the private sector was often deprived of the opportunity of any credit facility.

Now, in the context of HMG pursuing a policy of fiscal discipline, the budget deficit has declined and the monetization of the deficit has been considerably minimized too. This trend will be continued during the Eighth Plan. Similarly, as the credit extension to public enterprises on government guarantee adversely affects the soundness of the financial institution and of the commercial banks in their finances, a policy will be adopted to follow the usual market techniques for providing loans to government undertakings. The banking sector will assist through credit extension in the efficiency and productivity enhancing activities of the private sector in domestic or foreign trade.

Expansion of Branch Offices

The expansion of branches entails an unnecessary increased burden of expenditure on the commercial banks and financial institutions causing an adverse impact on their profits. In view of this experience, the branches will be extended on a commercial basis only to economically viable and appropriate places. Expanding the activities of the branches running in loss,' efforts will be made to operate them in profit. The branches which fail to show any profit, even after functional adjustments will either be merged with the nearest banking office or dissolved. However, appropriate programmes may be introduced to provide some banking services even in the areas without banking offices or without any feasibility of any economic activities expanding within a short period. These programmes may include the introduction of Post-Office Saving Bank, Mobile Savings Bank, Mobile Credit Bank and Cooperative programmes, etc.

Strengthening of Banking and Financial Institutions

Necessary steps aimed at appropriate allocation of' Financial resources will be taken in the following subjects on the basis of the position of the economy. These steps will strengthen the financial position of the banks.

a. Transparent rules on directed loans,

b. Sufficiency of the deposits of banks and financial institutions,

c. Simplification and transparency of laws and regulations relating to banks and financial institutions,

d. A congenial situation for an entry of new financial institutions and the exit of existing ones,

e. Development of the second market,

f. Diversification in financial instruments,

g. Non interference in the activities of banks and financial institutions from the government.

Finance Company

The establishment and development of finance companies will be emphasized for (fie creation and extension of a Competitive financial environment, Appropriate programmes will be formulated for a convenient supply of financial resources from banks to such financial institutions to meet their short term needs. The development of these institutions in Nepal has not taken place to a desired extent. In this context, the commercial banks should come to the aid of these institutions so that they may be able to mobilise their own medium and long-term resources in the future. The structure of a finance company determines the extent of its activities. Smaller companies of this nature will confine themselves to discounting the commercial bills, bills of exchange and cheques whereas the financing of long term projects will require the assistance of large companies. The Eighth Plan will launch programmes to establish and extend as far as possible such finance companies which may be capable of making arrangements for long term financial resources.

Commercial Banks and Financial Institutions

In the present context of the commercial banks being the only prominent institutions in the Nepalese economy to mobilise the collection of scattered monetary savings among the common people, the establishment of financial institutions may provide further assistance in the monetary collection work. These financial institutions will, at the same time, be both competitive with and complementary to commercial banks. In urban sectors with sound financial bases the finance companies will compete with banks, but in areas with relatively scarce financial bases, these companies will play a role complementary to banking activities.

These finance companies classified as non-banking agencies can engage in various activities including providing loans to clients for personal use and are thus provisioned under the Company Act. However, the Nepal Rastra Bank in the capacity of a monetary authority will inspect and supervise their activities in a subtle manner. Special provisions will be made in the early years of the Eighth Plan with regard to the framework of their sources and utilisation of resources in large urban areas and the rural sector.

Credit Policy of Commercial Banks

Improving upon the traditional collateral-oriented credit policy the commercial banks have now begun extending loans in accordance with the merit of the project or programme. This policy of programme oriented credit extension will be further encouraged. However, it is equally important to make this kind of credit extension risk-free for the commercial banks. Therefore, an efficient monitoring unit will be formed to supervise whether the extended credit is utilised productively and meaningfully in keeping with the purpose or not. A health report of the project will be prepared and made available. The credit amount applied for by the projects will be disbursed in installment basis.

Collateral Arrangements

The practice of extending loan against collateral cannot be stopped immediately. Although the share of such loans in total bank credit extension can be lowered comparatively, providing loans on the collateral of gold and silver or food products has their significance in the economy. The provision of loans on the collateral of a stock of agricultural produce alone can do away with the compulsion of exporting food grains at lower prices. Therefore, the system of accepting the stock of products as collateral for loans needs to be encouraged. However, such loans will be extended only upon ascertaining the quality and quantity of products in the stock and making proper warehousing arrangements for them.

Computerization of Commercial Banks

In the initial stage, computerization will entail additional expenditure and training in computer technology will be equally necessary. The replacement of traditional accounting system, auditing and supervision by a new technology may create a psychological impact among employees of their relative significance having been decreased. Therefore, the banks should proceed with computerization on a phased basis by emphasizing on the positive aspects of the computers that they do not make employees redundant but instead enhance the work quality, lighten the employees' operational burden and even create more personnel requirements through the expansion of the banking operation. The Eighth Plan will accordingly orient the banking business towards modern technology.

Strengthening of Institutional Intermediaries

The availability of financial resources is a prerequisite for exploiting the possibilities of economic development. To expand the activities of the existing banks and financial institutions, it is necessary to augment the use of new instruments, to introduce new technology in their operation and to develop a new management system in their organisation. Moreover, it is also equally important to establish additional institutions in keeping with the demand of the economy. Therefore, these aspects will be given special emphasis in the Eighth Plan in order to achieve extensive financial soundness of the economy. Similarly, due attention will be paid to savings and credit management through the development and expansion of financial institutions. This will extend support to the efforts of controlling the rate of inflation. The organisational structures of various institutions will be reconciled with the emergent changes in the economic structure.

Establishment of a Rural Bank

During the Eighth Plan period, rural banks will be established with a view to attaining sustainable economic development through an intensive increase in rural economic activities. The activities of these banks will definitely support the programmes aimed at raising the standard of living of the people living in abject poverty below the absolute poverty line and reduce the regional disparities. These banks will operate in the rural sector and extend credit facilities to small and cottage industries, income generating and productive agricultural activities and small scale business and trade. Upon the establishment of these banks, various rural sector programmes such as priority sector credit and small farmer's credit and those of the commercial banks, too, will be conducted through them.

5

Funneling Financial Data into Failure Probabilities

Along with most of the rest of us, U.S. commercial banks enjoyed the good economic times of the 1990s. Since 1992, the banking sector's average return on assets has easily topped the 1 percent benchmark that banking analysts apply to individual institutions as an indicator of healthy earnings. Recently, however, several indicators have pointed toward emerging weakness. For example, Standard & Poor's composite index of bank stocks has not kept pace with the S&P 500, meaning that publicly traded banks have not been performing as well as other publicly traded businesses. In addition, the yields on bank subordinated debt have risen relative to the yields on similarly rated corporate bonds, meaning that holders of sub debt perceive an increase in the likelihood of default. Finally, the business press has begun to note loan quality problems at large banks. Problems in the banking sector are not just a concern for bankers. Healthy banks are essential to the smooth operation of the economy. Commercial banks enhance economic efficiency by channeling surplus funds from household savers to business investors. Banks also serve as a key link in the chain that runs from the Federal Reserve to the macroeconomy. The Fed changes the level of bank reserves by buying and selling Treasury securities in the open market. Banks respond to changes in the level of their reserves by expanding or contracting their loan portfolios. A weak banking sector can limit the impact of monetary policy actions on the supply of credit and hamper the ability of bank-dependent firms to get credit. Indeed, in the early 1930s, nearly 9,000 banks failed, leading to a sharp contraction of the money supply and to a virtual dry-up of bank credit.

GETTING A HANDLE ON BANKING CONDITIONS

Measuring the overall condition of the banking sector can be tricky. Because only large banks issue stock or subordinated debt that is actively traded in financial markets, trends in the prices of bank securities say little about the condition of small banks. Moreover, looking at accounting ratios-such as returns on assets or loan delinquency rates-can sometimes provide misleading signals because of the trade-off between bank risk and return. For example, a bank may choose to specialize in making high risk loans, meaning that it will suffer from a high number of bad loans, but will also enjoy high interest income. Looking at interest income or delinquencies in isolation does not, therefore, provide a complete picture of the bank's condition. To gauge the overall condition of the bank, it is necessary to combine various measures of risk and profitability into one measure. Summarizing these measures across the entire banking sector would then shed some light on overall banking conditions.

Statistical models are typically used in bank supervision to generate measures of overall bank conditions. Bank supervisors use these models to monitor the condition of individual banks between visits by bank examiners. The typical model incorporates accounting measures of credit risk, liquidity risk, capital protection and earnings strength to estimate the likelihood that a bank will fail in the coming years. Because failure prediction models have such a strong track record of detecting emerging problems, supervisors use them to increase exam frequency at selected banks and to plan regularly scheduled exams. Failure probabilities from these models can be summarized either by taking the average of all individual bank failure probabilities-the mean probability-or by selecting the middle number from a rank ordering of individual bank failure probabilities-the median probability. The accompanying chart tracks the mean and median failure probabilities since 1984.

Looking Back

The trends in mean and median failure probabilities suggest that banking conditions have been quite good for several years now. The mean failure probability rose to almost 8 percent in 1986 but has remained below 1 percent since 1994. In 1986, the median failure probability reached 0.36 percent but has stayed below 0.05 percent since 1992. The improvement in banking conditions since the early 1990s can be traced to several factors. For one thing, the U.S. economy enjoyed a long, robust expansion during the 1990s. Record economic growth and low unemployment kept mean and median failure probabilities down by boosting loan demand and interest income without increasing nonperforming loans. Another factor behind the low failure probabilities is the major shake-out that took place in the banking industry during the last decade when thousands of inefficient or poorly performing banks either exited the market or merged with larger, healthier institutions. In fact, the total number of U.S. commercial banks dropped steadily from 14,426 at year-end 1983 to 8,302 banks in the third quarter of 2000.

Where Do We Go from Here?

Although banking conditions appear strong by historical standards, the banking sector is still not immune to the effects of a weakening economy. If the economy continues to softenas many forecasters predict-the downward trend in bank risk could easily reverse itself. During the 199091 recession, for example, the mean failure probability rose from 3.73 percent in the second quarter of 1990 to 4.08 percent in the first quarter of 1991. That said, banking conditions today are much stronger than they were prior to the 1990-91 recession. Indeed, the same 35 basis point increase in failure probabilities would bump today's mean probability to only 1.00 percent, which is still quite low by historical standards.

In short, despite some evidence of emerging weakness in banks and the prospect of an economic slowdown or outright recession, the banking sector as a whole seems much better equipped to weather adverse shocks than at almost any time in recent history.

6

Monetary and Credit Policy Operations

Monetary management had to contend with testing challenges on several fronts during 2004-05. First, an increase in domestic prices in the first half of the year, driven largely by a sustained increase in international commodity prices including fuel, and an unsatisfactory and uneven South-West monsoon posed serious concerns about price stability. Second, the situation was complicated by a large overhang of domestic liquidity generated by capital inflows. Third, financial markets had to be sensitised to the expected upturn in the interest rate cycle. The Reserve Bank had to, therefore, strike a fine balance between reining in inflationary expectations, encouraging the impulses of growth and ensuring financial stability. This called for a calibrated strategy of liquidity management in conjunction with fiscal measures to cushion the impact of international commodity prices on domestic inflation. The Market Stabilisation

Scheme (MSS) was introduced in April 2004 to provide the monetary authority an additional instrument of liquidity management and sterilisation. Several measures were also initiated to maintain asset quality of the banking system at a time of rapid credit growth. Initiatives to improve the credit delivery system, especially in respect of agriculture and small and medium enterprises, gathered further momentum during the year.

MONETARY POLICY OPERATIONS

Monetary Measures

The repo/reverse repo rates signal the Reserve Bank's monetary policy stance in the short term. The fixed reverse repo rate, the price at which the Reserve Bank absorbs liquidity under the LAF, was increased by 25 basis points to 4.75 per cent, effective October 27, 2004 and by a further 25 basis points to 5.00 per cent, effective April 29, 2005. The repo rate, the price at which the Reserve Bank injects liquidity under the LAF, remained unchanged at 6.0 per cent during the year. The spread between the repo rate and the reverse repo rate was thus reduced by 25 basis points each on two occasions (to 125 basis points with effect from October 27, 2004 and 100 basis points with effect from April 29, 2005).

The cash reserve ratio (CRR) was increased to 5.0 per cent in two stages of 25 basis points each with effect from September 18, 2004 and October 2, 2004, partly to absorb liquidity from the system but more importantly, to curb inflationary expectations. The Reserve Bank continues to pursue its mediumterm objective of reducing the CRR to the statutory minimum level of 3.0 per cent. At the same time, it retains the option to use the CRR flexibly in both directions for liquidity management, in addition to other instruments.

THE WORKING AND OPERATIONS OF THE RESERVE BANK OF INDIA

Liquidity Management

The instruments used for sterilisation operations in India underwent changes during 2004-05. It was recognised that the finite stock of Government paper with the Reserve Bank could potentially circumscribe the scope of outright OMOs for sterilising capital flows. Outright OMOs for sterilization purpose were last carried out in January 2004. Accordingly, LAF, essentially an instrument of day-to-day liquidity management, had to be relied upon for sterilisation as well during 2004-05.

The sterilisation operations were also constrained by several other factors. First, under the Reserve Bank of India Act, 1934 the Reserve Bank is not allowed to borrow beyond its paid-up capital of Rs.5 crore without collateral. Second, in the past, the Reserve Bank had augmented its ability to carry out OMOs by converting non-marketable special securities funded from Treasury Bills into marketable paper. With the full conversion of the entire stock of such paper in September 2003, the Reserve Bank was unable to resort to such operations. Third, the Reserve Bank cannot issue its own paper under the extant provisions of the Reserve Bank of India Act, 1934 and such an option has generally not been favoured in India.

Central bank bills/bonds would impose the entire cost of sterilisation on the Reserve Bank's balance sheet. Besides, the existence of two sets of risk-free paper – gilts and central bank securities – tends to fragment the market. Fourth, as the Government cannot statutorily receive interest on surplus balances with the Reserve Bank, its surpluses are 'invested' in its own securities held by the Reserve Bank to avoid costs for the Government in terms of idle funds. This arrangement, however, diminishes the availability of the stock of Government securities for sterilisation operations and overall liquidity management.

The constraints on sterilization operations induced a four-fold change in the strategy of sterilisation during 2004-05. First, the MSS was introduced in April 2004 to provide the Reserve Bank with an additional instrument of liquidity management and to relieve the LAF from the burden of sterilisation operations. The total outstanding amount absorbed under the MSS at end-March 2005 amounted to Rs.64,211 crore. The papers issued under the MSS comprised dated Government securities (Rs.25,000 crore), 91-day Treasury Bills (Rs.19,248 crore) and 364-day Treasury Bills (Rs.19,963 crore). Concomitantly, the balances under LAF reverse repos fell over the course of the year. Second, the Reserve Bank hiked reserve requirements for the first time after consistently reducing them for three years. Third, the reverse repo rate was hiked after three years of reduction to signal the Reserve Bank's monetary policy stance. Finally, the Union Budget for 2005-06 has proposed to introduce legislation to amend the Reserve Bank of India Act, 1934 to enable the Reserve Bank to lend or borrow securities by way of repo, reverse repo or otherwise.

MONETARY POLICY STANCE FOR 2005-06

The Reserve Bank's stance of monetary policy in 2005-06 was set out as conditional upon macroeconomic prospects, global developments and the balance of risks. First, the outlook for growth which should be noticeably better than the previous year, may get moderated by developments in the international oil markets which remain tight. Second, while supply factors would continue to dominate the price situation, demand management would invite close attention. Third, adequate credit growth would need to be ensured for productive sectors while closely assessing the implications for demand management and price stability. In these circumstances, liquidity management would become critical. The interest rate outlook would have to take into account these domestic challenges but the increasing integration also warrants some attention to global factors. Fourth, the smooth completion of the significantly higher borrowing programme of the Centre, particularly in a year of strong credit demand, needs to be factored in. Finally, while the external sector is expected to continue to exhibit strength and resilience in 2005-06, globally transmitted unanticipated shocks cannot be ruled out.

It was assumed that with a normal monsoon, the growth in agriculture could be around three per cent. Further, it was expected that industry and services would maintain their current growth momentum while absorbing the impact of oil prices. The real GDP growth during 2005-06, on the basis of these assumptions, was placed around 7.0 per cent for the purpose of monetary policy formulation. Consistent with the real growth of GDP and inflation, the projected expansion of money supply (M3) for 2005-06 was placed at 14.5 per cent. In tune with this order of growth in M3, the increase in aggregate deposits of scheduled commercial banks was set at Rs.2,60,000 crore which is higher by 15.0 per cent over its level in the previous year. Non-food bank credit including non-SLR investments of banks was projected to increase by around 19.0 per cent, which was expected to adequately meet the credit needs of all the productive sectors of the economy.

Quarterly Review of Monetary Policy

In its First Quarter Review (July 26, 2005), the Reserve Bank noted that the stance of monetary policy would depend on the macroeconomic developments including the global developments and the overall balance of risks. Factors such as increased global uncertainties, high and volatile international prices of oil, incomplete pass-through of oil prices domestically, upward trajectory of the policy rate in the US, overhang of liquidity, high credit growth, sustained industrial growth and possible capacity pressures, enlargement of trade deficit, infrastructural constraints and delayed monsoon could prompt a change in the stance of policy. On the other hand, it needs to be recognised that the oil price hike has been managed well with a combination of monetary and fiscal measures, overhang of liquidity has reduced with the increase in the absorptive capacity of the economy, excess liquidity remains sterilised, visible liquidity under LAF has reduced, money supply growth is within the projected trajectory, credit flow is getting broadbased industrial growth has revived after a long period of sluggishness, pick up in investment demand is evident, investment climate remains favourable, corporate earnings and profits have been sustained, current level of inflation remains moderate both at the wholesale level and retail level, globally monetary policy continues to be somewhat accommodative and global inflation during 2005 is projected to be moderate despite high oil prices. It is apparent that there are several global uncertainties but there are domestic factors, which indicate a confidently growing economy in a stable environment. While global factors are getting to be increasingly significant for India, the domestic factors still dominate and the latter point to favouring stability to maintain growth momentum at this juncture while being ready to respond to evolving circumstances. Accordingly, the overall stance of monetary policy for the remaining part of the year 2005-06 will continue to be as set out in the Annual Policy Statement of April 2005, but the Reserve Bank would respond, promptly and effectively, to the evolving situation depending on the unfolding of risks.

CREDIT DELIVERY

Credit delivery to small borrowers, particularly to the agriculture and smallscale industries (SSI) sector, is critical to the growth of the economy. The Reserve Bank has been proactively promoting a conducive credit culture by removing bottlenecks in credit delivery and providing adequate and timely finance at reasonable rates without procedural hassles to different sections of the economy. The policies relating to rural credit have been designed to bring about economic and social change in the rural areas, especially for the benefit of poorer sections of the society.

The Reserve Bank undertook several measures to improve credit delivery to the priority sector during 2004-05. More categories of advances were brought under the ambit of the priority sector lending: In order to encourage direct lending to priority sector, investments made by banks on or after April 1, 2005 in special bonds issued by certain specified institutions have been made ineligible for classification under priority sector lending. Such investments which have already been made by banks up to March 31, 2005 would cease to be eligible for classification under priority sector lending in a phased manner. Investments made by banks on or after July 1, 2005 in venture capital have been made ineligible for classification under priority sector lending. Such investments which have already been made up to June 30, 2005 would cease to be eligible for classification under priority sector lending with effect from April 1, 2006. In brief, monetary management during 2004-05 had to contend with a spurt in inflation during the first half of the year. The Reserve Bank continued with its policy of active management of liquidity through OMOs including LAF, MSS and CRR. Various monetary measures supported by fiscal measures were successful in stabilising inflationary expectations. The Reserve Bank continued with efforts to improve credit delivery to small borrowers, particularly to the agriculture and small scale industries. The overall stance of monetary policy for 2005-06 is provision of appropriate liquidity to meet credit growth and support investment and export demand in the economy while placing equal emphasis on price stability; to pursue an interest rate environment that is conducive to macroeconomic and price stability and maintaining the momentum of growth; and to consider measures in a calibrated manner in response to evolving circumstances with a view to stabilizing inflationary expectations.

DEVELOPMENT AND REGULATION OF FINANCIAL MARKETS

Generally stable and liquid financial market conditions during 2004-05 and positive sentiment generated by the macroeconomic fundamentals enabled the Reserve Bank to persevere with the development and integration of the money, the debt and the foreign exchange markets. In view of the abundant global liquidity, high levels of leveraging and uncertainty characterizing international financial markets, ensuring a domestic environment that avoids excessive and destabilising volatility became a key objective for the Reserve Bank during the year. Efforts to convert the call money market into a pure interbank market were accompanied by several initiatives to deepen the collateralised segments of the money market in order to enable non-bank participants to access/ deploy funds. The Reserve Bank continued to develop the

Government securities market by expanding the menu of products available, enlarging the investor base and improving the technological infrastructure. Orderly conditions in the foreign exchange market and the significant two-way exchange rate movements during the year facilitated a measured liberalisation of external current and capital account transactions in 2004-05.

MONEY MARKET

The process of transforming the call/notice money segment into a pure inter-bank market with a view to facilitating the transmission of monetary policy - in pursuance of the recommendations of the Committee on Banking Sector Reforms (Chairman: Shri M. Narasimham) (1998) - was completed in August 2005. This has been supported by the development of a repo market outside the Reserve Bank in which nonbank participants are allowed to trade their surplus/deficit liquidity. Prudential limits have been placed on borrowings and lendings of banks and Primary Dealers (PDs) in the call/notice market. Furthermore, in order to smoothen the transition through 2004-05, the Reserve Bank assured the market that in case of a genuine difficulty, a higher amount may be allowed to be lent in the call/notice money market for a specific period on a case-by-case basis.

Collateralised borrowing and lending obligations (CBLOs) were operationalised as a money market instrument through the Clearing Corporation of India Limited (CCIL) on January 20, 2003. With a view to developing the market for this instrument, the Reserve Bank introduced automated value-free transfer of securities between market participants and the CCIL during 2004-05.

A repo market outside the liquidity adjustment facility (LAF) has been assiduously developed by the Reserve Bank to provide an avenue for bank and non-bank participants to trade funds after the conversion of the call/notice money market into a pure inter-bank market. In order to broaden the market, nonscheduled urban cooperative banks (UCBs) and listed companies with gilt accounts with scheduled commercial banks were allowed, subject to eligibility criteria and safeguards, to participate in the repo market outside the Reserve Bank. An electronic trading platform for market repo operations in Government securities, in addition to the existing voice based system, would also be facilitated.

The minimum maturity period of certificates of deposit (CDs) was reduced from 15 days to 7 days effective April 29, 2005 to align it with the minimum maturity of commercial paper (CP) and fixed deposits with banks.

The Reserve Bank undertook several measures to further develop the CP market during 2004-05. The Reserve Bank reduced the minimum maturity period of CP from 15 days to 7 days in the Midterm Review of October 2004 in order to provide an option to issuers to raise short-term resources through CP as also an avenue for investors to invest in quality short-term paper. Issuing and paying agents (IPAs) are required to report issuance of CP on the NDS platform within two days from the date of completion of the issue to provide transparency and also facilitate benchmarking of CP issues. Following the supply of relevant software, IPAs have been advised to start reporting of CP issuance data through NDS platform with effect from April 16, 2005. Also, with effect from July 1, 2005 the data on CP issuance are being made available on the Reserve Bank's website.

GOVERNMENT SECURITIES MARKET

The Reserve Bank stepped up efforts to further deepen and broaden the Government securities market during the year. The measures to improve functional efficiency through improved technological infrastructure were accompanied by an assessment of the risk management systems in place under the new institutional arrangements.

The Fiscal Responsibility and Budget Management (FRBM) Act, 2003 prohibits the Reserve Bank from participating in primary issuances of Government securities with effect from April

1, 2006, except under exceptional circumstances. Consequently, open market operations (OMOs) would become a more active policy instrument necessitating a review of processes and technological infrastructure consistent with market advancement. In order to address these emerging needs and equip the Reserve Bank as well as the market participants appropriately, an internal Technical Group on Central Government Securities Market was constituted. The recommendations of the Group include proposals to enlarge liquidity and improve pricing in the market, reorientation of PD system post-FRBM, standardisation of transactions in Government securities to T+1 basis, and allowing banks to carry out PD business departmentally. The recommendations of the Group relating to restructuring the underwriting obligations of PDs, allowing PDs exclusivity in primary auctions, introduction of 'When Issued Market' and short selling in Government securities would be considered in consultation with the Government.

Several initiatives were taken to develop the technological infrastructure for the efficient functioning of the Government securities market. The anonymous, order-driven trading in Government securities introduced in select stock exchanges in January 2003 has had limited success. A Working Group on Screen Based Trading in Government Securities (Chairman: Dr. R. H. Patil) recommended operationalisation of a screen-based trading system in the NDS. Accordingly, a screen based trading system was operationalised with effect from August 1, 2005 initially for the Reserve Bank regulated NDS members.

FOREIGN EXCHANGE MARKET

The Reserve Bank continued with its policy of liberalisation of external transactions with a view to deepening the foreign exchange market. Resident individuals were allowed a greater degree of freedom in terms of access to foreign exchange. Measures initiated in respect of corporates included liberalisation of norms relating to external commercial borrowings (ECBs) and dispensation of prior approval of the Reserve Bank for cross-border transfer of equity. Several measures were also undertaken to encourage exports, including overseas deployment of funds from the Exchange Earners' Foreign Currency (EEFC) accounts. This was backed by steps to provide easier access to import financing, especially with the enlargement of limits of the authorized dealers (ADs) in respect of trade credits. Import of gold, especially for jewellery exports, has also been liberalised further. Benefits for non-resident Indians (NRIs) include easier access to housing loans for acquisition of property in India.

Cancellation and rebooking of all eligible forward contracts booked by residents, irrespective of tenor, has been allowed. Banks are allowed to approve proposals for commodity hedging in international exchanges from their corporate customers. The closing time for inter-bank foreign exchange market in India has been extended by one hour up to 5.00 p.m. The Reserve Bank would disseminate additional information including traded volumes for derivatives such as foreign currency-rupee options to the market. Other recommendations relating to writing of covered options by corporates and hedging of economic risk of corporates in respect of their domesticoperations arising out of changes in the landed cost of the imported substitutes of the commodities they consume/ produce would be considered. The sequencing with regard to implementation of these measures would take into account the enabling conditions for further progress towards capital account convertibility, liberalisation in other sectors of the economy and the trend in overall balance of payments.

To sum up, the Reserve Bank continued with its efforts to increase the depth and width of the various segments of the financial market during 2004-05 with a view to enhancing allocative efficiency and ensuring financial stability. Notably, the process of converting the call money market into a pure inter-bank market was completed by August 2005. A series of measures in the foreign exchange market were aimed at further liberalisation of the current and capital account transactions. In the Government securities market, efforts continued towards improving the technological infrastructure. In the context of the FRBM Act 2003 and with a view to moving towards functional separation between debt management and monetary operations, the Reserve Bank initiated attempts to restructure/reorient the PD system. The Reserve Bank will pursue its efforts to further develop, integrate and provide vibrancy to the various segments of the financial markets.

FINANCIAL REGULATION AND SUPERVISION

The conduct of financial regulation and supervision by the Reserve Bank in 2004-05 was guided by the need for ensuring financial stability. The overriding objective has been to maintain confidence in the financial system by enhancing its soundness and efficiency. For this purpose, the Reserve Bank evaluates system-wide risks and promotes sound business and financial practices. It also conducts inspections and analyses of institution-wise risks. Over the years, the Reserve Bank has progressively aligned the regulatory framework with international best practices with country-specific adaptation. During the year, in addition to fine-tuning the prudential guidelines, the Reserve Bank focussed on encouraging market discipline and ensuring good governance with an emphasis on "fit and proper" owners and diversified ownership.

Steps to implement Basel II norms were carried forward through the Capital Adequacy Assessment Process (CAAP). With regard to Regional Rural Banks, the focus of regulation and supervision was on consolidation, efficiency and expansion of areas of business. Efforts were carried forward during the year to develop urban cooperative banks into a sound, well managed network of financial institutions providing quality banking services to the widest sections of society. Regulatory issues in the context of integrating development finance institutions into the financial system engaged the Reserve Bank in 2004-05. As regards non-banking financial companies (NBFCs), the focus during the year was on strengthening supervisory oversight and disclosure standards.

REGULATORY FRAMEWORK FOR THE INDIAN FINANCIAL SYSTEM

The Reserve Bank is vested with regulatory and supervisory authority over commercial banks and urban cooperative banks (UCBs), development finance institutions (DFIs) and nonbanking financial companies (NBFCs). As on March 31, 2005 there were 289 commercial banks, 1,872 UCBs, 8 DFIs and 13,187 NBFCs.

The Board for Financial Supervision (BFS) has been constituted as a Committee of the Central Board of the Reserve Bank since November 1994 and is headed by the Governor with a Deputy Governor as Vice Chairperson and other Deputy Governors and four Directors of the Central Board as members. In respect of State and district central cooperative banks, while the Reserve Bank is the regulator, the supervision is vested with the National Bank for Agriculture and Rural Development (NABARD). Insurance companies and mutual funds are regulated by the Insurance Regulatory and Development Authority (IRDA) and the Securities and Exchange Board of India (SEBI), respectively.

During the year (July 2004 – June 2005), the BFS held 12 meetings and examined 105 inspection reports. Various issues which received the attention of the BFS included ownership and governance in banks; further progress towards international best practices in prudential norms; greater deregulation and rationalisation of banking policies; and compliance with Know Your Customer (KYC) norms. Strengthening the financial system for global integration in the light of the ongoing liberalisation of the exchange and payments regime assumed priority for the BFS in 2004-05. Greater interregulatory coordination and improving the quality of public services rendered by banks were concurrent objectives.

REGULATORY AND SUPERVISORY INITIATIVES

Scheduled Commercial Banks

The BFS formulated a draft comprehensive policy framework with regard to ownership of and governance in private sector banks and placed it in the public domain on July 2, 2004. Based on the feedback and inputs received from the public, and in consultation with Government, the Reserve Bank released detailed guidelines on February 28, 2005 stipulating diversified ownership and restrictions on cross holding by banks. Based on the recommendation of the Working Group to evolve guidelines for voluntary mergers involving banking companies, the guidelines laying down the process of merger, determination of swap ratios, disclosures, the stages at which Boards will get involved and norms for buying/selling of shares by promoters before and during the process were finalised and sent to all scheduled commercial banks in May 2005.

The Reserve Bank has accepted the adoption of the New Capital Adequacy Framework (Basel II) in principle. The pace of approaching the various levels of sophistication under the Basel II standards would be decided by the Reserve Bank depending upon the preparedness of the banks. Accordingly, commercial banks in India (excluding RRBs) are required to adopt the Standardised Approach for credit risk and Basic Indicator Approach for operational risk as on March 31, 2007. After adequate skills are developed, some banks would be allowed to migrate to the Internal Rating Based (IRB) Approach.

In terms of the New Capital Adequacy Framework, banks will be allowed to adopt/migrate to the advanced approaches only with the specific approval of the Reserve Bank. Banks aiming to adopt the advanced approaches should first make an objective self assessment of their fulfilment of the minimum criteria prescribed under Basel II. Banks that meet the minimum requirements for adopting advance methods may approach the Reserve Bank with a road map that has approval of their board of directors for migration to these approaches. In order to ensure a smooth transition to Basel II in a non-disruptive manner, a consultative approach has been adopted. The Reserve Bank appointed a Steering Committee comprising senior officials from 14 banks. On the basis of the recommendations of the Steering Group, draft guidelines on implementation of the New Capital Adequacy Framework were formulated and issued to banks on February 15, 2005.

Banks were advised of the applicability of the Accounting Standard (AS) 11 in respect of the effects of changes in foreign exchange rates for compliance. A minimum framework for disclosures on risk exposures in derivatives was required to be furnished by banks as a part of the 'Notes on Accounts' to the balance sheet with effect from March 31, 2005.

With a view to increasing the options available to banks for dealing with non-performing assets (NPAs), guidelines were issued on sale/purchase of NPAs on July 13, 2005. The guidelines broadly cover the areas on procedure for purchase/sale of NPAs by banks including valuation and pricing aspects, prudential norms and disclosure requirements.

Based on the recommendations of the Committee on Procedures and Performance Audit on Public Services (CPPAPS) (Chairman: S.S.Tarapore), efforts were renewed in 2004-05 for facilitating improvements in customer service in banks. All public sector/private sector banks and select foreign banks were advised in August 2004 to constitute Customer Service Committees of their boards with a view to strengthening the corporate governance structure in the banking system and bringing about ongoing improvements in the quality of customer service.

Formulation of a comprehensive deposit policy, addressing issues such as the treatment on death of a depositor for operation of his account, the product approval process, the annual survey of depositor satisfaction and the tri-enniel audit of such services were issues which were placed in the ambit of the functioning of these Committees. They would also play a pro-active role with regard to complaints/grievances resolved by the Banking Ombudsmen. Banks were advised to ensure that the awards of the Banking Ombudsmen are implemented immediately and with active involvement of Top Management.

Co-operative Banks

It has been the endeavour of the Reserve Bank to ensure that the UCBs emerge as a sound and healthy network of jointly owned, democratically controlled and ethically managed banking institutions providing need based quality banking services, essentially to the middle and lower middle classes and marginalised sections of the society. Accordingly, in 2004-05, the Reserve Bank continued its efforts to integrate the urban cooperative banking system with the rest of the banking system. Major policy initiatives undertaken by the Reserve Bank in 2004-05 with a view to further strengthening the urban banking sector relate to legislative and structural changes, regulatory measures on scheduled and non-scheduled urban cooperative banks and computerisation of returns.

Scheduled UCBs generally have a large deposit base and hence descheduling weak scheduled banks or taking them into liquidation may have a significant systemic impact. Accordingly it was decided to draw up a programme for their restructuring and rehabilitation in a time-bound manner. As the restructuring involves generation of funds internally and through external sources (Government), discussions are underway among the various regulators to put in place a package that would ensure turnaround in a reasonable timeframe.

Development Finance Institutions (DFIs)

Consolidation in the banking sector has also encompassed the Development Finance Institutions (DFIs) which have been the traditional providers of long-term finance in India. The complexities involved in harmonising the role and operations of the DFIs were examined and the Reserve Bank enabled the reverse-merger of a large DFI with its commercial banking subsidiary. Another large DFI also converted into a bank.

Non-Banking Financial Companies (NBFCs)

Supervisory oversight over nonbanking financial companies (NBFCs) continued to be based on a four-pronged strategy comprising: a) on-site inspection based on CAMELS methodology, b) offsite monitoring supported by state-of-the art technology, c) market intelligence and d) reports of statutory auditors. The emphasis was on developing NBFCs into a financially strong sector with improved skills and technology. The policy changes made by the Reserve Bank during the year related to issue of credit cards, preparation of balance sheets, premature withdrawal of deposits, quarterly returns for NBFCs not accepting/holding public deposits and having an asset size of Rs.500 crore and above, cover for public deposits and policy changes for RNBCs.

MACRO-PRUDENTIAL INDICATORS REVIEW

In line with international best practices for monitoring the stability of the financial system, the Reserve Bank has been compiling macro-prudential indicators (MPIs), comprising both aggregated micro-prudential indicators (AMPIs) relating to the health of individual financial institutions and macro economic indicators (MEIs) associated with financial system soundness. India is one of the few countries which has volunteered to participate in the coordinated compilation of the financial soundness indicators for December 2005 under the aegis of the International Monetary Fund.

The MPI review for 2004-05 indicates that capital ratios were well above minimum requirements across the financial system in India with a distinct improvement in asset quality. This was accompanied by some erosion in earnings and profitability indicators, except for development finance institutions, and an increase in operating costs. The salient features of the MPI review for 2004-05 are set out below.

Capital Adequacy

The aggregated capital ratio of scheduled commercial banks at end- March 2005 was marginally lower than at end-March 2004. The small decline in CRAR of scheduled commercial banks over the year could be attributed to the increase in total risk weighted assets relative to capital, for the first time since March 2000. Higher growth in the advances portfolio of banks and higher risk weights made applicable for housing loans - the most rapidly increasing retail loans component - contributed to the increase in risk-weighted assets. The core capital (Tier-I) ratio of banks increased from 8.1 per cent at end-March 2004 to 8.5 per cent at end-March-2005 as some banks raised resources from the capital market, mostly at substantial premium. Only two banks could not meet the prescribed CRAR requirements at end March 2005.

Asset Quality

The declining trend in gross and net NPAs for scheduled commercial banks that set in during 2002-03 continued during 2004-05 with the net NPA ratio going below two per cent for the first time. The fact that the provisioning for NPAs was much lower during 2004-05 indicates that the decline was due to increased recovery and overall reduction in asset slippage. An improved industrial climate also contributed to better recoveries. Only four banks had net NPAs in excess of 10 per cent of their net advances. Similarly, the net NPA to capital ratio steadily declined from 21.3 per cent at end-March 2004 to 14.4 per cent by end-March 2005 reflecting the increase in capital, coupled with rapid decline in net NPAs.

Earnings and Profitability Indicators

The earnings and profitability indicators for the financial system showed mixed movements during 2004- 05. The cost-income ratio of PDs increased sharply during 2004-05 reflecting low net income on account of upward shifts in the yield curve and the return on total assets turned negative during the year. The return on total assets of scheduled UCBs declined marginally from 0.4 per cent to 0.3 per cent in 2004- 05. FIs posted a turnaround and their return on total assets moved from (-)0.2 per cent in 2003-04 to 1.1 per cent in spite of narrowing of spreads. The replacement of high cost borrowings by low cost borrowings resulted in higher net profits for most FIs. As regards scheduled commercial banks (SCBs) too, movements in performance indicators are mixed. While operating expenses and net interest income as proportion to total assets show little or no quarterly variation over 2003-04 and 2004-05 across bank groups, there was some erosion in profitability and capital.

Outlook

Financial stability has moved to centre-stage nationally as well as in discussions relating to the future of the global monetary and financial system. Accordingly, financial stability in India is an integral responsibility of the Reserve Bank. Reflecting the various regulatory and supervisory initiatives taken by the Reserve Bank in consonance with the pace and sequencing of financial deepening and benchmarking against international best practices, the Indian banking system is emerging as a well-capitalised financial system even by international standards with low levels of loan delinquency. Domestic financial markets have been orderly and functioning smoothly and the ability of the financial intermediaries to deal in various segments of the financial market spectrum is improving almost continuously.

The Reserve Bank will continue to strengthen its regulatory and supervisory framework with a view to ensuring a sound, efficient and vibrant financial system in the country. Implementation of Basel II will initially require more capital for banks in India due to the fact that operational risk is not captured under Basel I, and the capital charge for market risk was not prescribed until recently. Given the fact that commercial banks in the country are scheduled to start implementing Basel II with effect from end-March 2007, the Reserve Bank will focus on supervisory capacity-building measures to identify the gaps and to assess as well as quantify the extent of additional capital which may be required to be maintained by such banks. Finally, while recognising the importance of consolidation, competition and risk management to the future of banking, the Reserve Bank will continue to lay stress on corporate governance and financial inclusion.

PUBLIC DEBT MANAGEMENT

Public debt management by the Reserve Bank in 2004-05 was guided by the twin objectives of minimisation of cost over time and lengthening of the maturity profile of debt for both the Centre and the States in a scenario of upward shifting yield curves. The market borrowing programme of the Central and State Governments was successfully completed in easy liquidity conditions. The weighted average cost of market borrowings of the Centre as well as the States increased marginally after eight years of consecutive decline, reflecting the hardening of interest rates attributable to uncertainty surrounding international oil prices, the upturn in global interest rates, buoyant domestic growth and sharp spikes in domestic inflation. The weighted average maturity of the primary issuances of Centre and States under the market borrowing programme during the year declined marginally. The Central Government did not avail of overdraft during 2004-05.

The utilisation of WMA by State Governments was also lower as compared with the previous year. Issuances of Floating Rate Bonds (FRBs) continued as part of the endeavour to provide a diversified pool of instruments to investors and in a scenario of firming yields, they facilitated the hedging of interest rate risk. The proposed re-introduction of the Capital Indexed Bonds (CIBs) in 2005-06 would help to widen the investor base and provide the holders with an inflation risk free return on their investment.

CENTRAL GOVERNMENT

The Centre maintained surplus cash balances in its current account with the Reserve Bank during most part of the year, mainly due to substantial inflows on account of prepayment of high cost debt by the States under the debt swap scheme (DSS) and other receipts. Investment of the Central Government's surplus cash balances in dated securities was discontinued temporarily from April 8, 2004 in order to shore up the existing stock of securities for the conduct of monetary policy. With the introduction of the Market Stabilisation Scheme (MSS) to absorb liquidity, investment of surplus balances was partially restored for investments up to Rs.10,000 crore from June 12, 2004. This limit was increased to Rs.20,000 crore, effective October 14, 2004. As at end-March 2005, the Central Government's surplus cash balances in the form of investment balance (Rs.20,000 crore) and cash balance (Rs.6,202 crore) amounted to Rs.26,202 crore, almost the same as at end-March 2004 (Rs.26,669 crore). During the fiscal year, the Central Government took recourse to WMA on several occasions till September 9, 2004 but maintained surpluses thereafter.

Comfortable liquidity conditions and lower than budgeted market borrowings facilitated a smooth completion of the market borrowing programme of the Central Government. The Central Government raised a gross amount (excluding issuances under the MSS) of Rs.1,06,501 crore (a net amount of Rs.46,050 crore) through the issuance of dated securities and 364-day TBs during the year, significantly lower than Rs.1,47,636 crore (net Rs.88,816 crore) raised during the previous year (excluding Rs.14,434 crore issued under the debt buy back scheme). This was on account of a number of factors. First, the Central Government had privately placed securities amounting to Rs.16,500 crore with the Reserve Bank to prepay relatively high cost external debt during 2003-04; however, no prepayment was effected in 2004-05. Second, the higher amount of market borrowings in 2003-04 resulted in a sharp increase in surplus cash balances to Rs.26,669 crore as at end-March 2004 from Rs.8,905 crore as at end-March 2003; during 2004-05, on the other hand, such cash balances exhibited a marginal decline. Third, investments in 14-day Intermediate TBs emerged as a major source of financing in 2004-05 as compared with 2003-04.

Finally, the DSS lowered the Centre's market borrowing requirement both in 2003-04 and in 2004-05. However, while the impact of the DSS was offset by prepayment of external debt and buildup of surplus cash balances during 2003- 04, there was no such offsetting factor in 2004-05, resulting in lower market borrowings.

According to the issuance calendar for the first half (April- September) of 2004-05, dated securities for face value of Rs.59,000 crore were to be issued through auctions. As against this, auctions of dated securities amounting to Rs.54,000 crore were conducted; the auction of Rs.5,000 crore scheduled in April 2004 was cancelled. On September 20, 2004, an indicative calendar for issue of dated securities for the second half (October -March) of 2004-05 for Rs.44,000 crore was issued; of this, Rs.26,000 crore were auctioned, while the balance scheduled auctions for Rs.18,000 crore were cancelled. The weighted average yield of the dated securities issued during 2004-05 worked out to 6.11 per cent as compared with 5.71 per cent during the previous year. The weighted average maturity of the dated securities issued during 2004-05 worked out to 14.13 years as compared with 14.94 years during 2003-04.

STATE GOVERNMENTS

During 2004-05, the average utilisation of special WMA, normal WMA and overdrafts by the State Governments was lower than the previous year. The improvement in the overall cash position of the States was also reflected in the spurt in investments in 14-day Intermediate Treasury Bills.

State Governments, excepting Kerala, Arunachal Pradesh, Mizoram, Nagaland, Tripura and Uttaranchal resorted to WMA for a fewer number of days as compared with 2003-04. The recourse to overdrafts by the State Governments also showed improvement over the previous year. As many as 13 States did not avail overdrafts in 2004-05.

Effective April 1, 2005 the aggregate normal WMA of the State Governments, which is based on the recommendations of the Ramachandran Committee, was revised upwards by 9.8 per cent. The increase is due to the higher average revenue receipts of the States in the preceding three years. The WMA limit for non-special category States was revised upwards by 9.4 per cent for the year 2005-06. In the case of special category States, there was an increase of 13.5 per cent. The Advisory Committee on Ways and Means Advances to the State Governments (Ramachandran Committee; January 2003) had recommended that the formula and the limits of WMA to State Governments may be reviewed in totality after receipt of the recommendations of the Twelfth Finance Commission (TFC). Accordingly, an Advisory Committee on Ways and Means Advances to the State Governments was constituted in May 2005.

The net market borrowings allocated to the States for 2004-05 amounted to Rs.36,935 crore, including additional allocation of Rs.18,805 crore under the DSS. Taking into account repayments of Rs.5,123 crore, the gross allocation amounted to Rs.42,058 crore in 2004-05. As against this, gross market borrowings during 2004-05 by the State Governments were lower at Rs.39,101 crore. An amount of Rs.16,943 crore was raised under the DSS during 2004-05. The gross borrowing also included an additional amount of Rs.1,387 crore for prepayment of loans from the NABARD under the RIDF Scheme.

In the twelfth Conference of State Finance Secretaries held on August 1, 2003, it was decided that the Reserve Bank would provide technical assistance in the preparation of a model fiscal responsibility legislation for the State Governments. Accordingly, a Group was constituted in October 2003 with select Finance Secretaries of State Governments and a representative of the Government of India, Ministry of Finance, as members. The Report of the Group was submitted on January 22, 2005. As decided in the 14th Conference of State Finance Secretaries held on August 13, 2004 the Report of the Group has been placed on the Reserve Bank's website.

Outlook

The market borrowing programme of the Central Government during 2005-06 is budgeted to be much higher than in the previous year. Furthermore, the interest rate cycle is turning up internationally. The Reserve Bank expects to conduct debt management within the monetary projections set out in the Annual Policy Statement for 2005-06 consistent with the objectives of minimisation of cost and rollover risk. The reintroduction of capital indexed bonds is expected to widen the choice for investors while lowering the cost of borrowings to the Government in the long run. The initiatives by the Reserve Bank towards further deepening and widening the Government securities market with innovative instruments and new participants would pave the way for healthy and smooth conduct of debt management and borrowing requirements. The steps taken towards improving the liquidity of State Government loans are expected to ease hurdles encountered by State Governments in their access to the market. State Governments' efforts towards ensuring sustainability of debt position will be an abiding concern of the Reserve Bank in the conduct of public debt management operations in 2005-06.

CURRENCY MANAGEMENT

The Reserve Bank's currency management operations pursued the objectives of ensuring adequate availability of banknotes and coins, improving the quality of banknotes in circulation and upgrading customer service, including public awareness. Steps were taken during 2004-05 towards progressive mechanisation of verification, processing and sorting of banknotes at currency chests and, in general, enhancing efficiency of all underlying processes constituting the currency management function. This enabled the Reserve Bank to reduce annual expenditure on security printing. As part of anti-counterfeiting measures during 2005, banknotes with additional/new security features will be issued in a phased manner. The Reserve Bank's Monetary Museum was inaugurated by the President of India on November 18, 2004, and opened to the public on January 1, 2005.

BANKNOTES IN CIRCULATION

During 2004-05, the value of banknotes in circulation registered a growth of 12.2 per cent as compared with 15.8 per cent during the previous year. In terms of volume, however, there was a reduction of around four per cent, mainly due to change in denomination-wise mix of banknotes based on region-wise and currency chest-wise demand, increasing number of automated teller machines and a gradual rise in the number of users of ebanking. The ratio of currency to broad money (M3) increased marginally (15.7 per cent) from its level in the previous year.

CLEAN NOTE POLICY

There has been a marked improvement in the quality of banknotes in circulation due to various measures initiated by the Reserve Bank and the Government of India. These measures include speedier disposal of soiled banknotes; discontinuance of the practice of stapling of banknote packets; appeal to the members of the public not to fold and write on the banknotes; gradual phasing out of Ashoka Pillar series banknotes from circulation; mopping up of soiled and mutilated banknotes of lower denominations; increased mechanised processing capacity at the Reserve Bank offices; progressive mechanisation in the currency chests; regular removal of soiled banknotes from the currency chests; and regular supply of adequate quantity of fresh banknotes on a timely basis. During 2004- 05, Rs.100 denomination banknotes constituted the largest share of soiled banknotes that were processed and disposed off, followed by Rs.10 and Rs.50 denominations.

Mechanisation of verification, processing, sorting and disposal of soiled banknotes through on-line shredding has been a thrust area in currency management. With a view to augmenting banknote processing capacity, six Currency Verification and Processing Systems (CVPS) machines and one Shredding and Briquetting Systems (SBS) are proposed to be installed at Lucknow in addition to the existing 48 CVPS and 27 SBSs installed at 18 Issue Offices. The banknotes processed on these machines increased from 3,290 million pieces during 2003-04 to 5,672 million pieces in 2004-05 through better utilisation of these machines by the Reserve Bank offices by diversion of soiled banknotes from offices with higher accumulation to offices having spare capacity and extended hours of CVPS operations, achieving and even exceeding the rated capacity of these machines and by judicious distribution of soiled banknotes among Regional Offices of the Reserve Bank so as to avoid both accumulation of soiled banknotes and underutilisation of CVPS machines.

The value of counterfeit banknotes detected during 2004-05 declined marginally in relation to 2003-04. The number of counterfeit banknotes detected in Rs.500 and Rs.100 denominations declined considerably. On the other hand, there was an increase in detection of Rs.1000 denomination banknotes. Security features of banknotes are reviewed continuously and updated from time to time in order to take advantage of latest innovations and with the objective of making counterfeiting difficult. Mahatma Gandhi series banknotes in denominations of Rs.100 and Rs.10 with enhanced security features were introduced in 1996, followed by Rs.50 and Rs.500 in 1997, Rs.1000 in the year 2000 and Rs.20 and Rs.5 in 2001. Introduction of additional/ improved/new security features is envisaged for denominations of Rs.50, Rs.100, Rs.500 and Rs.1000 to be put into circulation during 2005-06. The changes in security features, inter alia, include: increase in grammage; reduction in font size of numerals and shift in colour from new green to new blue optically variable ink (OVI) font in Rs.500 and Rs.1000 denominations; one-side Intaglio printing; electrolyte watermark in addition to Mahatma Gandhi portrait watermark; colour shift magnetic machine readable security thread for denominations of Rs.100 and above; and dual coloured fluorescent fibres in banknotes of all denominations.

During the year, the Reserve Bank stepped up efforts for improvement of customer services in matters relating to issue of coins, acceptance of coins from the public and exchange of soiled and mutilated banknotes. Scheduled commercial banks were directed to issue coins, accept coins and soiled banknotes in transactions or for exchange without any restriction. Efforts were continued to provide timely and efficient customer service not only at the Reserve Bank Offices but also at bank branches. The Reserve Bank revised the Citizens' Charter and placed it on the website. All Issue offices have implemented the major recommendations of the Committee on Procedures and Performance Audit on Public Services (Chairman: Shri S.S. Tarapore) on services relating to individuals on currency management.

The President of India Dr. A.P.J. Abdul Kalam inaugurated the Reserve Bank of India Monetary Museum on November 18, 2004. The President noted in the visitor's book, " It is a beautiful idea and well presented. Hearty congratulations." The Reserve Bank's Monetary Museum aims at documenting, preserving and presenting India's monetary heritage. The Museum was opened to the public from January 1, 2005. The Museum is the first of its kind in the country and aims at depicting the history of currency and the evolution of money in India. The Museum exhibits collections of Indian coinage, paper currency as well as financial instruments and curiosities down the ages.

Outlook

The Reserve Bank would continue to conduct its currency management operations with a view to ensuring optimal customer service through an adequate supply of good quality and secure banknotes and coins in the country. Clean banknotes and intensified anti-counterfeiting measures will be a concurrent objective, alongside continuous upgradation of security features. The Reserve Bank intends to implement the Integrated Computerised Currency Operations and Management

System (ICCOMS) in all its offices and major currency chests during 2005-06. It is expected that the modernisation of the technological infrastructure, the diffusion of IT initiatives in computerisation of bank branch operations and the advances in the communication facilities will improve customer satisfaction and create the necessary environment for ongoing improvements in currency management. The Reserve Bank will continue to ensure production and circulation of high quality banknotes and coins, to influence banknote circulation to meet the needs of the consumers, and to contribute to the integrity and security of the banknotes.

Efforts will continue to ensure availability of coins and banknotes to the consumers in their day-to-day cash transactions; to minimise the risk of counterfeits; to withdraw, authenticate and sort banknotes which are not fit to be re-issued; to examine the existing technological options as well as innovations to increase the circulation life of banknotes; to ensure printing of banknotes to very strict quality rules/ standards; to make currency operations ISO accredited; to review the banknotes and coins handling practices including recycling of banknotes and coins; to adopt/ develop improved banknote security features, and to contribute to the integrity and security of the banknotes by providing regular training in this area to the professional handlers of cash, by promoting the security features to consumers through the public information materials, and by processing lodgement of higher denomination banknotes within the shortest possible time to help improve counterfeit detection. Strategic plans that are in place will be continuously reviewed as part of an on-going process to take the Reserve Bank's currency management to a level to meet the ISO requirements and specifications.

PAYMENT AND SETTLEMENT SYSTEMS AND INFORMATION TECHNOLOGY IN THE RESERVE BANK

A key element of financial sector reforms in India has been building the appropriate technological infrastructure for the smooth functioning of the financial system. At the core of this drive is the development of a sound and efficient payment and settlement system. During 2004-05, the thrust of the Reserve Bank's policy initiatives was on widening the range of electronic payment products and building a sound institutional framework for regulation and supervision. The stabilisation of the Real Time Gross Settlement (RTGS) system was a significant development. The establishment of the National Financial Switch by the Institute for Development and Research in Banking Technology (IDRBT) was another noteworthy development. A Payment and Settlement System Vision Document was released in May 2005 for charting the direction for the medium term.

PAYMENT SYSTEMS

The overall turnover of various payment and settlement systems rose by 27.4 per cent during 2004-05. The turnover in respect of RTGS transactions increased sharply. In terms of value, turnover in RTGS now constitutes the largest item, followed by foreign exchange clearing and high value clearing among the Systematically Important Payment Systems (SIPS).

A substantial increase in repo transactions (outside the Reserve Bank's LAF) and transactions in foreign exchange clearing conducted by the Clearing Corporation of India Limited (CCIL) resulted in a sizeable expansion in the value of turnover under the Negotiated Dealing System (NDS) and the foreign exchange clearing system. The Reserve Bank has taken a number of steps in the recent period to strengthen the institutional, technological and procedural framework for the payment and settlement systems. The Vision Document for Payment and Settlement Systems (2005-08) encapsulates these initiatives and lays out a road map for the future.

Retail payment systems recorded considerable increase in volume and value during 2004-05. These systems include the cheque clearing system - the predominant mode for retailpayments (both the MICR and Non-MICR clearings)-electronic systems i.e., the Electronic Clearing Service (ECS - Debit and Credit), Electronic Funds Transfer (EFT), the Special EFT (SEFT) and cardbased systems (credit, debit, ATM and smart cards). ECS is now available at 44 centres. In order to facilitate electronic modes of payment, banks are providing innovative products to their customers by developing new products and integrating them with ECS/EFT/SEFT/RTGS at the back-end for settlement .

The Electronic Funds Transfer (EFT) System has been in existence since 1997 covering 15 centres where the Reserve Bank manages the clearing houses. In order to increase the coverage of the scheme and to provide for funds transfers in a quicker manner, a variant of EFT called the Special EFT (SEFT) scheme was introduced with effect from April 1, 2003. SEFT is available across branches of banks that are computerised and connected through a network so that electronic messages can travel to the receiving branch in a straight through manner. In the case of EFT, all branches of banks in the 15 locations are part of the scheme irrespective of whether they are networked or not. Therefore, in EFT there are last mile issues impacting its efficiency. In order to broad base the facilities of EFT and to provide for integration with the Structured Financial Messaging Solution (SFMS) of the Indian Financial Network (INFINET), it was decided to implement a new variant of the EFT called the National EFT (NEFT). The NEFT uses SFMS for EFT message creation and transmission from a branch to the bank's Gateway and to the NEFT Centre, considerably enhancing the security in funds transfer operations.

SETTLEMENT SYSTEMS

The paper-based clearing remains the most important retail settlement system in terms of volume with a share of 66 per cent in the total transactions recorded during 2004-05. MICR-based clearing operations have emerged as an efficient method of processing paper-based instruments. During 2004-05, one more centre (Dehradun) commenced MICR based clearing using state-of-the-art reader sorter-based processing capabilities, taking the total number of MICR centres to 40. These centres account for about 70 per cent of the total cheque volumes and value. In view of the criticality of the MICR clearing, back-up centres have been set up by the State Bank of India at each of the four metropolitan centres where the Reserve Bank is managing and operating the clearing houses. The MICR Cheque Processing Centre (CPC), set up by banks at other centres, have been advised to identify nearby CPCs to operate as back-up centres. In order to increase efficiency in the existing paperbased instruments, the Cheque Truncation System (CTS) has been undertaken in the National Capital region on a pilot basis. The technical evaluation phase of the project is over and the commercial evaluation is in progress.

Financial Switch

The National Financial Switch (NFS) to facilitate apex level connectivity of other ATM switches has been set up by the Institute for Development and Research in Banking Technology (IDRBT). The NFS started operation from August 28, 2004. The implementation of RTGS has made it possible for large value payments to be transacted in a faster, efficient, and secure manner. After the stabilisation of RTGS, the need for continuing the deferred net settlement (DNS) based inter-bank clearing was examined and it was decided that the inter-bank clearing should be done away with. Accordingly, the inter-bank clearing was discontinued in Mumbai in November 2004, followed by other centres.

High Value Clearing

High Value Clearing is a value added service where select branches located in close proximity to the clearing house/service branch/central business/ commercial district present instruments with value of Rs.1 lakh and above deposited by their customers within the specified cut-off time to the clearing house. High Value Clearing at some centres has been extended to cover the entire jurisdiction of the clearing house. The settlement is carried out through the Magnetic Media Based Clearing System (MMBCS). The return clearing is also held on the same day which results in the final settlement being concluded on that day.

INFORMATION TECHNOLOGY IN THE RESERVE BANK

Information technology (IT) has brought about a fundamental change in the way businesses function the world over. The financial sector has undergone a metamorphosis in its operations, driven primarily by information technology. The Reserve Bank has had a significant role to play in large scale IT implementation in the banking sector. Within the Reserve Bank, initial efforts aimed at mechanisation of activities in the 1980s expanded in the 1990s into computerisation of critical operations of the Reserve Bank. The year 2004-05 marked a phase of consolidation, with renewed thrust towards putting in place comprehensive systems following the Generic Architecture within the Reserve Bank and providing solutions to enhance the efficiency of the payment and settlement systems in India.

Outlook

During 2005-06, the priority of the Reserve Bank would be the strengthening of institutional framework for regulation and supervision of payment and settlement systems. As a part of this initiative, the Reserve Bank has constituted the Board for Regulation and Supervision of Payment and Settlement Systems (BPSS) as a Committee of its Central Board. The functions and powers of BPSS include policy formulation relating to the regulation and supervision of all types of payment and settlement systems, setting standards for existing and future systems, authorisation of the payment and settlement systems and determination of criteria for membership to these systems. A new department called Department of Payment and Settlement System (DPSS) has also been constituted in the Reserve Bank. The National Payments Council, functioning since 1999, received recognition of a Technical Advisory Committee to the BPSS. The direction provided in the Vision Document would provide a road map for streamlining and refining the payment systems in the medium- term. The definitive role of IT in the functioning of the Reserve Bank as also for the entities comprising the financial sector is gaining greater significance. Technology would bridge the gaps in terms of reach and coverage of systems and will also enable better decision making based on accurate information, reduced costs and overall improvement in operational efficiency. IT based initiatives would focus on meeting the three pronged objective of better house keeping, improved customer service and overall systemic efficiency.

HUMAN RESOURCE DEVELOPMENT AND ORGANISATIONAL MATTERS

The function of human resource development in the Reserve Bank is driven by the goal of enhancing the efficiency of the organisation by nurturing a motivated staff in an organisational culture that facilitates a congruence between personal goals with those of the institution, thereby fostering a sense of pride and belonging. During 2004-05, the Reserve Bank continued with its efforts to upgrade its human resources (HR) to face the challenges arising out of globalisation and advances in technology. Human resource development initiatives in the Reserve Bank focused primarily on designing appropriate HR systems, processes and practices, capacity building to bridge HR gaps in functional areas, developing skills, fostering personal and professional growth and drawing out qualities of leadership and team building. Concomitant measures were initiated to ensure transparency in operations and to improve customer service.

TRAINING AND SKILLS ENHANCEMENT

Three training colleges of the Reserve Bank, viz., the Bankers' Training College (BTC), Mumbai, the Reserve Bank Staff College (RBSC), Chennai and the College of Agricultural Banking (CAB), Pune cater to the training needs of the officers of the Reserve Bank and the banking industry. The BTC was established to train the personnel of commercial banks and other financial institutions in India. The College caters mainly to the training requirements of middle and senior level officers. The RBSC was established to impart training to the Reserve Bank's own officers in junior and middle management cadres and specialised development of officers in the senior management cadre. The CAB was originally set up with a focus on training the senior and middle level officers of rural and co-operative credit sectors. In recent years, the CAB has diversified into areas relating to nonbanking financial companies, human resource management and Information Technology (IT). An In-house Working Group was constituted during the year to review the overall functioning of the three training colleges, their target groups and other related matters with a view to enhancing the utility of the training programmes, avoiding unnecessary costs and bringing about improvements in their functioning. The four Zonal Training Centres (ZTCs) focus exclusively on training of Class III and IV staff of the Reserve Bank. The total number of participants in programmes conducted by all the Colleges and ZTCs increased during 2004-05.

Customer Service Measures

Efforts were made to introduce innovative measures for better customer service in the fields of currency management, foreign exchange, banking matters, clearing mechanism and in evaluation of customer satisfaction. To assess the quality of currency in circulation, officials of some regional offices paid incognito visits to major market localities and interacted with shopkeepers, vegetable vendors, cashiers in departmental stores/ restaurants, post offices and a few noncurrency chest branches of banks. Meetings were also held with senior officials of banks maintaining currency chests. Problems of forged notes, reverse flow of coins and exchange facility to the public were some of the other issues discussed during such meetings. Commercial banks were advised to open special counters for exchange of soiled and mutilated notes on Sundays and holidays and accept coins of all denominations tendered through their counters either for exchange or for deposit in accounts. Training programmes/workshops were conducted to educate the officials of various banking and non-banking organisations such as anti-economic offences cells of state Crime Investigation Departments (CIDs), urban co-operative banks' federations, frontline staff of various Government departments such as electricity boards, police, regional transport, central railway and post offices regarding the features of genuine notes and difference between forged notes and genuine notes. Some Regional Offices launched education campaigns on currency management related issues, such as security features of genuine notes and availability of exchange facility for currency notes and coins, through issue of press releases, advertisements, display of banners, distribution of handouts and interviews in the local electronic media for awareness of the general public. Jammu Regional Office imparted training to the officials of Shri Mata Vaishno Devi regarding detection of forged notes, which was appreciated by the Shrine's Board authorities. As a measure to eliminate middlemen and also to obviate the need for carrying back large amounts of cash, Kanpur regional office commenced, effective July 2004, crediting the exchange value of coins exchanged by bulk quantity users through ECS.

7

Credit Policy: Indecent Exposure

Financial institutions are stepping up their credit risk management policies and implementing new measures to control credit limits. Geoff Bedser defines how these changes should be made.

There has been an unprecedented amount of interest in the past few months in how banks formulate and operate their credit risk management policies. At the end of July, the Basle Committee on Banking Supervision issued a consultative paper, which outlines 17 basic principles to be followed in the credit risk management process.

All but two of these principles are directly concerned with implementing a credit policy. The paper, Principles for the management of credit risk, places much emphasis on the responsibility of senior management to formulate, agree and implement a structured credit policy. Some of the main areas covered by the paper concern credit approval processes, credit administration processes and procedures and the application of controls on problem areas. The paper also contains recommendations on how a bank should define its overall credit risk management strategy, which forms the starting point for a credit policy.

Banks seem to have realised it is in their interest to run a sensible, structured credit policy. For too long, too many of them have set credit limits in a disorganised, fragmented fashion. They have either used outmoded methodologies to calculate exposures against limits or have spent considerable time and effort to arrive manually at a global, consolidated view of their exposures. The problems encountered during the worldwide economic turmoil of late 1998 led many such banks to appreciate the benefits of a rational, pragmatic credit policy that can be implemented using the most appropriate systems and approaches.

Although the Basle paper says lending is the most obvious source of credit risk, it also emphasises that, in practice, credit risk arises from banking and trading activity both on and off the balance sheet. If anything, the paper does not emphasise enough the potential credit risk impact of off-balance sheet and other trading activity. Comments on this paper are required by November 30, which suggests that final rules are likely to be implemented by the middle of next year.

While the risk policy principles proposed by the Basle Committee are commendable, the key issue for most banks is how they should actually be put into practice.

When a bank's credit committee (or similar body) comes to approve a credit line, it is essential that committee members have a thorough understanding of every aspect of the counterparty or borrower. An experienced credit analyst should be responsible for collating the relevant information from a variety of sources, including credit rating agencies, annual reports, market briefings and other sources, such as the Internet.

This approach highlights the importance not only of the basic ratings information provided by credit rating agencies, but also of more detailed profiles of banks and companies, provided by the organisations themselves. This is especially important in emerging markets, where there is a lack of accurate ratings data. Additionally, the information provided by rating agencies may not be kept up to date with the speed of downgrades, as happened during Russia's financial crisis of August 1998. Even all the available information is no real substitute for first-hand knowledge gained by credit analysts and managers.

The essential output from the credit approval process is the setting of the bank's credit limits. Some recent discussions have concluded that credit limits are insufficiently flexible and limit the scope of a bank's traders, and that they should be replaced by sophisticated return on risk measures. Using this approach, traders are allowed to deal up to any level, provided they generate an adequate return to compensate for the risk taken. The greater the value of the trades, the higher the return demanded. But this can give rise to extra dangers by encouraging excessive leverage, and is too reliant on the use of value-at-risk measures. Limits are still needed to protect against event risk.

The vast majority of banks are not yet advanced enough in the use of return on risk methodologies, and are unlikely to be so for some time. For most banks, therefore, limits will still be vital to control the risk in all credit-related activity.

To monitor their banking and trading activity in a controlled fashion and on a global basis, banks must set multiple limits – by product, operational unit and customer subsidiary – for every customer or customer group. These limits are additional to the overall limits traditionally applied by banks for a whole customer group. For example, for a particular customer, there may be limits at several levels in a bank's product hierarchy. Similarly, there may be separate limits for each subsidiary (or branch) of a customer that the bank trades a particular product with.

To maintain control over these multiple limit levels, the highest level limits applied to a particular customer group are considered to be 'master' limits and all other limits in the group are 'sub' limits. This distinction is important because it helps to monitor exposures across counterparty groups and to treat excesses. The total of the sub limits can, and often should, be greater than the master limit, as this enhances trading flexibility.

It is also increasingly important to set limits according to the residual maturity of the underlying transactions. Figure 2 shows how, within an overall limit (with a top residual maturity ceiling of five years) of £600,000, there are further limits of £250,000 for business with a residual maturity of more than one month and of £150,000 for business with a residual maturity of more than one year. Such an approach provides maximum control over riskier, longer-term loans, while still allowing larger volumes of short-term business.

Banks must also continue to set and adhere to limits reflecting the economic and political risks associated with a particular country. In practical terms, country limits are only needed for areas where such risks are considered significant, such as emerging markets. To be useful, country limits must be set lower than the sum of the limits of the individual customers based in that country.

The Basle Committee proposals state that banks should set limits by industry sector, geographic region and, overall, for specific products, as well as using traditional customer and country limits. In practice, these limits will tend to be more advisory than the customer limits, and may not necessarily be set for every geographic region. Traditionally, many banks have monitored their total exposures within these categories, but have not felt the need to set ceilings on their exposures to industry sectors, geographic regions or products. Today, however, with a greater understanding of the risk of contagion in, say, a particular industry, banks are realising the value of such limits.

Just as important as setting limits is calculating accurate exposures against them. A surprising number of banks set limits and hold them on spreadsheets, isolated from the exposure. Others may have a system to monitor limits and exposures, but continue to use the most basic methodologies to measure the exposure against their limits. For example, many banks still measure exposures against foreign exchange and derivative limits on the basis of the principal amounts involved, rather than of the replacement cost of each trade, or using a statistical approach. This means the exposures may be incorrect, and that the limits set to accommodate these types of exposures will be far higher than they should.

Banks must define the approaches to be used for calculating exposures against limits as part of their credit policy. The methodologies vary according to the type of product, and the availability of information in a bank's computer systems. For current accounts and lending, the ledger balance provides an adequate measure. There has been some debate as to whether accruals should be measured as part of the exposure. Some banks have asserted they should not, as they would simply write off the interest if necessary. However, in principle, accruals should be considered as part of the credit exposure, since the default of the counterparty would almost certainly lead to the loss of the interest income. Admittedly, many banks currently have problems making this information available to their credit risk management system.

For issuer exposures on bonds and equities, the current market value forms the ideal exposure value. For unsettled trades on these products, the counterparty exposure should be based on the replacement cost of the trade, that is, the difference between the agreed sale or purchase price and the current market price.

More sophisticated measures are necessary for foreign exchange and derivatives. The most common acceptable approach is to calculate the exposure based on the replacement cost of the trade, plus an add-on value based on its nominal value. This add-on value is designed to reflect the potential for future adverse movements in the replacement cost. Traditionally, most banks have adopted a very broad-brush approach to determining the factors used in the add-on calculation. Many have used a similar approach to that used for capital adequacy purposes, where the add-on factor varies according to one of three time-bands and one of five broad product categories. Banks need to take a more sophisticated approach to setting add-on factors, using a wider range of time bands and product categories, and varying the add-on factors according to the currencies involved. These factors should be based on the historical volatility of interest and exchange rates in each currency. However sophisticated the setting of add-on factors, this approach can never be a match for the use of a statistically based credit exposure calculation engine, employing techniques such as Monte Carlo simulation. This method can determine a full future profile over time of the exposure for a portfolio (see figure 3). The greatest exposure in the future profile, measured at a 95% or 99% confidence level, is normally used for comparison with the credit limit.

In most cases, this value is likely to be considerably lower than the traditional exposure. Stress tests should also be applied to credit exposures, using a range of real and hypothetical scenarios.

Once the exposure has been calculated, defined administration processes must be set up to monitor exposures against limits; review credit facilities prior to their approaching renewal; check the legal validity of elements, such as netting agreements; and update internal credit risk ratings. These should be used to identify potential problem customers as early as possible. Senior management should be informed, ideally at least monthly, of all new, increased and renewed limits.

As well as monitoring exposures to individual customers, banks must have a policy for monitoring concentrations of exposures in individual products, industries, countries, regions and connected counterparties. The key reason for monitoring concentration risk is the potential for adverse economic movements that may have a harmful effect on a whole area. Provided information is available on a global basis, a bank can perform this type of monitoring simply, using straightforward enquiry tools that summarise its exposure to, say, different industry sectors, on a percentage basis.

Over the Limit

The other key area where clear, enforceable procedures are vital is when managing excesses, ie, when an exposure breaches the limit. A credit manager – rather than the relationship manager that deals directly with the customer – must take responsibility for approving an excess, to avoid any conflict of interests. There should also be an escalation process in place so that exceptionally large excesses are referred to the head of credit rather than to individual credit managers (see figure 4). Senior management should be informed – on at least a weekly basis – of all excesses, and should ensure an appropriate course of action is taken, normally via a formal summary report.

Credit risk monitoring and implementing a credit policy should not be the responsibility of the credit department alone. Senior management and members of the board must also take responsibility. They need to be able to understand the key issues quickly, which requires a clear presentation of the information. They should receive summary printed reports, and should be encouraged to use on-line systems capable of accessing the underlying information, to investigate any specific concerns rapidly and easily.

Too often, these basic principles are being ignored because banks are either not fully aware of the risks they are running or are not able to control those risks. For too long, in credit risk management, banks have relied on the knowledge inside people's heads, but this approach is no longer adequate. Robust, global systems – which can facilitate the setting of limits, undertake all the necessary calculations and provide the triggers for monitoring – are essential. The skills of good quality credit personnel will remain important, especially in the credit approval process and in taking the correct actions when problems arise. The ideal solution is a mixture of the right system, the right advice to help implement that system and the right people in the bank to get the best out of the system, together with a coherent credit policy and clear procedures for its application.

Annual Credit Policy: RBI Keeps all Rates Intact

In its credit policy for 2007-08, the Reserve Bank of India has kept all the interest rates unchanged to sustain the investment boom. The RBI has lowered its growth forecast to 8.5 per cent from 8.5-9 per cent as it expects global GDP to decline in 2007. Inflation targets have also been revised downward to 5 per cent from last year's targets of 5-5.5 per cent and RBI's medium term inflationary target is now 4-4.5 per cent. The RBI has also announced important operational tools for moving towards capital account convertibility. Among them Indian companies can invest in foreign companies upto 300 per cent of their net worth, hedging for individuals and remittances up to $100,000 v/s. USD 50,000 earlier.

Domestic producers and users will also be allowed to hedge their price risk on international commodity exchanges for copper, aluminia, zinc, and even aviation turbine fuel. Indian companies will also be allowed to rebook and cancel their forward contracts.

Highlights of Credit Policy 2007-08: The RBI is looking at a GDP growth of 8.5 per cent assuming no oil, domestic shocks for the FY08, while it is aiming to keep the inflation target for FY08 at 5 per cent as against 5.5 per cent for FY07, whereas the medium term inflation target has been set at 4-4.5 per cent

* The GDP forecast has been lowered on expected decline in global GDP growth
* The target money supply growth is set at 17-17.5 per cent for FY08 v/s 15 per cent for FY07. The growth in aggregate deposits stood at Rs4.9 lakh crore.
* The risk weight for housing loan up to Rs20 lakh has been cut to 50 per cent from 75 per cent
* Infrastructure constraints identified as the single most concern for the economy
* The RBI aims to curb credit flow to business at at 24-24.5 per cent in the FY08
* The RBI expressed that the "socially tolerable" rate of inflation has come down
* It revealed that the bank loans to real estate grew 66.7 per cent till December 2006 and housing loans grew 30 per cent, while those for infrastructure by 21.7 per cent till December 2006
* The overseas investment limit for Indian companies has been kept up to 300 per cent of their networth, from 200 per cent for FY07. The overseas investment limit for MFs has been raised to $4 billion from $3 billion
* The interest rate ceiling on foreign currency deposits has been lowered to 75 bps minus the LIBOR rate, whereas the interest rate ceiling on NRE (a) deposits has been lowered by 50 bps to LIBOR
* The RBI will allow for the repayment of ECBs (external commercial borrowings) up to $400 million v/s $300 million without prior approval
* The listed companies can invest overseas up to 35 per cent of their net worth vs 25 per cent earlier
* The non-food credit growth forecast is set at 24-25 per cent in FY08 vs 29 per cent in the last 3 years.
* The FY08 trade and current account deficits have been seen at the same level as in FY07
* Individuals can book forward contracts up to $100,000 annually, up from $50,000
* The RBI believes that the financial sector warrants use of prudential tools in support of monetary policy
* The RBI aims to facilitate dynamic forex hedging by individuals. The domestic producers/users have been allowed to hedge price risk on internal commodity exchanges. Hedging price risk will be allowed for aviation turbine fuel (ATF), aluminum, copper, lead, nickel, zinc, etc

* The forward contract limits for exporters & importers have been hiked to 75 per cent from 50 per cent. Companies can cancel & rebook forward contracts for hedging overseas equity investments. SME's can cancel & rebook forward contracts too
* Listed companies can make portfolio investments abroad up to 35 per cent of net worth v/s 25 per cent earlier
* BPOs setting up call centers abroad can remit cost of equipment
* The RBI intends to introduce non-competitive bidding for state government loan auctions. It also mulls re-issuance of state government securities
* The RBI believes that Repos in corporate bonds after trading platform in corporate bonds stabilize. The base rate for new floating rate bonds will be average yield in last 3 182-day T-bill auctions
  # The risk weights for loans up to Rs1 lakh against gold and send this article to a friendsilver have been reduced to 50 per cent v/s 125 per cent earlier
  # Rural reconstruction banks will be allowed corporate agencies for distribution of all insurance products
  # The RBI plans to introduce credit guarantee schemes for distressed farmers
  # The interest rate ceiling on deposits paid by NBFC's has been raised to 12.5 per cent from 11 per cent

RBI CREDIT POLICY: REFOCUSING ON INFLATION

The RBI has raised both the repo and the reverse repo rates by 25 basis points and most analysts expect further hikes over the next year. Does this mean that the era of benign interest rates are over?

Central banks all over the world are generally fixated on controlling inflation, even at the cost of economic growth. The US Fed is famous (or notorious, depending which side you are on), for its obsession with inflation control and has often been accused of pushing the economy to phases of lower growth through its hawkish interest rate policies. The RBI, as befitting the central bank of a developing country starved of economic growth, has traditionally given more importance to growth. The latest credit policy review came after some optimistic statements from the finance ministry on inflation and the need to keep interest rates low for sustaining the growth momentum. The finance minister was less convinced about the need for a rate hike as he stated publicly that inflation was within manageable limits. The finance ministry was of the opinion that the effect of high oil prices had more or less been absorbed.

Going by the language of the mid-term review announced yesterday, the RBI clearly differs with the government on both inflation and the impact of oil price. The central bank believes that higher oil prices, considered a temporary phenomenon in early reports, have become a more permanent component in inflation management. The RBI is also of opinion that the pass-through effect of higher oil prices are not fully reflected in the prices of intermediate and final goods. Hence, the central bank seems to have decided to focus more on inflation rather than growth.

The RBI clearly admits that it would be difficult to keep year end inflation at the targeted 5 to 5.5 per cent without necessary policy responses. Hence, it has decided to act ahead of the problem. As a deputy governor of the bank put it, inflation is like toothpaste – once you let it ooze out, it is very difficult to push back. Though the next policy review is due only in January 2006, the RBI has stated that it is ready to take further measures as the risk unfolds.

Given this more aggressive stand on inflation, most analysts were expecting a rate hike of 25 basis points. Some were even predicting a 50 basis point increase. Commercial banks had also braced themselves for the increase and bank stocks had begun to decline ahead of the policy announcement.

As expected, the RBI raised the reverse repo rate, the rate at which it borrows money from the system, by 25 basis points taking it to 5.25 per cent. The repo rate, the rate at which the RBI lends money to the system, has also been raised by a matching margin to 6.25 per cent. The second move was not as widely expected as the first and is being seen as a sign of this new found aggressiveness.

To prevent the market from reading too much into the hikes in repo and reverse repo rates, the RBI has left both the bank rate and cash reserve ratio (CRR) unchanged. The bank rate, currently at 6 per cent, is a token or signaling rate which does not have any operational significance. However, it has some psychological significance as it is used as a reference rate indicating the medium term interest outlook of the central bank. By keeping the bank rate stable, the RBI is allowing itself the flexibility to roll back if economic growth is affected in future. A decent balancing act.

Are Cheap Loans a Thing of the Past?

So, is this the end of the low interest rate phase which the corporate sector and retail consumers had become used to?

In the short term, there would definitely be some pressure on interest rates. Most commercial banks have already stated that they are reviewing the interest rates though none has announced a rate hike so far. An across the board hardening of rates is very unlikely in any case.

For corporate borrowers, the era of sub-PLR borrowings may be coming to an end. PLR or prime lending rate is the benchmark lending rate of a commercial bank. Banks have been lending to blue chip companies at rates which are lower than the PLR. However, this is unlikely to have any significant impact on the investment plans of large companies as multiple avenues of fund raising are open to these companies. Indian companies are increasingly relying on external financing, like external commercial borrowings and foreign currency bonds. In September alone, Indian companies had raised over $1 billion through this route.

For retail consumers, there could be a marginal upward revision on interest rates on home loans and consumer durable loans. This was happening anyway as the demand for retail loans is quite strong. Banks were struggling to meet the credit demand as the deposit side of their business was languishing. Consumers can take a marginal hike in their stride as long as income growth remains robust.

What could upset the RBI's Outlook?

The RBI is quite bullish on economic growth and has increased the GDP forecast to 7-7.5 per cent from the earlier 7 per cent. It sees no significant threat to the growth momentum and believes that the marginal increase in interest rates would not affect growth.

The most significant threat to growth, as of now, is high oil prices. Though prices have come down significantly from the recent record levels, the current levels are still not comfortable. The opinion is still divided as to whether the economy has learnt to live with high oil prices. Even the RBI and finance ministry has differing opinion on this.

Though it looks like crude oil prices are trending lower and industry expects it to settle between $40 and $50 per barrel over the next few years, an unexpected rise cannot be ruled out. Oil prices have become highly sensitive to news flows as financial investments in commodity futures have increased significantly. Any significant development affecting oil supplies could take the prices back to record highs.

A further rise in oil prices would push up prices further. Coupled with higher interest rates, this could stop the economic growth momentum in its tracks and upset RBI's fine balancing act. Other worries like slowing global growth, rising interest rates across the globe, etc, are significant but not threatening, at least as of now.

Managing the Asset Price Bubble

The RBI is acutely aware of the asset price inflation caused by the low interest regime which prevailed over the last few years. The bank has identified four sectors of the economy for close supervision of bank exposures. Close supervision of bank exposures to real estate, capital markets, NBFC's and venture capital have already been initiated by the bank. Among these, real estate is considered to be the one area where there are early signs of a bubble.

To ensure better ability to manage the risks, the RBI has increased the provisioning requirement on standard assets from 0.25 per cent to 0.40 per cent. This provision is a general provision on all advances made by banks, except priority sector advances. Most PSU banks keep this general provision at the required level while some private banks maintain higher provisions. The increase in provisioning is expected to cost the banking sector an additional Rs800 crore.

Banks' Exposure to Capital Markets

The RBI has changed the norms regarding banks' exposure to capital markets, a move which it said is part of a rationalisation process. Till now banks were allowed to have an exposure not exceeding five per cent of its total assets. Apart from direct exposure, bank advances to brokers and retail investors were also considered a part of this overall exposure.

Under the new guidelines, a bank's direct exposure to capital markets should be limited to 20 per cent of its net worth. Aggregate exposure, including advances to market participants, should not exceed 40 per cent of the net worth. RBI will continue to give a case by case approval to individual banks for increasing their capital exposure limits from these norms. In the past, some of the leading private sector banks had received this approval.

The initial reaction to the new guideline was that it would facilitate more liquidity flows from the banking sector into the capital markets, which would be contrary to the policy stance of the RBI. The aggregate exposure limits under the new regulations would not significantly higher than the earlier limits.

In any case, most of the banks have been reluctant to increase their exposure to the capital markets. The exposure of PSU send this article to a friendbanks was much lower even under the earlier regulations. The experience of Global Trust Bank, which had capital market exposures way beyond the prescribed norms, serves a cautionary note.

8

The Credit Expansion Process

This chapter and the following five comprise an analysis of the economic consequences of violating the general legal principles inherent in the irregular deposit contract. We examined the legal and historical consequences of such violations in chapters 1, 2, and 3 and will now focus on the process by which banks create loans and deposits from nothing and on the different implications this process has for society. The most serious consequence of banks' creation of loans is the following: to the extent loans are granted without the corresponding backing of voluntary saving, the real productive structure is inevitably distorted and recurrent economic crises and recessions result. We will explain the circulation credit theory of the business cycle and then critically analyze the macroeconomic theories of monetarism and Keynesian economics. In addition we will carry out a brief review of the recurring economic crises which have thus far assailed the world. The first of the two final chapters contains a theoretical study of central banking and free banking, and the second consists of an examination of the proposal of a 100-percent reserve requirement for banking.

INTRODUCTION

The economic theory of money, banking, and business cycles is a relatively recent development in the history of economic thought. This body of economic knowledge has followed the relevant events (the development of fractional-reserve banking and the recurring cycles of boom and recession) and corresponding legal formulations with *great delay*. As we have seen, the study of legal principles, the analysis of their loopholes and contradictions, the search for and correction of their logical defects, etc. took place much earlier in history and can even be traced back to classical Roman legal doctrine. In any case, in keeping with the evolutionary theory of institutions (legal, linguistic, and economic), according to which institutions emerge through a lengthy historical process and incorporate a huge amount of information, knowledge, and experience, the conclusions we will reach through our economic analysis of the monetary bank-deposit contract in its current form are hardly surprising. They largely coincide with and support inferences the reader may have already drawn (from a purely legal standpoint) in preceding chapters.

Our analysis of banking will be limited to the study of the monetary deposit contract, which in practice applies to socalled demand checking accounts, savings accounts and time deposits, whenever the last two permit the *de facto* withdrawal of the balance by the customer at any time. Hence, our study excludes numerous activities private banks presently engage in which are in no way related to the monetary irregulardeposit contract. For example, modern banks offer their customers *bookkeeping* and *cashier services.* They also buy and sell foreign currencies, following a *money-changing* tradition that dates back to the appearance of the first monetary units. In addition, banks accept *deposits of securities* and on behalf of their clients collect dividends and interest from the issuers, informing customers of increases in owner's equity, stockholders' meetings, etc. Moreover, banks *buy and sell securities* for their clients through discount houses and offer *safe deposit box* services at their branches. Likewise, on many occasions banks act as *true financial intermediaries,* attracting loans from their customers (that is, when customers are aware they are providing a loan to the bank, as holders of bonds, certificates, or true time "deposits") and then lending those funds to third parties. In this way, banks derive a profit from the *interest rate differential* between the rate they receive on loans they grant and the one they agree to pay to customers who initially give loans to them. None of these operations constitutes a monetary bank-deposit, a transaction we will examine in the following sections. As we will see, this contract undoubtedly represents the most significant operation banks carry out today and the most important from an economic and social standpoint.

As we have already pointed out, an economic analysis of the monetary bank-deposit contract provides one more illustration of Hayek's profound insight: whenever a universal legal principle is violated, either through systematic state coercion or governmental privileges or advantages conferred on certain groups or individuals, the spontaneous process of social interaction is inevitably and seriously obstructed. This idea was refined in parallel with the theory of the impossibility of socialism and has spread. Whereas at one point it was only applied to systems of so-called real socialism, it has now also come to be associated with all parts or sectors of mixed economies in which systematic state coercion or the "odious" granting of privileges prevails.

Although the economic analysis of interventionism appears to pertain more to coercive governmental measures, it is no less relevant and illuminating with respect to those areas in which traditional legal principles are infringed via the granting of favors or privileges to certain pressure groups. In modern economies there are two main areas where this occurs. Labor legislation, which thoroughly regulates employment contracts and labor relations, is the first. Not only are these laws the basis for coercive measures (preventing parties from negotiating the terms of an employment contract as they see fit), they also confer important privileges upon pressure groups, in many ways allowing them to act on the fringes of traditional legal principles (as unions do, for instance). The second area in which both privileges and institutional coercion are preponderant is the general field of money, banking, and finance, which constitutes the main focus of this book.

Although both areas are very important, and thus it is urgent that both be theoretically examined in order to introduce and carry through the necessary reforms, the theoretical analysis of institutional coercion and the granting of privileges in the labor field is clearly less complex. As a result, the awareness it arouses has spread faster and penetrated deeper at all levels of society. Related theories have been significantly developed and broad social consensus has even been reached regarding the need for reforms and the direction they should take. In contrast, *the sphere of money, bank credit and financial markets* remains a formidable challenge to theorists and a mystery to most *citizens.* Social relationships in which money is directly or indirectly involved are by far the most abstract and difficult to understand, and as a result the related knowledge is the most vast, complex, and elusive. For this reason, systematic coercion in this area by governments and central banks is by far the most harmful and pernicious.1 Furthermore, the insufficient formulation of monetary and banking theory adversely affects the development of the world economy.

This is evidenced by the fact that, despite theoretical advances and government efforts, modern economies have yet to be freed of recurring booms and recessions. Only a few years ago, despite all the sacrifices made to stabilize western economies following the crisis of the 1970s, the financial, banking and monetary field was invariably again plagued by the same reckless errors. As a result, the beginning of the 1990s marked the inevitable appearance of a new worldwide economic recession of considerable severity, and the western economic world has only recently managed to recover from it.2 And once again, more recently (in the summer of 1997), an acute financial crisis devastated the chief Asian markets, threatening to spread to the rest of the world. A few years later (since 2001) the three main economic areas of the world (the United States, Europe, and Japan) have simultaneously entered into a recession.

The purpose of the economic analysis of law and legal regulations is to examine the role the latter play in the spontaneous processes of social interaction. Our economic analysis of the monetary bank-deposit contract will reveal the results of applying traditional legal principles (including a 100-percent reserve requirement) to the monetary irregular-deposit contract. At the same time, it will bring to light the damaging, unforeseen consequences that follow from the fact that, in violation of these principles, bankers have been permitted to make self-interested use of demand deposits. Until now these effects have gone mainly unnoticed. We will now see how bankers' use of demand deposits enables them to *create* bank deposits (that is, money) and in turn, loans (purchasing power transferred to borrowers, whether businessmen or consumers) *from nothing*. These deposits and loans do not result from any real increase in voluntary saving by social agents. In this chapter we will concentrate on substantiating this assertion and some of its implications and in subsequent chapters will undertake the study of the economic effects of credit expansion (the analysis of economic crises and recessions). To continue the pattern set in the first chapters, we will first consider the effects from an economic and accounting perspective in the case of the loan or mutuum contract. In this way, by comparison, we will be better able to understand the economic effects of the essentially distinct monetary bankdeposit contract.

THE BANK'S ROLE AS A TRUE INTERMEDIARY IN THE LOAN CONTRACT

Let us begin by supposing a banker receives a loan of 1,000,000 monetary units (m.u.) from a customer. A true legal loan contract exists, stipulating that the customer is to give up the availability of 1,000,000 m.u. in the form of present goods (money) he could have spent, and that he is to do so for a period of time or term (the essential element of any loan contract) lasting one year. In exchange for these present goods, the banker agrees to return after one year a larger quantity than that originally received. If the agreed-upon interest rate is 10 percent, at the end of one year the banker will have to return 1,100,000 monetary units. The following book entry is made when the loan is received:

(1) **Bank A**

Debit	**Credit**
1,000,000 m.u. Cash (Input in the bank's cash asset account)	**Loan received 1,000,000 m.u. (Increase in liabilities)**

Economically speaking, this contract clearly involves a simple exchange of present goods (the availability of which is transferred from the lender to the bank) for future goods (which Bank A agrees to turn over to the lender at the end of one year). *Therefore, from a monetary standpoint there is no change*. Acertain number of monetary units simply cease to be available to the lender and become available to the bank (for a predetermined period of time). A mere transfer of 1,000,000 m.u. takes place, without any resulting variation in the total number of preexisting monetary units. We could view entry (1) as the journal entry made the day the contract is signed and 1,000,000 m.u. are handed over to the bank by the lender. We could also see it as Bank A's balance sheet, drawn up immediately following the transaction and registering on the left side (the asset side) 1,000,000 m.u. in the cash account and on the right side (the liability side) the debt of 1,000,000 m.u. contracted with the lender. Let us also suppose that Bank A carries out this operation because its managers plan in turn to loan 1,000,000 m.u. to Business Z, which urgently needs the money to finance its operations and is willing to pay 15 percent interest per year for the loan of 1,000,000 m.u. from Bank A.3 When Bank A loans the money to Business Z, an entry in Bank A's journal is made to reflect the output of 1,000,000 m.u. from the cash account and Business Z's debt to the bank, replacing the original cash asset. The entry is as follows:

(2) Bank A

Debit		Credit	
1,000,000	Loan granted (Accounts receivable)	Cash (Output from cash account)	1,000,000

In this case Bank A clearly acts as a *true financial intermediary*. Its managers recognize and take advantage of a business opportunity.4 Indeed, they see a chance to make a profit, since at one place in the market there is a lender willing to loan them money at 10 percent interest, and at another Business Z is willing to take out a loan at 15 percent, leaving a profit differential of 5 percent. Therefore, the bank acts as intermediary between the original lender and Business Z, and *its social function* consists precisely of recognizing the existing disparity or lack of *coordination* (the original lender wished to loan his money but could not find a creditworthy borrower willing to take it, while Business Z urgently needed a loan of 1,000,000 m.u. and its managers did not know where to find a suitable lender). The bank, by obtaining a loan from one and granting a loan to the other, satisfies the subjective needs of both and derives a *sheer entrepreneurial profit* in the form of the interest differential of 5 percent. At the end of a year, Business Z will return the 1,000,000 m.u. to Bank A, together with the agreed-upon 15 percent interest. The entries are as follows:

(3) Bank A

Debit		Credit	
1,000,000	Cash	Loan granted (Repayment)	1,000,000
150,000	Cash	Interest received from Business Z (Revenue for the year)	150,000

Soon afterward, Bank A must in turn honor the contract it entered into with the original lender, returning to him the 1,000,000 m.u. its managers had committed to pay at the end of one year, along with 10 percent interest. The entries are as follows:

(4) Bank A

Debit		Credit	
1,000,000	Loan received (Repayment)	Cash	$1,000,000
100,000	Interest payment (Expenses for the year)	Cash	$100,000

In other words, the bank repays the loan, records the output from its cash account of the 1,000,000 m.u. received from Business Z and adds to that sum the 100,000 m.u. (also charged to the cash account) in agreed-upon interest it pays the original lender. On the bank's income statement, this interest is registered as a charge in the form of interest payments made during the year. After these entries, at the end of the year, the bank's income statement would appear as follows:

(5) Bank A
Income Statement
(During the Year)

Expenses		Revenues	
Interest paid	100,000	Interest Received	150,000
Net income	50,000		
Total Debit	150,000	Total Credit	150,000

This income statement reflects an entrepreneurial profit for the year of 50,000 m.u., a net income derived from the difference between the year's revenue (150,000 m.u. in interest received) and the year's expenses (100,000 m.u. in interest paid). At the end of the year, Bank A's balance sheet would appear as follows:

(6) Bank A
Balance Sheet
(End of the year)

Assets		Liabilities	
Cash	50,000	Owner's equity (Profit for the year)	50,000
Total Assets	50,000	Total Liabilities	50,000

If we look at the balance sheet drawn up at the very end of the year, we see that the bank's assets include 50,000 m.u. available in the cash account that correspond to the year's profit, which has been placed in the corresponding owner's equity account (capital and retained earnings) under Liabilities.

The following points recapitulate our description in accounting terms of a banking activity based on receiving and granting a loan or mutuum: *one,* for one year the original lender relinquished the availability of 1,000,000 m.u, present goods; *two,* the availability of this money was transferred to Bank A for exactly the same time period; *three,* Bank A discovered an opportunity to make a profit, since its managers knew of a borrower, Business Z, which was willing to pay a higher interest rate than the one the bank had agreed to pay; *four,* the bank granted a loan to Business Z, relinquishing in turn the availability of 1,000,000 m.u. for one year; *five,* Business Z obtained the availability of the 1,000,000 m.u. for one year in order to expand its activities; *six,* therefore, for the period of one year, the number of m.u. did not vary, as they were simply transferred from the original lender to Business Z via the intermediary—Bank A—; *seven,* in the course of its activities, Business Z brought in a profit enabling it to make the interest payment of 150,000 m.u. (these 150,000 m.u. do not represent any money creation, but are simply obtained by Business Z as the result of its sales and purchases); *eight,* at the end of one year, Business Z returned 1,000,000 m.u. to Bank A, and Bank A paid the same amount back to the original lender, along with 100,000 m.u. in interest; *nine,* as a result, Bank Aobtained an entrepreneurial profit of 50,000 m.u. (the difference between the interest it paid the original lender and the interest it received from Business Z), a sheer entrepreneurial profit resulting from its legitimate business activity as intermediary.

As is logical, Bank A could have been mistaken in its choice of Business Z. It could have miscalculated the risk involved, or the ability of Business Z to return the loan and pay the interest.

Therefore, the success of the bank's activity in this case depends not only upon its bringing the operation with Business Z to a successful conclusion, but also on its own obligation (to return to the original lender 1,000,000 m.u. plus 10-percent interest) falling due *after* Business Z repays the loan to the bank, along with 15-percent interest.

In this way the bank can maintain its solvency and avoid any unfortunate incidents. Nevertheless, like any other business, banks are subject to possible entrepreneurial error. For example, Business Z could be unable to return on time the amount it owes the bank, or it could even suspend payments or go bankrupt, which would render Bank A insolvent as well, since it would be unable to in turn pay back the loan it received from the original lender.

However, this risk is no different from that inherent in any other business activity and can be easily reduced through the use of prudence and deliberation by the bank in its business activities. Moreover, for the length of the operation (throughout the year), the bank remains fully solvent and faces no liquidity problems, *since it has no obligation* to make any cash payments for as long as its loan contract with the *original lender remains in force.*

THE BANK'S ROLE IN THE MONETARY BANK-DEPOSIT CONTRACT

The economic events and accounting procedures involved in the monetary bank-deposit contract are substantially different from those examined in the preceding section, on the loan or mutuum. (We covered the loan contract first in order to better illustrate by comparison the essential differences between the two contracts.)

In the case of a *regular* (or sealed) deposit of a certain number of perfectly and individually marked monetary units, the person receiving the deposit need not record anything under Assets or Liabilities, because no transfer of ownership occurs.

However, as revealed by our study of the legal essence of the *irregular* (or open) deposit contract, this second contract represents a deposit of fungible goods, in which it is impossible to distinguish between the individual units deposited, and therefore a certain transfer of "ownership" does take place.

This occurs in the strict sense that the depositary is not obliged to return the very same units received (which would be impossible, given the difficulty of specifically identifying the units of a fungible good received), but others of equal quantity and quality (the *tantundem*). Nevertheless, even though a transfer of ownership may be established, *availability* is not transferred to the depositary, because in the irregular deposit contract he is obliged to continuously safeguard the *tantundem* of the deposit and therefore must always maintain available to the depositor units of an equal quantity and quality as those originally received (though they may not be the same specific units). Hence, the only justification a depositary has for entering a deposit contract in his account books lies precisely in the transfer of ownership entailed by the irregular deposit; however, it is important to point out that given the extremely limited sense in which this transfer of ownership occurs (it is not at all equal to a transfer of availability), at most the information should be recorded in mere "memorandum accounts" with purely informative purposes.

Let us imagine that we have traveled back in time to the dawn of fractional-reserve banking and that a depositor, Mr. X, decides to deposit 1,000,000 m.u. in Bank A (or if you prefer, any person today decides to open a checking account in a bank and deposit 1,000,000 m.u.). This second case involves a true deposit contract, though an irregular one, given the fungible nature of money. In other words, the essential cause or purpose of the deposit contract is the desire of Depositor X that Bank A *safeguard* the 1,000,000 m.u. for him. Mr. X believes that, despite having opened the checking account, he retains the *immediate availability* of 1,000,000 m.u. and can withdraw them at any time for whatever use he pleases, since he has made a "demand" deposit. *From an economic* standpoint, for Mr. X the 1,000,000 m.u. are fully available to *him at all times and therefore contribute to his cash balances*: that is, even though the monetary units were deposited in Bank A, from a subjective viewpoint they remain as available to Mr. X as if he carried them in his pocket. The entry corresponding to this irregular deposit is as follows:

Bank A

(7) Debit		Credit	
1,000,000	Cash	Demand deposit (made by Mr. X)	1,000,000

(This should be a mere memorandum entry.)

We see that, although Bank A is justified in making this book entry, since it becomes owner of the monetary units and stores them in its safe without distinguishing them from others, the reference entries should only affect information or memorandum accounts.

This is due to the fact that, though the ownership of the monetary units has been transferred to the bank, *it has not been completely transferred*, but remains totally restricted, in the sense that Depositor X still possesses the full availability of the monetary units.

Apart from this last observation, nothing unusual has yet happened from an economic or accounting standpoint.

A Mr. X has made an irregular deposit of money in Bank A. *Up to now* this contract has not resulted in any modification of the quantity of money in existence, which continues to be 1,000,000 m.u. and remains available to Mr. X who, for his own convenience, has deposited it in Bank A.

Perhaps depositing the money is convenient for Mr. X because he wishes to better safeguard his money, avoiding the dangers that await it in his own home (theft and losses), and to receive cashier and payment services from the bank.

In this way Mr. X avoids having to carry money in his pocket and can make payments by simply writing a sum down on a check and instructing the bank to send him a summary each month of all the operations carried out. These banking services are all very valuable and warrant the decision of Mr. X to deposit his money in Bank A. Furthermore, Bank A is fully justified in charging the depositor for these services. Let us suppose the agreed-upon price for the services is 3 percent per year of the quantity deposited (the bank could also charge a flat rate unrelated to the amount deposited, but for the purpose of illustration we will assume the cost of the services depends on the entire amount deposited), a sum with which the bank can cover its operating costs and also achieve a small profit margin.

If we suppose the operating costs are equivalent to 2 percent of the amount deposited, the bank will obtain a profit of 1 percent per year, or 10,000 m.u. If Mr. X pays this annual fee (30,000 m.u.) in cash, the following book entries would result from the rendering of the above-mentioned services:

Bank A

(8)

Debit		Credit	
30,000	Cash	Income from Client X in payment for services	30,000
20,000	Operating expenses paid by the bank in order to offer its services	Cash	20,000

At the end of the year, Bank A's income statement and balance sheet would be as follows:

(9)

Bank A
Income Statement
(During the year)

Expenses		Revenues	
Operating costs	20,000	Income from services rendered	30,000
Net Income	10,000		
Total Debit	30,000	Total Credit	30,000

Balance Sheet
(End of the year)

Assets		Liabilities	
Cash	1,010,000	Owner's equity (Profit for the year)	10,000
		Demand deposit	1,000,000
Total Assets	1,010,000	Total Liabilities	1,010,000

As we see, up to now there has been nothing unusual or surprising about the economic events or accounting processes resulting from the monetary irregular-deposit contract. The bank has made a small legitimate profit, derived from its role as a renderer of services valued by its customer at 30,000 m.u. Moreover, there has been no change in the quantity of money, and after all of the transactions, the bank's cash account has only increased by 10,000 m.u. This sum corresponds to the pure entrepreneurial profit derived by the bank from the difference between the price paid by the client for services (30,000 m.u.) and the operating cost of providing them (20,000 m.u.). Finally, given the depositor believes the money he deposited in Bank Aremains constantly available to him, a situation equal to or even better than his keeping the money in his own pocket or at home, he need not demand any additional compensation, as in the case of the loan contract, which is radically different. The loan contract required the lender to relinquish the availability of 1,000,000 m.u. of present goods (in other words, to *lend*) and to transfer the availability to the borrower in exchange for the corresponding interest and the repayment of the principal one year later.[6]

THE EFFECTS PRODUCED BY BANKERS' USE OF DEMAND DEPOSITS: THE CASE OF AN INDIVIDUAL BANK

Nevertheless bankers were soon tempted to violate the traditional rule of conduct requiring them to maintain the *tantundem* of monetary irregular deposits continuously available to depositors, and they ended up using at least a portion of demand deposits for their own benefit. In chapter 3 we covered the comments of Saravia de la Calle with respect to this human temptation. Now we must stress how overwhelming and nearly irresistible it is, given the *huge profits that result from yielding to it.* When bankers first began using their depositors' money, they did so shamefacedly and in secret, as shown by chapter 2's analysis of different historical cases. At this time bankers were still keenly aware of the wrongful nature of their actions. It was only later, after many centuries and vicissitudes, that bankers were successful in their aim to openly and legally violate the traditional legal principle, since they happily obtained the governmental privilege necessary to use their depositors' money (generally by granting loans, which initially were often given to the government itself.)[7] We will now consider the way bankers record the appropriation of demand deposits in their account books. Our study will begin with the case of an individual bank and will later extend to the banking system as a whole.

THE CONTINENTAL ACCOUNTING SYSTEM

Two accounting systems, the continental and the Anglo- Saxon, have traditionally been used to document the phenomenon we are studying. The continental system is based on the false notion that for the depositor, the irregular deposit contract is a true deposit contract, while for the banker it is a loan or mutuum contract. In this case, Mr. X makes a "demand" deposit of 1,000,000 m.u. in Bank A, and Bank A receives the money not as a deposit, but as a loan it can freely use, considering the depositor will not be aware of this use nor be affected by it. Moreover, while keeping only a portion of deposits on hand as a *security reserve*, the bank estimates it will be able to comply with depositors' withdrawal requests. These expectations are especially strong, given that under normal circumstances it is highly unlikely customers will attempt to withdraw an amount exceeding the security margin or reserve ratio. Experience appears to show this is true, and the trust the bank has earned through years of properly safeguarding clients' deposits contributes to the unlikelihood of such a predicament, as does the fact that many withdrawals are offset by new deposits. If we suppose the banker considers a 10-percent security reserve (also called a "reserve ratio") sufficient to satisfy possible demands for deposit withdrawals, then the other 90 percent of demand deposits, or 900,000 m.u., would be available to him to use to his own benefit. Using the European accounting system, this economic event would be represented in the following way:8 When Mr. X makes the demand deposit, a book entry identical to number (7) is made, though this time it is not considered a memorandum entry.

Bank A

(10) Debit		Credit	
1,000,000	Cash	Demand deposit (made by Mr. X)	1,000,000

Once the bank yields to the temptation to appropriate most of the *tantundem*, which it should keep on hand and available to the depositor, the following entry is made:

Bank A

(11) Debit		Credit	
900,000	Loan to Z	Cash	900,000

At the moment the banker appropriates the money and loans it to Z, an economic event of great significance occurs: 900,000 m.u. are created *ex nihilo,* or out of nothing. Indeed, Mr. X's essential motive for making a demand deposit of 1,000,000 m.u. was the custody and safekeeping of the money, and with good reason he subjectively believes he retains the complete availability of it, just as if he had it in his pocket, and in a sense better. To all intents and purposes, Mr. X still has 1,000,000 m.u. in cash as if the money were physically "in his possession," since according to his contract it remains fully available to him. From an economic standpoint, there is no doubt the 1,000,000 m.u. Mr. X deposited in Bank A continue to contribute to his cash balances. However, when the bank appropriates 900,000 m.u. from deposits and loans them to Z, it simultaneously generates additional purchasing power from nothing and transfers it to Z, the borrower, who receives 900,000 m.u. It is clear that, both subjectively and objectively, Z enjoys the full availability of 900,000 m.u. beginning at that point and that these monetary units are transferred to him.9 Therefore, *there has been an* increase in the amount of money in circulation in the market, due to beliefs held simultaneously and with good reason by two different economic agents: one thinks he has 1,000,000 m.u. at his disposal, and the other believes he has 900,000 m.u. at his disposal. In other words, the bank's appropriation of 900,000 m.u. from a demand deposit results in an increase equal to 900,000 m.u. in the aggregate balances of money existing in the market. In contrast, the loan or mutuum contract covered earlier involves no such occurrence. We should also consider the location of the existing money in the market from the time the banker appropriates the deposit. The number of monetary units in the market has clearly grown to 1,900,000, though these units exist in different forms. We say there are 1,900,000 m.u. because different economic agents subjectively believe they have at their disposal 1,900,000 m.u. to exchange in the market, and money consists of all generally-accepted mediums of exchange.

Nevertheless the form of the money varies: Borrower Z possesses it in a different form from Mr. X, who made the deposit. Indeed, Z has available to him 900,000 *physical* monetary units (which we could call *commodity money* or, nowadays, *paper money* or *fiat money*), while Depositor X has a checking account containing a deposit of 1,000,000 m.u. Considering the bank has kept 100,000 m.u. in its vault as a security reserve or reserve ratio, the difference between 1,900,000 m.u. and the 1,000,000 m.u. existing in physical form is equal to the amount of money the bank created from nothing. (A total money supply of 1,900,000 m.u. minus 900,000 physical m.u. in Z's possession and 100,000 physical m.u. in the bank's vault equals 900,000 m.u. which do not physically exist anywhere.) As this money lacks the corresponding backing and exists due to the confidence Depositor X has in Bank A, it is called *fiduciary money* (or, better, *fiduciary media*). It is important to emphasize that to all intents and purposes demand deposits are like *physical* units; that is, they are perfect *money substitutes.* The depositor can use them to make payments at any time by issuing a check on which he writes the sum he wishes to pay and giving instructions to the bank to make the payment. The portion of these perfect money substitutes, or demand deposits, which is not fully backed by physical monetary units in the bank's vault (the 900,000 m.u. not backed by reserves in the present example) is called *fiduciary media.*10

Demand deposits backed by cash reserves at the bank (100,000 m.u. in our example) are also called *primary deposits,* while the portion of demand deposits not backed by the bank's reserves (fiduciary media) is also called a *secondary deposit or derivative deposit.*

Once banks had violated the legal principle that no one may appropriate a deposit made with them for safekeeping, and had ceased to guard 100 percent of the *tantundem*, it was natural for them to try to justify their activity and defend themselves with the argument that they had actually received the money *as if* it were a loan. In fact, if a banker considers the money received a loan, then there is nothing improper in his conduct, and from the economic and accounting viewpoint described in the previous section, he is only playing the legitimate, necessary role of intermediary between lenders and borrowers. Nonetheless, an essential difference arises here: the money is not handed over to the bank as a loan, but as a deposit. In other words, when Mr. X made his deposit, he did not have the slightest intention of relinquishing the availability of present goods in exchange for a somewhat higher figure (considering interest) of future goods.

Instead, his only desire was to improve the custody and safekeeping of his money and to receive other peripheral services (cashier and bookkeeping services), while at all times retaining the full, unaltered availability of the *tantundem.* This absence of an exchange of present goods for future goods is precisely what indicates we are faced with a radically different economic event, one that involves the creation *ex nihilo* of 900,000 m.u. of fiduciary media or derivative deposits when the bank loans 90 percent of the money it has in its vault.

In addition it is important to understand clearly that if the bank uses the money to grant a loan to Z, as we have supposed in our example and is usually the case, this loan does entail the exchange of present goods for future goods, *though* it is not backed anywhere in the market by a necessary, previous *increase of 900,000 m.u. in voluntary saving.* Indeed, the bank creates from nothing money it loans to Z in the form of present goods, while no one has been first obliged to increase his savings by the amount of the loan. Mr. X, the original depositor, continues to subjectively believe he possesses the full availability of the 1,000,000 m.u. he deposited in the bank; that is, he thinks he has at his disposal 1,000,000 m.u. of a completely liquid asset (money). At the same time, Borrower Z receives for his investments 900,000 m.u. of new liquidity which has not come from anyone's savings. In short, two different people simultaneously believe they have at their full disposal the same liquid asset of 900,000 m.u., which correspond to the portion of the deposit of 1,000,000 m.u. which the bank loaned to Z (derivative deposit). At this point it is obvious banks generate liquidity which is invested without any prior saving. This phenomenon constitutes the main cause of recurring economic crises and recessions, and we will examine its crucial economic importance in the following chapters.

Once the bank has given the loan to Z, the bank's balance sheet appears as follows:

(12)

Bank A
Balance Sheet
(End of the year)

Assets		Liabilities	
Cash	100,000	Demand deposit	1,000,000
Loans granted	900,000		
Total Assets	1,000,000	Total Liabilities	1,000,000

Clearly, the banker will tend to deceive himself, thinking he has received his depositors' money as a loan. Furthermore, it will never occur to him that by granting the loan to Business

Z he has created 900,000 m.u. *ex nihilo*, nor much less that he has granted a loan without the prior backing of an actual increase in saving by anyone. Moreover, the banker will consider the natural counteraction between withdrawals and new deposits, and in accordance with his "experience," he will deem his decision to maintain a cash or security reserve of 10 percent adequate and the resulting cash reserve of 100,000 m.u. more than sufficient to satisfy requests for *normal* deposit withdrawals by customers.12 The whole structure is made possible by customers' faith that the bank will honor its future commitments. The bank must build up this faith through the impeccable custody and safekeeping of the money for an extended period of time, without any misappropriation.

It is understandable that a banker may not be familiar with economic theory and therefore not recognize the fundamental economic events we have just described. It is more difficult to excuse the fact that his misappropriation of deposits constitutes a violation of traditional legal principles which, in the absence of a theory to explain the social processes involved, serve as the only safe guide to follow in order to avoid severe social damage.

However, any intelligent person, banker or not, would surely be able to see some *signs* of what is really happening. Why is it necessary for the banker to maintain *any* reserve ratio? Does he not realize that when he acts legitimately as true intermediary between lenders and borrowers he need not maintain any? Does he not understand, as Röpke states, that his bank is "an institution which, finding it possible to hold less cash than it promises to pay and living on the difference, regularly promises more than it could actually pay should the worse come to the worst"?14 In any case, these are simply indications which any practical person could understandably interpret in a wide variety of ways. Legal principles exist for precisely this reason. They act as an "automatic pilot" for behavior and facilitate cooperation between people, though given the abstract nature of these principles, we may not be able to identify their exact role in the processes of social interaction.

As Mises correctly indicates, as long as confidence in the bank is preserved, the bank will be able to continue using the majority of deposited funds, and customers will remain unaware that the bank lacks the necessary liquidity to meet all of its commitments. It is as if the bank had found a permanent source of financing in the creation of new money, a source it will continue to tap as long as the public retains its faith in the bank's ability to fulfill its commitments. In fact, as long as these circumstances last, the bank will even be able to use its newly created liquidity for covering its own expenses or for any other purpose besides granting loans. In short, the ability to create money *ex nihilo* generates wealth the banker can easily appropriate, provided customers do not doubt his good conduct. The generation of this wealth is detrimental to many third parties, each of whom suffers a share of the damage caused by the banker's activities. It is impossible to identify these individuals, and they are unlikely to recognize the harm they suffer or to discover the identity of the perpetrator.

Though private bankers may often be unaware that their ability to create new money *ex nihilo* (by using customers' deposits to grant loans) constitutes a source of huge profits, and although they may naively believe they are merely loaning a part of what they receive, the majority of their profits still derive from a general process in which they are immersed and the implications of which they do not completely comprehend.

We will see this point confirmed later when we study the effects of fractional-reserve banking in terms of the entire *banking system.* One thing bankers understand perfectly, however, is that by loaning most of the funds clients deposit, they make a *much larger* profit than they would if they acted only as legitimate intermediaries between lenders and borrowers—entries (1) to (6)— or as mere providers of bookkeeping and cashier services— entries (8) and (9). In fact on the loan made to Z, Bank A will earn an interest rate of 15 percent of the amount of the loan; that is, 135,000 m.u. The entry is as follows:

Bank A

(13)	Debit	Credit	
135,000	Cash	Revenue from interest on loans	135,000

If we suppose the bank performs the cashier and bookkeeping services described earlier, which are typical of checking accounts and generate an operating cost of 20,000 m.u. in our example, then by covering these costs with interest income it is even able to provide these services free of charge. The following entry is made to record the operating costs:

Bank A

(14)	Debit	Credit	
20,000	Operating costs of services	Cash	20,000

Although the bank would be completely justified in continuing to charge 30,000 m.u. (3 percent of the amount deposited) for its services, and although it may offer these services free to its depositors to attract more deposits and to pursue the more or less covert objective of using these deposits to grant loans, it still makes a very large profit, equal to the 135,000 m.u. it receives in interest, minus the 20,000 m.u. it pays in operating costs. In fact the bank's profit of 115,000 m.u. is more than *double* the legitimate profit it would make as a mere financial intermediary between lenders and borrowers and more than ten times what it would bring in by charging its customers for cashier and bookkeeping services. The bank's income statement would hence appear as follows:

(15)

Bank A
Income Statement
(During the year)

Expenses		Revenues	
Operating costs	20,000	Interest received	135,000
Net Income	115,000		
Total Debit	135,000	Total Credit	135,000

After carrying out all of the operations, the bank's balance sheet would appear as follows:

(16)

Bank A
Balance Sheet
(End of the year)

Assets		Liabilities	
Cash	215,000	Owner's Equity (Profit for the year)	115,000
Loans granted	900,000	Demand deposits	1,000,000
Total Assets	1,115,000	Total Liabilities	1,115,000

ACCOUNTING PRACTICES IN THE ENGLISH-SPEAKING WORLD

English banking practices reflect fewer reservations about plainly recording in the accounts the creation *ex nihilo* of fiduciary media. Indeed, as Hayek states, "English banking practice credits the account of the customer with the amount borrowed before the latter is actually utilized."17 In English-speaking countries, when a customer makes a demand deposit of 1,000,000 m.u. at a bank, the first account entry made corresponds exactly to that made in the continental system:

Bank A

(17) Debit	Credit	
1,000,000 Cash	Demand deposits	1,000,000

The difference between the Anglo-Saxon and the continental system lies in the entry the English-speaking banker makes upon deciding to grant a loan to Z, and hence to make self-interested use of 900,000 m.u. the banker holds in his vault in excess of his security reserve.

In Anglo-Saxon banking practices, an entry is made to record the loan under Assets, and at the same time a checking account in favor of the borrower is opened under Liabilities for the sum of the loan (900,000 m.u.). The entry looks like this:

Bank A

(18)	Debit	Credit	
900,000	Loans granted	Demand deposits	900,000

Thus, in this respect the English custom is much more straightforward and appropriate to the actual economic events than the continental custom. Anglo-Saxon accounting practices distinctly reflect the *ex nihilo* creation of 900,000 m.u. which results when demand deposit funds are loaned to Z. After the loan is granted, the bank's balance sheet appears as follows:

Bank A
Balance Sheet

(19) Assets		Liabilities	
Cash	1,000,000	Demand deposits	1,900,000
Loans	900,000		
Total Assets	1,900,000	Total Liabilities	1,900,000

In keeping with the English custom, this balance sheet clearly reveals that the moment the bank grants a loan of 900,000 m.u., it simultaneously generates deposits *ex nihilo* for the sum of 900,000 m.u. In other words, the bank places at the disposal of the borrower up to 900,000 m.u., which raises the balance of demand deposits to 1,900,000 m.u. Of this amount, 1,000,000 m.u. correspond to physical monetary units; that is, to primary deposits. The other 900,000 m.u. reflect fiduciary media created from nothing; in other words, derivative or secondary deposits.

If we again suppose for the sake of argument that the banker regards as a *loan* the money placed with him on demand deposit, then because this loan derives from a monetary irregular-deposit contract, which by definition stipulates no term for the return of the money (as it is "on demand"), the "loan" in question would clearly have no term. Furthermore, if the depositors trust the bank, the banker will rightly expect them to withdraw only a small fraction of their deposits under normal conditions. As a result, even though the "loan" he has supposedly received from his depositors is "on demand," the banker may with good reason consider it a "loan" *he will never have to return*, since it ultimately lacks a term. Obviously if the banker receives a loan believing he will never have to return it (and in most cases he does not even have to pay interest on it, though this is not fundamental to our argument), then rather than a loan, we are dealing with a *de facto gift* the banker gives himself and charges to the funds of his depositors. This means that although for accounting purposes the bank recognizes a debt (parallel to the loan granted) in the form of "demand deposits" (derivative or secondary deposits for the sum of 900,000 m.u.), under ordinary circumstances what the bank actually does is to create from nothing a perennial source of financing which the banker supposes *he will never have to return.* Therefore, despite the impression the account books give, the banker ultimately appropriates these funds and considers them his property. In short, banks amass tremendous wealth, mainly by generating means of payment to the detriment of third parties. The harm done is very generalized and diluted, however, and takes the form of a gradual relative loss of purchasing power. This phenomenon occurs constantly and stems from the banking system's *ex nihilo* creation of means of payment. This continuous transfer of wealth to bankers persists as long as the banking business suffers no disruptions and assets keep increasing bankers' balances in the form of loans and investments backed by the corresponding deposits created from nothing.

The full recognition of this never-ending source of financing and of the enormous wealth banks have accumulated to the detriment of other citizens (money which still contributes to the banks' balances, disguised as active investments backed by "deposits") will prove very important in the last chapter, when we propose a model for changing and reforming the current banking system. Though these funds in fact only benefit banks and governments, and though from an economic and accounting standpoint they belong to alleged depositors, in all reality *they do not belong to anyone*, since these depositors view their deposits as perfect money substitutes.

Therefore, as we will see when we study the process of banking reform, these resources could be used to pursue important goals in the public interest. Such goals might include eliminating the remaining public debt or even financing a process of social-security reform to accomplish a transition from a pay-as-you-go public system to an entirely private system based on investment. Let us return now to our example. As Borrower Z gradually uses his money by writing checks on the account opened for him by the bank, the two banking systems, the Anglo-Saxon and the Continental, would begin to reflect the bank's account records in an increasingly similar way. Let us suppose the borrower withdraws his loan in two portions, one on each of two separate, consecutive occasions. On the first occasion (t1) he withdraws 500,000 m.u., and on the second (t2), 400,000 m.u. The accounting entries would appear as follows:

Bank A (t_1)

(20) Debit		Credit	
500,000	Demand deposits (part of the loan withdrawn by Z)	Cash	500,000

Bank A (t_2)

(21) Debit		Credit	
400,000 Demand deposits (the remainder of the loan)		Cash	400,000

After the borrower withdraws the entire loan, the bank's balance sheet looks like this:

(22)

Bank A
Balance Sheet

Assets		Liabilities	
Cash	100,000	Demand deposits	1,000,000
Loans	900,000		
Total Assets	**1,000,000**	**Total Liabilities**	**1,000,000**

This balance sheet corresponds exactly with balance sheet (12), which we obtained using continental accounting methods and which comprises demand deposits of 1,000,000 m.u. made by customers and backed by 100,000 m.u. in cash (the reserve ratio or requirement) and 900,000 m.u. in loans granted to Z. Therefore once the borrower withdraws his entire loan, the accounting records of both systems are identical: 1,900,000 m.u. exist in the market, of which 900,000 m.u. correspond to fiduciary media (the portion of demand deposits which are not backed by cash balances at the bank, in this case 1,000,000 m.u. minus 100,000 m.u.) and 1,000,000 m.u. are physical monetary units (the 100,000 m.u. in the bank's vault and the 900,000 m.u. that have been handed over to Borrower Z and which he has already used for his own purposes).

The main advantage of the Anglo-Saxon accounting system is that it demonstrates, as Herbert J. Davenport pointed out in 1913, that banks "do not lend their deposits, but rather, by their own extensions of credit, *create* the deposits." In other words, banks *do not act as financial intermediaries* when they loan money from demand deposits, since this activity does not constitute mediation between lenders and borrowers.

Instead banks simply grant loans against deposits they create from nothing (*fiduciary media*) and which therefore have not first been entrusted to them by any third party as deposits of physical monetary units. Not even under the continental accounting system are banks financial intermediaries, since true original depositors turn their money over for custody and safekeeping, not as a loan to the bank. Furthermore we have already shown that by reducing to a fraction the number of monetary units they keep on hand (reserve ratio), banks create fiduciary media in proportion to the total sum of their unbacked deposits. Thus, by a somewhat more abstract analysis, the continental accounting system leads us to the same conclusion as the Anglo-Saxon system: rather than credit intermediaries, banks are creators of loans and deposits, or fiduciary media. Nevertheless, the process is much more obvious and easier to understand when evaluated according to Anglo-Saxon accounting criteria, because from the beginning this method reflects the fact that the bank creates deposits *ex nihilo* and grants loans against them. Therefore, no abstract intellectual exercise is required to understand the process.

From the perspective of economic theory, the chief disadvantage of both accounting systems is that they reflect a *much lower* volume of deposit creation and loan concession than truly exists. That is, they reveal only a fraction of the total volume of deposits and loans which the banking system *as a whole* is capable of creating. Only when we consider the effects of fractional-reserve banking from the standpoint of *the overall banking system* will this important fact be confirmed. However, first it is necessary to identify the limits to deposit creation and loan concession by an isolated bank.

AN ISOLATED BANK'S CAPACITY FOR CREDIT EXPANSION AND DEPOSIT CREATION

We will now consider the limits to an isolated bank's capacity to create loans and expand deposits from nothing. The following variables are involved:

d: the money originally deposited in the bank's vault;

$d1$: the money or reserves which leave the bank as a result of loans it grants;

x: the bank's maximum possible credit expansion starting from d;

c: the cash or reserves ratio maintained by the bank, in keeping with the banker's experience and his careful judgment on how much money he needs to honor his commitments; and

k: the proportion of loans granted which, on average, remain unused by borrowers at any given time.

From the above definitions it is clear that the reserves which leave the bank, $d1$, will be equal to the loans granted multiplied by the percentage of these loans which is used by borrowers; that is:

[1] $d1 = (1 - k)x$

In addition, if we consider that the money which leaves the bank, $d1$, is equal to the amount originally deposited, d, minus the minimum amount kept on reserve, cd, in relation to the money originally deposited, plus ckx, in relation to the percentage of loans which on average remains unused, then we have:

[2] $d1 = d - (cd + ckx)$

If we now replace dl in formula [2] with the value of dl in [1], we have:

$(1 - k)x = d - (cd + ckx)$

Next we work to solve the equation, factor out common factors and isolate x:

$(1 - k)x = d - cd - ckx$ $(1 - k)x + ckx = d - cd$ $x(1 - k + ck) = d(1 - c)$

Therefore the maximum credit expansion, x, an isolated bank could bring about *ex nihilo* would be:

$x = d\ (1 - c)\ 1 - k(1 - c)$

Or to put it another way:

[3] $x = d\ (1 - c)\ 1 + k(c - 1)$

As formula [3] makes clear, the reserve ratio, c, and the average percentage of loans which remain unused, k, have opposite effects on an isolated bank's capacity to create loans and deposits. That is, the lower c is and the higher k is, the higher x will be. The economic logic of formula [3] is therefore very plain: the higher the reserve ratio estimated necessary by the bank, the fewer the loans it will be able to grant; in contrast, if the reserve ratio or requirement remains unchanged, the fewer the loaned funds the bank believes, on average, will be withdrawn by borrowers, the more money it will have available for expanding loans.

Up until now we have assumed k to be the average percentage of loans unused by borrowers. However, according to C.A. Phillips, k can include other phenomena which have the same ultimate effect.21 For instance, k can stand for the very great likelihood that, in a market where few banks operate, a borrower will make payments to some other customers of his own bank. It is assumed that when this happens, these customers will deposit their checks in their own accounts at the same bank, thus keeping money from leaving the bank. This phenomenon has the same ultimate effect as an increase in the average percentage of loans unused by borrowers. The fewer the banks operating in the market, the higher k will be; the higher k is, the less money will leave the bank; the less money leaves the bank, the greater the bank's capacity for expanding loans.

One of the strongest motivations behind the trend toward bank mergers and acquisitions which has always been obvious in fractional-reserve banking systems is precisely the desire to increase k.22 In fact, the more banks merge and the larger their subsequent market share, the greater the possibility that the citizens who receive the banks' fiduciary media will be their own customers. Therefore both k and the corresponding capacity to create loans and deposits from nothing will be increased and the resulting profit much greater. The value of k is also increased when monetary deposits are made in other banks, which in turn expand their loans, and their borrowers ultimately deposit in the original bank a significant portion of the new money they receive. This phenomenon also causes an increase in the bank's monetary reserves and therefore in its capacity for credit expansion.

For example, if we suppose that the reserve ratio or requirement, *c*, is 10 percent; that the proportion of loans which remain unused, *k* (which also includes the effects of a larger number of bank customers, as well as other factors), is 20 percent; and that the sum of the original deposits, *d*, made in the bank is equal to 1,000,000 m.u.; then, by substituting these values into formula [3] we obtain:

$$[4] \quad x = \frac{1{,}000{,}000\,(1 - 0.1)}{1 + 0.2\,(0.1 - 1)} = 1{,}097{,}560 \text{ m.u.}$$

Therefore we see that a bank which accepts 1,000,000 m.u. in demand deposits, and which maintains a reserve ratio of 10 percent and a *k* of 20 percent will be able to grant loans not only for the sum of 900,000 m.u., as we assumed for the purpose of illustration in entries and following, but for a considerably larger amount, 1,097,560 m.u. Hence, even in the case of an isolated bank, the capacity for credit expansion and *ex nihilo* deposit creation is 22 percent greater than we initially supposed in entries and following.23 As a result, we should modify our earlier accounting entries to reflect that, in keeping with the Anglo-Saxon accounting system, when $c=0.1$ and $k=0.2$, the bank will be able to expand its credit by 1,097,560 m.u., instead of the 900,000 we assumed before (that is, the bank's capacity for credit expansion is 22 percent greater). The modified journal entries and corresponding balance sheet would appear as follows (compare with initial entries 18 and 19):

Bank A

(23)	Debit	Credit	
1,000,000	Cash	Demand deposits (checking accounts)	1,000,000
1,097,560	Loans granted	Demand deposits (newly-created deposits)	1,097,560

These entries correspond to an original deposit of 1,000,000 m.u. and an isolated bank's *ex nihilo* creation of loans and deposits for the sum of 1,097,560 m.u. The value of *k* (0.2) indicates that, on average, borrowers only withdraw 80 percent of the funds they are lent. When this withdrawal is made (and even if a greater amount is withdrawn, when some of the final recipients of the money are also customers of the original bank and deposit their money there), the following entry is recorded: Former continental accounting methods are more complex. However, it is possible to arrive at balance sheet (25) by supposing that the statement $k=0.2$, instead of referring to the percentage of loan funds unused (which, as we know, this system does not reflect), represents the proportion of the public which does business regularly with the bank and therefore will deposit funds back into it. In this case, the entries would appear as follows:

Bank A

(26) Debit		Credit	
1,000,000	Cash	Demand deposits	1,000,000

Upon loaning 900,000 m.u., the bank would make the following entry:

Bank A

Debit		Credit	
900,000	Loans	Cash	900,000

Bank A

Bank A

(24) Debit		Credit	
878,048	Demand deposits (80% of 1,097,560)	Cash	878,048

The bank's balance sheet would appear as follows:

If we suppose that 20 percent of the 900,000 m.u. which leave the bank's vault will again be deposited in the same bank, and that 90 percent of that amount will then be loaned, etc., the entries appear as follows:

(27) Debit		Credit	
180,000	Cash	Demand deposits	180,000

When 90 percent of this amount is loaned:

Bank A

(28) Debit		Credit	
162,000	Loans	Cash	162,000
32,400	Cash	Demand deposits	32,400
29,160	Loans	Cash	29,160
5,832	Cash	Demand deposits	5,832
5,248	Loans	Cash	5,248

We have supposed that 20 percent of each loan granted has returned to the bank's vault, given that the final recipients of that proportion of funds loaned are customers of the bank.

Therefore, a balance sheet drawn up according to the continental system would look like this:

(25)

Bank A
Balance Sheet
c=0.1 and *k=0.2*

Assets		Liabilities	
Cash	121,952	Demand deposits	1,219,512
Loans	1,097,560		
Total Assets	1,219,512	Total Liabilities	1,219,512

THE CASE OF A VERY SMALL BANK

Let us now consider a particular type of isolated bank: a very small or "Lilliputian" bank; that is, one in which $k=0$

(29)

Bank A
Balance Sheet
(By the continental system)
c=0.1 k=0.2

Assets		Liabilities	
Cash	121,824	Demand deposits	1,218,232
Loans	1,096,408		
Total Assets	1,218,232	Total Liabilities	1,218,232

These figures are practically identical to those in balance sheet. They do not match exactly because our example stops at the third repetition of the loan-deposit process. If we had continued to follow the process, the numbers in balance sheet would have become more and more similar to those in, and they eventually would have matched exactly.

This means borrowers immediately withdraw the entire amount of their loans, and those to whom they make payments are not customers of the same bank as the borrowers. If $k=0$, then by substituting this value into formula [3] we obtain formula [5]:

[5]

$x = d(1 - c)$ And since in our example d = 1,000,000 m.u. and c = 0.1, then:

x = 1,000,000(1 – 0.1) = 1,000,000 . 0.9 = 900,000 *m.u.*

This is precisely the sum of deposits or fiduciary media created *ex nihilo* which appears in entries (11) and (18). Nevertheless, we saw in the last section that in practice, even if k is only slightly larger than 0, an isolated bank can create a considerably larger amount of fiduciary media. (If k=0.2, it can create 22 percent more, or 1,097,560 m.u. instead of the 900,000 m.u. in the first example.) This is true whether the bank uses the continental accounting system or the Anglo-Saxon system, and the sum created may even exceed the total of original deposits in the isolated bank.

With this in mind, it is easy to understand why banks compete as fiercely as they do to attract the largest possible number of deposits and customers. Bankers try to obtain as much money as possible in the form of deposits, because they are capable of expanding credit for an even greater amount than the volume of their deposits. Thus, the greater the volume, the more the bank will be able to expand the corresponding credit. Bankers try to attract as many customers as they can, because the more customers they have, the larger k will be; and the larger k is, the greater their capacity to expand loans and generate deposits. Most importantly, bankers are technically unable to discern whether their growth policies lead to a broadening of their individual spheres of activity at the expense of other banks, or whether their policies ultimately result in a generalized increase in credit expansion involving the entire banking system, or whether both occur at once.

Banks expand credit and deposits on their own and also participate in processes which bring about even greater credit and deposit expansion in the banking system as a whole. Moreover, in this process banks strive to play an increasingly important role with respect to other banks, and as a result they continually provide fresh impetus to credit expansion on the level of individual banks and in the banking system as a whole. In any case, k is a crucial factor in determining a bank's earning power. Competition between banks keeps k significantly below 1, however each bank fights to continually raise the value of its k factor. To do so banks take advantage of their opportunities (with respect to geographic expansion, the ability to exclude or take over competitors and the development of competitive advantages). Though a k factor equal to one is impossible for an isolated bank (except in the case of a monopolistic bank), k values significantly greater than zero are very common, and under almost all circumstances, banks make a supreme effort to increase k. Among other phenomena, this explains the constant pressure they face to merge with other banks.

For illustrative purposes, we have compiled the following table of different combinations of reserve ratios, c, and percentages of loans unused or customers banking with the same institution, *k*, which allow an isolated bank to alone double its money supply (by substituting these values into formula [3], we obtain $x=d$).

Reserve ratio "*c*"	Percentage of loans unused "*k*"
	$k = \frac{c}{1-c} \quad (x = d = 1)$
2 percent	2.04 percent
5 percent	5.26 percent
7 percent	7.52 percent
13 percent	14.94 percent
15 percent	17.64 percent
17 percent	20.48 percent
20 percent	25.00 percent

In some cases banks even pay interest to their checking-account holders in order to attract and keep new deposits. As a result, they ultimately reduce the large profit margins reflected in entry (15). This does not affect our essential argument nor banks' capacity to create deposits, their main source of profit. In the words of Mises, in this competitive process "some banks have gone too far and endangered their solvency." Mises, *Human Action*, p. 464.

CREDIT EXPANSION AND EX NIHILO DEPOSIT

Creation by a Sole, Monopolistic Bank

Let us now suppose that $k=1$. We are dealing either with a sole, monopolistic bank in which borrowers are obliged, because there is no other, to maintain as deposits all funds they are lent; or a situation exists in which all final recipients of payments made by borrowers of the bank are also clients of the bank. (This "ideal" goal would be reached at the merger of all remaining megabanks.) When we substitute the value $k=1$ into formula [3], we obtain:

$$[6] \quad x = \frac{d\,(1-c)}{c}$$

Returning to our example in which d=1,000,000 m.u. and c=0.1, if we substitute these values into the formula, we obtain:

$$[7] \quad x = \frac{1{,}000{,}000\,(1-0.1)}{0.1} = \frac{1{,}000{,}000 \cdot 0.9}{0.1} = \frac{900{,}000}{0.1} = 9{,}000{,}000\ m.u.$$

In this case, the bank could alone create *ex nihilo* loans and deposits or fiduciary media for the sum of 9,000,000 m.u., which means it could multiply its total money supply by ten (1,000,000 m.u. originally deposited, plus 9,000,000 m.u. in the form of fiduciary media or deposits created from nothing to back the loans granted by the bank).

Following the example of Bresciani-Turroni, and assuming all payment transactions are carried out between customers of the same bank (given that it is monopolistic, or because certain circumstances exist which produce this situation), we will now use accounting records to show the process leading to this result.

We will now follow the traditional continental system (as opposed to the Anglo-Saxon) in which all payments are registered in the cash account. The following represents the journal at moments t1, t2, t3, . . . t9, etc., and reflects the bank's practice of repetitively granting its own clients loans for an amount equal to 90 percent of the funds it receives in cash.

The clients withdraw the full amount of the loan, but because they have no account in any other bank (or there is no other bank in society), they ultimately deposit the money they receive back into the same bank. This permits the bank, in turn, to grant new loans and generate new deposits, and the process is repeated again and again:

(30)

Bank A
(Journal of the year's operations)

Debit	Credit	
t_1 1,000,000 Cash	Demand deposits made by Mr. X	1,000,000
t_2 900,000 Loans to U	Cash	900,000

Let us suppose that U withdraws the entire amount of his loan and pays his creditor, A. A is also a customer of U's bank and deposits the 900,000 m.u. he receives. The following entries result:

Debit	Credit	
t_3 900,000 Cash	Demand deposits made by A	900,000
t_4 810,000 Loans to V	Cash	810,000

We will assume that Borrower V withdraws his money and pays Creditor B, who is also a customer of the bank and deposits his money back into it. This repetitive process continues, producing the following journal entries:

	Assets	Liabilities	
t_5	810,000 Cash	Demand deposits made by B	810,000
t_6	729,000 Loans to Y	Cash	729,000
t_7	729,000 Cash	Demand deposits made by C	729,000
t_8	656,000 Loans to Z	Cash	656,000
t_9	656,000 Cash	Demand deposits made by D	656,000

This occurs again and again, until at the end of the year the bank's total deposits equal:

[8] $$1{,}000{,}000 + 1{,}000{,}000 \times 0.9 + 1{,}000{,}000 \times 0.9^2 + 1{,}000{,}000 \times 0.9^3 + 1{,}000{,}000 \times 0.9^4 + \ldots = 1{,}000{,}000(1 + 0.9 + 0.9^2 + 0.9^3 + 0.9^4 + \ldots)$$

The above expression represents the sum of the terms in a geometrical progression. The terms increase and have a common ratio of 0.9.

In our example, r=0.9 and a=1,000,000 m.u., and hence the sum of the terms would be equal to:

[13] $$\frac{a}{1-r} = \frac{1{,}000{,}000}{1-0.9} = \frac{1{,}000{,}000}{0.1} = 10{,}000{,}000 \text{ m.u.}$$

If we keep in mind that d represents the 1,000,000 m.u. originally deposited, and that r=1-c; that is, r=1-0.1=0.9, then clearly the sum of all the bank's deposits (original and secondary) would be:

[14] $$\frac{d}{1-(1-c)} = \frac{d}{c}$$

Thus, the total volume of deposits in a monopolistic bank (or in a bank where all those who receive money from the bank's borrowers also ultimately have their accounts) would be equal to the value of the original deposits, d, divided by the reserve ratio, c.

Formula [14] is the simplest version of the so-called *bank multiplier*, and it is identical to formula [27], which yields the same result for a banking system of multiple small banks and appears to have been worked out for the first time by Alfred Marshall in 1887.28

We could use the following formula to calculate the net credit expansion the bank brings about *ex nihilo* (in other words, the deposits or fiduciary media generated from nothing to make the credit expansion possible):

[15] $$x = \frac{d}{c} - d = \frac{d}{c} - \frac{dc}{c}$$

Now we factor out common factors:

[16] $$x = \frac{d(1-c)}{c}$$

The above formula coincides with [6].

In fact, when d=1,000,000 m.u. and c=0.1, in the case of a monopolistic bank, the net credit expansion would be equal to:

[17] $$x = \frac{1{,}000{,}000(1-0.1)}{0.1} = 9{,}000{,}000 \text{ m.u.}$$

Therefore the balance sheet of Bank A, a monopolistic bank, would ultimately appear as follows:

(31)

Bank A
(Monopolist)
Balance Sheet

Assets		Liabilities	
Cash	1,000,000	Demand deposits	
Loans to U	900,000	By X	1,000,000
Loans to V	810,000	By A	900,000
Loans to Y	729,000	By B	810,000
Loans to Z	656,000	By C	729,000
.	.	By D	656,000
.	.	.	.
.	.	.	.
Total Assets	10,000,000	Total Liabilities	10,000,000

With only 1,000,000 m.u. in original deposits safeguarded in its vault, Bank A, a monopolist, has expanded credit by granting loans for the sum of 9,000,000 m.u. and creating from nothing 9,000,000 m.u. in new deposits or fiduciary media to back these loans.

9

Credit Expansion and New Deposit Creation by the Entire Banking System

We have already observed the great capacity isolated banks have for creating fiduciary loans and deposits. In fact, they are normally able to double their money supply on their own. We will now see how the fractional-reserve banking system as a whole generates *ex nihilo* a much larger volume of deposits and brings about much greater credit expansion.

Indeed, in this respect the fractional-reserve system produces effects resembling those of a monopolistic bank.

We will base our demonstration on the most general case, a banking system comprised of a group of normal banks, each of which maintains cash reserves, c, of 10 percent. Also, on average, the customers of each fail to withdraw 20 percent of loans granted (or 20 percent of fiduciary media return to the bank because a significant number of the final recipients are also clients of the bank). Hence, k=20 percent.

Let us suppose that Mr. X deposits 1,000,000 m.u. in Bank A. The bank would then make the following entry in its journal:

Bank A

(32)	Debit	Credit	
1,000,000	Cash	Demand deposits (made by X)	1,000,000

Bank A would then be able to create and grant loans to Z for a sum determined by the formula in [3]. The following entry would result:

Bank A

(33) Debit		Credit	
1,097,560	Loans to Z	Demand deposits	1,097,560

And since k=0.2, 80 percent of loans granted would be withdrawn, resulting in the following entry:

Bank A

(34) Debit		Credit	
878,048	Demand deposits	Cash	878,048

The balance sheet of Bank A following these entries would look like this:

(35)

Bank A
Balance Sheet
c=0.1 and k=0.2

Assets		Liabilities	
Cash	121,952	Demand deposits	1,219,512
Loans	1,097,560		
Total Assets	1,219,512	Total Liabilities	1,219,512

Let us suppose that when Z withdraws his deposit he pays Y, who is a customer of Bank B and deposits the money there. Three entries parallel to the above three would result. Formula [3] would again be used to determine the amounts.

Bank B

(36) Debit		Credit	
878,048	Cash	Demand deposits (made by Y)	878,048
963,710	Loans to V	Demand deposits	963,710
770,969	Demand deposits	Cash	770,969

After these operations, Bank B's balance sheet would appear as follows:

(37)

Bank B
Balance Sheet
c=0.1 and *k*=0.2

Assets		Liabilities	
Cash	107,079	Demand deposits	1,070,789
Loans	963,710		
Total Assets	1,070,789	Total Liabilities	1,070,789

If we imagine that V pays his debts to U, who in turn deposits the money he receives in his bank, Bank C, then the following journal entries would result:

Bank C

(38) Debit	Credit	
770,969 Cash	Demand deposits (made by U)	770,969
846,185 Loans to R	Demand deposits	846,185
676,948 Demand deposits	Cash	676,948

The bank would make this last entry when R withdraws 80 percent (*k*=0.2) of his loan from Bank C to pay his creditors (T, for example). Once these operations have been completed, Bank C's balance sheet would appear as follows:

(39)

Bank C
Balance Sheet
c=0.1 and *k*=0.2

Assets		Liabilities	
Cash	94,021	Demand deposits	940,206
Loans	846,185		
Total Assets	940,206	Total Liabilities	940,206

And if Creditor T, upon receiving the money he was owed, deposits it in his own bank, Bank D, these entries would result:

(40)

Bank D

Debit		Credit	
676,948	Cash	Demand deposits (made by T)	676,948
742,992	Loans to S	Demand deposits	742,992
594,393	Demand deposits	Cash	594,393

The bank would make this last entry in its journal when S pays his creditors. At this point, Bank D's balance sheet would appear as follows:

(41)

Bank D
Balance Sheet
c=0.1 and k=0.2

Assets		Liabilities	
Cash	82,555	Demand deposits	825,547
Loans	742,992		
Total Assets	825,547	Total Liabilities	825,547

The process continues in this way, and the chain of deposits and loans extends to all banks in the system. Once the effects of the original deposit of 1,000,000 m.u. have completely disappeared, the total deposits created by the banking system would be the sum of the following sequence:

$$1{,}219{,}512 + 1{,}219{,}512 \times 0.878 + 1{,}219{,}512 \times 0.878^2 + \ldots$$

[21]

$$= a + ar + ar^2 + \ldots = \sum_{n=0}^{\infty} ar^n; \text{ where } a = 1{,}219{,}512$$

$$\text{and the common ratio } r = (1-k)\,\frac{(1-c)}{1+k(c-1)}$$

AFEW ADDITIONAL DIFFICULTIES

When Expansion is Initiated Simultaneously by All Banks

In light of the fact that in this context we are forced to offer a simplified view of the processes of credit expansion, it is now necessary to make a few supplementary points and clarifications. To begin with, the expansion process we have described originates entirely from an increase in money deposited at the original bank (in our example, d represents 1,000,000 m.u. deposited in Bank A). Nevertheless, both historically, as banking developed, and currently, all processes of credit expansion have been characterized by the fact that the new money reaches the banking system not through one single bank, but through many (if not, to a larger or smaller extent, through all the banks in the system). As Richard G. Lipsey reveals, credit expansion such as we have described, which takes place *ex nihilo* and is backed by the creation of the necessary bank deposits, *will recur as often as 1,000,000 m.u. are deposited in any of the different banks. Therefore, the widespread expansion process is, in practice, much more substantial and qualitatively more complicated, since it originates simultaneously at many banks and from many deposits.* In our example alone, which involved a reserve ratio of 10 percent, loans for the sum of 9,000,000 m.u. were ultimately created, an amount nine times larger than the original deposit, and as a result the total money supply was multiplied by ten. The main conclusion to be drawn is that if all banks simultaneously receive new deposits of money, they will be able to expand credit without having to decrease their cash reserves, because although they grant loans which could lead to a withdrawal of cash (as we have supposed up until now in the accounting entries), they simultaneously receive the deposit of a portion of the money loaned by other banks. Hence *in practice, significant decreases in each bank's reserves will not necessarily occur, and each bank, while maintaining its reserves practically intact, will be able to make loans and therefore create deposits without serious risk.*

This theoretical argument has prompted various authors, among them Murray N. Rothbard, to write about the process of credit expansion in the banking system from the viewpoint that an isolated bank does not lose reserves when it grants new loans. Instead, while maintaining the volume of its reserves intact, it makes every attempt to make new loans for a multiple determined by the inverse of the reserve ratio. The argument for explaining the bank multiplier in this way, even in the case of an isolated bank, is that the bank will attempt to avoid reducing its reserves in the process of granting loans (i.e., the banker will not wish to keep 100,000 m.u. and loan 900,000). Instead, it is much more advantageous for the bank to maintain its reserve ratio by loaning a much larger amount of money and keeping the initial cash reserves unaltered (that is, by holding 1,000,000 m.u. in cash and creating *ex nihilo* 9,000,000 m.u. in new loans). In practice, the level of cash reserves can be ensured if the credit expansion process takes place *simultaneously* at all banks. This is because the decrease in cash a bank experiences upon granting loans will tend to be compensated for by the reception of new deposits originating in loans made by other banks. When the expansion process is presented in this way, it is not often easily understood by nonspecialists, nor even by professionals in the banking sector, who are accustomed to considering their "business" mere intermediation between depositors and borrowers. However, clear evidence that the approach of Rothbard and others is totally correct lies in the fact that for our purposes it makes no difference whether we study the case examined up to this point (an original deposit, extended throughout the banking system, of 1,000,000 m.u. in Bank A), or we consider a banking system comprised of ten banks, each of which simultaneously receives a deposit of 100,000 m.u. (i.e., a total of 1,000,000 m.u. divided among ten banks). In the latter case, each bank will keep unaltered 100,000 m.u. in cash, making it possible for the banks to expand their loans and create *ex nihilo* new fiduciary media for the sum of 900,000 m.u. Each bank will be able to maintain stable cash reserves of 100,000 m.u. if possible reductions in these reserves as the result of loans granted are offset by new deposits originating from loans made by other banks. Therefore if all of the banks bring about expansion simultaneously, each one is able to maintain its cash reserves unaltered, and with a reserve ratio of 0.1, create from nothing, in the form of loans backed by new fiduciary media, up to nine times its initial deposits. Let us examine this process of simultaneous expansion in terms of accounting entries. We will assume that each of ten banks receives 1,000,000 m.u. in new, original deposits of money. The ten banks are all of the same size, and each has a reserve ratio, c, of 10 percent, and (to keep it simple) a k equal to zero. Let us also suppose that each bank has a market share of 10 percent. In other words, each bank receives the business of 10 percent of all the customers in the market in which it operates. Moreover, these customers are randomly distributed. If these banks simultaneously begin to expand credit according to the process described in entries (42) and following, it is obvious that any one of them, for example Bank A, will eventually receive deposits coming from loans granted by the other banks. If all of the banks expand credit simultaneously, Bank A's journal entries would appear as follows:

Bank A

Debit	Credit
1,000,000 Cash	Demand deposits 1,000,000
900,000 Loans	Demand deposits 900,000
900,000 Demand deposits	Cash 900,000

This decrease in cash would be counteracted by a demand deposit from a final recipient of a loan granted, for example, by Bank B, resulting in the following entries:

Bank A

	Debit	Credit
	900,000 Cash	Demand deposits from loans granted by Bank B 900,000
(51)	810,000 Loans	Demand deposits 810,000
	810,000 Demand deposits	Cash 810,000

Bank A would eventually recuperate these 810,000 m.u. in the form of a deposit originating from loans granted, for example, by Bank C. The journal entries would look like this:

(52) Bank A

Debit	Credit	
810,000 Cash	Demand deposits from loans granted by Bank C	810,000
729,000 Loans	Demand deposits	729,000
729,000 Demand deposits	Cash	729,000

As this process continues, Bank A would receive deposits from the recipients of loans granted by Banks D, E, F, G, H, I, and J. We have greatly simplified the process in our explanation. In reality, the bank receives, on average, 10 percent of the ten loans of 900,000 m.u. granted in the first stage by each bank in the system. It then receives 10 percent of the ten loans of 810,000 m.u. made by each of the banks in the second phase, 10 percent of the ten loans of 729,000 m.u. made by each in the third phase, etc.

Hence, if we suppose that each of ten banks receives 1,000,000 m.u. in original deposits, and the banks expand credit simultaneously, the balance sheet of any of them, Bank A, for instance, would appear as follows:

(53) Bank A
Balance Sheet
$c=0.1$ and $k=0$

Assets		Liabilities	
Cash	1,000,000	Demand deposits (primary)	1,000,000
Loans	9,000,000	Demand deposits (secondary)	9,000,000
Total Assets	10,000,000	Total Liabilities	10,000,000

Therefore, the balance sheet of each bank would coincide with the one we discovered when we assumed k was equal to one (a monopolistic bank or one whose clients are the ultimate recipients of the loans it grants). This is due to the fact that although in this case there is no monopoly, the loss of cash each bank initially experiences upon expanding credit is eventually offset by deposits originating in loans expanded by the other banks.

We may conclude from balance sheet (53) that each banker need not reduce his cash reserves to expand his bank's credit; instead, if the rest of his colleagues expand their credit at the same time, he can maintain his level of cash reserves unaltered and proceed directly to grant loans for a sum equal to a multiple of his reserves. (In our case, each banker holds 1,000,000 m.u. in cash reserves and creates from nothing 9,000,000 m.u. in loans backed by 9,000,000 m.u. in secondary deposits.) Therefore Rothbard's interpretation of the process is correct even in the case of an isolated bank, when each of the other banks in the system also receive original deposits (that is, a proportional amount of the new money created in the system) and all expand their credit simultaneously. The cash each bank would theoretically lose by granting loans is counteracted by deposits received from recipients of loans expanded by the banker's colleagues. Thus each bank can alone expand its credit for the sum of 9,000,000 m.u. In turn, the system's total expansion would be equal to 90,000,000 m.u., and the amount of total deposits or the money supply would be 100,000,000 m.u.

We can achieve numerical results identical to those in simply by supposing that an original deposit of 1,000,000 m.u. is made at Bank A and is divided equally among the ten banks in the system, each of which receives 100,000 m.u. Those 100,000 m.u. would remain unaltered in each bank's vault. Each bank could expand its credit by 900,000 m.u., and therefore the entire banking system could generate 9,000,000 m.u. in new loans and a total of 10,000,000 m.u. in primary and secondary deposits.

Obviously this last example, which wraps up our accounting analysis of the expansion of loans and deposits by isolated banks and banking systems, is the most realistic. In the current monetary system, increases in the money supply filter throughout the system and reach practically all banks, permitting them to expand their credit simultaneously according to the processes we have studied. In addition, there are clear historical indications that banks have never emerged alone, but in groups. Even Saravia de la Calle mentions that bankers established themselves in groups, offering "guarantors and acting as guarantors for each other."34 This means that by the time of the sixteenth-century Castilian markets, bankers were already aware of the intimate relationship and strong community of interests uniting them in terms of the success or failure of their businesses, and they realized they needed to support one another mutually.

With respect to the gold standard and a money supply based on the discovery of new gold mines and on the development of extraction techniques, we can assume that new money originating from substantial, new discoveries would initially reach only a few bankers, and from there it would extend throughout the rest of the banking system. Therefore, it would not set off a process of simultaneous expansion, but a gradual process by which the money would filter throughout the entire system.

We can conclude that if there are many banks and many new deposits, and the banks expand their credit simultaneously following the processes we have studied, even an isolated bank will be able to maintain a stable level of reserves and by itself expand loans and deposits for a multiple of this level, an amount determined by the inverse of the reserve ratio (when $k=0$).35 Therefore it is obviously only in the account books that deposits back the wealth bankers appropriate upon expanding their credit. From an accounting (but not a legal) standpoint, the formal ownership of these loans corresponds to the deposit-holders, since under normal circumstances they consider their deposits money (perfect money substitutes) they can use in their transactions without ever having to withdraw them in physical monetary units. Nonetheless, it is clear that the assets generated by the banking system do not actually belong to anyone. To a large extent, however, they could be considered the property of banks' shareholders, directors and administrators, the people who actually take advantage of many of the economic benefits of this wealth, with the additional advantage of not appearing as the owners, since the account books indicate that the depositors own the wealth. In other words, under normal conditions, deposits come from loans and are merely a secondary result, reflected in the account books, of the wealth banks accumulate and retain indefinitely. We will return to this topic later in the book, in a discussion on banknotes and in the last chapter, where we present our proposal for a process of banking reform.

FILTERING OUT THE MONEY SUPPLY FROM THE BANKING SYSTEM

Another complexity derives from the fact that in reality, each time loans are granted and deposits are created and withdrawn, a certain percentage of the money supply "filters" out of the system and is kept by individuals who do not wish to deposit it in a bank. The larger the percentage which physically "filters" into the pockets of individuals at each stage and remains outside the banking system, the smaller the bank's expansive capacity to generate new loans. In a system of small banks (in which $k = 0$) with a reserve requirement of 10 percent ($c = 0.1$), if f refers to the proportion of the money supply that filters out of the banking system and $f = 0.15$, then when Bank A loans 900,000 m.u., the amount of money which would return to the banking system would be equal to $(1 - f)$ 900,000 = (1 – 0.15) 900,000 = 0.85 x 900,000 = 765,000 m.u. Therefore if we are dealing with a system of small banks and we assume that $k=0$, $c=0.1$ and $f=0.15$, we can use the following formulas:

If DN refers to the total net deposits, which are comprised of gross deposits, DG, minus the total sum of money, F, that filters out of the banking system, then:

[29] $DN = DG - F$

The total sum of money that filters out of the banking system will logically be equal to f times the total sum of gross deposits, DG, where f is the percentage of money which filters out of the system. That is:

[30] $F = fDG$

In turn, the amount of money initially deposited is equal to the sum of net deposits multiplied by the corresponding reserve ratio plus the total sum which has filtered out of the system:

[31] $d = DN \, . \, c + F$

If we substitute into this equation the value of DN in formula

[29] and the value of F in [30], we obtain:

[32] $d = (DG - F) \, . \, c + fDG$

If we replace F in the equation with fDG, we obtain:

[33] $d = (DG - fDG)c + fDG$

Then we factor out DG:

[34] $d = DG\ (c - cf + f)$

And therefore:

[35] $$D_G = \frac{d}{c - cf + f}$$

As $DN = DG(1\text{-}f)$,

[36] $$D_N = D_G(1-f) = \frac{d(1-f)}{c - cf + f} = \frac{d(1-f)}{c(1-f) + f} = \frac{d}{c + \dfrac{f}{1-f}}$$

This would be the formula for the net deposits created by the banking system. The credit expansion brought about by a banking system out of which some money filters would be equal to:

[37] $$x = D_N - d = \frac{d}{c + \dfrac{f}{1-f}} - d$$

If we substitute a value of zero for f in the preceding formulas,we are left with the same equations we have used until now to determine the total volume of deposits and the total credit expansion:

[38] $$D_N = \frac{d}{c} = \frac{1{,}000{,}000}{0.1} = 10{,}000{,}000$$

and

[39] $$x = \frac{d}{c} - d = \frac{d(1-c)}{c} = \frac{1{,}000{,}000(0.9)}{0.1} = 9{,}000{,}000$$

Let us see to what value credit expansion is reduced if, as before, $d = 1{,}000{,}000$ m.u. and $c = 0.1$, while in addition 15 percent of the money supply filters out of the banking system ($f = 0.15$).

$$[40] \quad D_N = \frac{1{,}000{,}000}{0.1 + \frac{0.15}{1 - 0.15}} = \frac{1{,}000{,}000}{0.1 + \frac{0.15}{0.85}} = \frac{0.85 \times 1{,}000{,}000}{0.085 + 0.15} = \frac{850{,}000}{0.235} = 3{,}617{,}021$$

Hence, in a banking system where 15 percent of the money supply filters out of the system, the total sum of deposits would be 3,617,021 m.u., instead of 10,000,000 m.u., as is the case when $f = 0$.

The net credit expansion would be equal to x = 3,617,021 - 1,000,000 = 2,617,021, instead of the 9,000,000 m.u. which are created when no money filters out of the system. Therefore, when the percentage of money which filters out is greater than zero, the capacity of the banking system to create loans and generate deposits *ex nihilo* decreases noticeably.

THE MAINTENANCE OF RESERVES EXCEEDING THE MINIMUM REQUIREMENT

Another complication which produces effects similar to those covered in the preceding section takes place when banks hold cash reserves exceeding the minimum requirement. This tends to occur at certain stages in the economic cycle in which banks behave relatively more prudently, or they are obliged to increase their reserves due to difficulties in finding enough creditworthy borrowers willing to request loans, or both. This occurs, for example, in the phases of economic recession that follow credit expansion. At any rate, the maintenance of cash reserves exceeding the necessary level reduces the system's capacity for credit expansion in the same way as f, a percentage of the money supply which filters out of the banking system.

DIFFERENT RESERVE REQUIREMENTS FOR DIFFERENT TYPES OF DEPOSITS

Finally, another complication we could consider derives from the fact that in many countries the reserve requirement for demand deposits differs from the requirement for time deposits, even though as we know, in practice the latter are often true demand deposits. Although the formulas we have considered up until now could be worked out again for both deposit types, the degree of complexity involved would not be worth the slight additional value the analysis could afford, so we have chosen not to do so here.

THE PARALLELS BETWEEN THE CREATION OF DEPOSITS AND THE ISSUANCE OF UNBACKED BANKNOTES

The economic analysis of the issuance of unbacked banknotes, an operation which emerged long after the discovery of fractional-reserve banking, is not one of the main purposes of this book.39 However it could be useful at this point to consider in some detail the accounting and legal aspects of the issuance of unbacked banknotes, since as we will demonstrate, its effects are identical to those produced by banks' creation of loans and deposits from nothing.

Let us imagine that banking is just beginning to emerge, and banks act as true depositaries of money as stipulated in an irregular deposit contract. As long as the general legal principles we studied in chapters 1 through 3 are upheld, banks will accept monetary units (usually gold or any other type of commodity money) and keep them in their vaults, and in return they will give depositors deposit certificates, receipts or banknotes for the entire sum deposited. A bank which correctly honors its commitments will make the following entry in its journal:

Bank A

(54)	Debit	Credit	
Cash	1,000,000	Deposit receipts or banknotes	1,000,000

If the bank fulfills its commitments for a lengthy period of time and people completely trust it, it is certain that the public will gradually begin to use the banknotes (or the deposit slips or receipts the bank issues in exchange for monetary units deposited) as if they were the units of commodity money themselves, thus converting the banknotes into monetary units (perfect money substitutes, to use Mises's terminology). Given that money is a present good people need and use only as a medium of exchange and not for their own consumption, if depositors trust the bank, their use of banknotes as money could be prolonged indefinitely (they would not need to go to the bank and withdraw the monetary units they originally deposited). When this situation arises, bankers may start to feel tempted to issue deposit receipts for an amount exceeding the sum of monetary units actually deposited. Clearly if bankers succumb to this temptation, they violate universal legal principles and commit not only the crime of counterfeiting (by issuing a false receipt unbacked by a corresponding deposit), but the crime of fraud as well, by presenting as a means of payment a document that in reality lacks all backing.40 Nevertheless, if people place enough trust in the bank and the banker knows from experience that a reserve ratio, c, of 0.1 will permit him to honor his commitments under ordinary circumstances, he will be able to issue up to nine times more in new false deposit receipts or banknotes. His corresponding journal entry will appear as follows:

Bank A

(55)	Debit	Credit	
9,000,000	Loans	Banknotes	9,000,000

We have assumed the bank uses the counterfeit bills to grant loans, but it could use them for any purpose, for example to purchase any other asset (like lavish buildings) or simply to pay day-to-day expenses. If the bank uses the bills to grant loans, its balance sheet will appear as follows:

(56)

Bank A
Balance Sheet

Assets		Liabilities	
Cash	1,000,000	Banknotes	10,000,000
Loans	9,000,000		
Total Assets	10,000,000	Total Liabilities	10,000,000

Total Assets 10,000,000 Total Liabilities 10,000,000 If people trust the bank, borrowers will agree to receive their loans in bills, which will circulate as if they were money. Under these conditions the banker may even believe, with good reason, that no one will ever return these bills to the bank to withdraw the original money deposited. The moment the banker decides this is the case, his judgment may manifest itself as an accounting entry identifying the 9,000,000 false bills put into circulation by the bank as part of the year's profit, which the banker may freely appropriate. The following journal entries will be made:

Bank A

(57) Debit		Credit	
1,000,000	Cash	Banknotes	1,000,000
9,000,000	Loans	Banknotes	9,000,000
9,000,000	Banknotes	Profit	9,000,000

These accounting entries reflect the fact that the banker is sure he will never have to return the sum of the bills, since his bills circulate as money. The bank's balance sheet will look like this:

(58)

Bank A
Balance Sheet

Assets		Liabilities	
Cash	1,000,000	Banknotes	1,000,000
Loans	9,000,000	Profit (equity)	9,000,000
Total Assets	10,000,000	Total Liabilities	10,000,000

From this balance sheet we can conclude that once the banknotes have acquired the nature of monetary units, no one will ever return them to the bank to withdraw the money deposited, since the bills circulate freely and are considered money themselves. Only 1,000,000 of the banknotes issued are recorded in the Liabilities column, because 10 percent is sufficient to comply with ordinary requests for conversion. Hence this balance sheet amounts to an acknowledgment of the fraud the bank commits when it issues bills for an amount exceeding the sum of money deposited. Bankers have never thus recorded in their account books the issuance of unbacked banknotes, as it would fully reveal the fraud they commit. By their deceitful actions they harm third parties, whose money drops in value due to the increase in the money supply, not to mention economic crises and recessions, an effect we will consider later. Nonetheless this last balance sheet is clearly more honest, in the sense that at least it demonstrates the banker's maneuver and the fact that the issuance of unbacked bills constitutes an endless source of financing which permits bankers to appropriate a very large volume of wealth. The reader will surely have noticed that records (54) through (55) are identical to ones we studied with respect to deposits. In fact the nature of banknotes is identical to that of secondary deposits and both produce the same economic effects. They actually represent the same operation and result in identical accounting records. Both activities generate considerable assets for banks, who gradually take this wealth from all economic agents in the market through a process the agents cannot understand or identify, one which leads to small decreases in the purchasing power of the monetary units all use in society. Credit expansion is backed by the creation of new deposits or bills, and since these are considered money in themselves, from the subjective point of view of the public, they will never be withdrawn under normal conditions. In this way banks appropriate a large volume of wealth, which from an accounting standpoint they guarantee with deposits or bills that permit them to disguise the fact that economically speaking they are the only beneficiaries who completely take advantage *de facto* of these assets. Thus they have found a perennial source of financing which will probably not be demanded from them, a "loan" they will never have to return (which is ultimately the same as a "gift"). From an economic point of view, bankers and other related economic agents are the ones who take advantage of these extraordinary circumstances.

They possess the enormous power to create money, and they use this power continually to expand their assets, open new offices, hire new employees, etc. Furthermore they have managed to keep their activities relatively hidden from most of the public, including economists, by backing their created loans with liability accounts (deposit accounts or banknote accounts) that do not coincide with their actual equity. In short, bankers have discovered their *Philosopher's Stone* (much like the one soughtafter in the Middle Ages), which enables them to create new monetary units from nothing, and thus to generate hidden wealth, harming and deceiving third parties in the process. In account books depositors are formally recognized as the owners of such wealth, but in practice it does not belong to anyone (however, economically speaking, it belongs to the bankers themselves). As we mentioned before, the recognition of this fact is fundamental to our arguments in the last chapter, where we propose a plan for reforming the banking system. The wealth banks have gradually accumulated can and must be returned to the citizens. Through a process of privatization, it should become available for different uses of great importance to society (for example, to help pay off the national debt, or make a transition to a private Social Security system based on investment).

The parallels between the issuance of unbacked banknotes and credit expansion backed by secondary deposits created *ex nihilo* are now evident. Indeed all of the arguments offered in the preceding pages hold true for banknotes as well as for demand deposits. With that in mind, let us briefly consider a few entries. For example, when loans are granted against the issuance of banknotes:

Bank A

(59) Debit		Credit	
1,000,000	Cash	Banknotes	1,000,000
900,000	Loans	Banknotes	900,000

In this case the bank grants loans from nothing by simply issuing "false" bills and giving them to borrowers. In the worst of cases, if these borrowers return the bills to the bank to withdraw units of commodity money from the vault, the bank's balance sheet will look like this:

(60)

Bank A
Balance Sheet

Assets		Liabilities	
Cash	100,000	Banknotes	1,000,000
Loans	900,000		

If we suppose that the borrowers pay this money to other people, who eventually take it to another bank, for instance Bank B, which also issues banknotes without backing, Bank B would make the following journal entries:

Bank B

(61) Debit		Credit	
900,000	Cash	Banknotes	900,000
810,000	Loans	Banknotes	810,000

Bank B's balance sheet would appear as follows:

(62)

Bank B
Balance Sheet

Assets		Liabilities	
Cash	90,000	Banknotes	900,000
Loans	810,000		
Total Assets	900,000	Total Liabilities	900,000

The process continues in this manner and spreads throughout the system. If we suppose that the reserve ratio, *c*, for banknotes is equal to 0.1 and $k = 0$, we know the system will be able to create from nothing:

$$[41] \quad \frac{d(1-c)}{c} = \frac{1{,}000{,}000(0.9)}{0.1} = 9{,}000{,}000$$

monetary units in the form of bills unbacked by original money (gold or any other type of commodity money). We would have obtained the same result in the case of a monopolistic bank, one that enjoys the trust and business of everyone, with a reserve ratio, *c*, of *0.1* and a *k* of 1. In this case the credit expansion, *x*, would be equal to:

$$[42] \quad x = \frac{d(1-c)}{1+k(c-1)}$$

and when $k = 1$, x equals: $\frac{d(1-c)}{c}$ banknotes created *ex nihilo*. If we suppose that all the banks issue bills simultaneously and receive new original monetary units at the same rate, then by maintaining its cash reserves unaltered, a single bank will be able to generate banknotes equal to:

$$\frac{d(1-c)}{c}$$

This is the same formula we applied to deposits. The following entries will be made:

Bank A

(63) Debit		Credit	
1,000,000	Cash	Banknotes	1,000,000
9,000,000	Loans and other uses	Unbacked banknotes	9,000,000

We could also reproduce all of the accounting entries for the more general case in which $k > 0$ (in our previous example $k = 0.2$). If $c = 0.1$, then for each 1,000,000 m.u. a bank receives, it will be able to create from nothing new banknotes for a sum equal to:

$$[43] \quad \frac{d(1-c)}{1+k(c-1)}$$

That is, the bank will have the capacity to create 1,097,560 m.u. in the form of unbacked bills. One by one we could duplicate for banknotes all of the results we obtained for bank deposits, which shows that there is no economic difference between the issuance of unbacked bills and the *ex nihilo* expansion of bank-credit backed by deposits generated from nothing. The only substantial difference is of a legal nature, since according to universal legal principles, the issuance of unbacked bills implies counterfeiting and the crime of fraud, while the monetary bank-deposit contract only involves misappropriation. Nonetheless there are some differences regarding the way the operation is carried out. Banknotes take the form of bearer bonds and each has a particular face value, allowing the notes to be transferred from one person to another without it being necessary for the bank to make any accounting entry in its books (and as a result the cost of bank transactions decreases).

In contrast deposits offer customers the advantage of being able to write an exact figure on a check without needing to hand over a specific number of bills of a set value. However the fact that the banker must follow the transactions conducted and record them in his books constitutes a disadvantage. Still, apart from these legal differences and differences in form, from an economic standpoint the two operations are essentially identical and produce the same effects. As we will see later, however, when the theory of money was first being developed, theorists only recognized the immorality of the creation of unbacked banknotes and the serious harm it causes.

They did not initially realize nor respond to the fact that the expansive creation of loans backed by deposits generated from nothing has exactly the same effects. This explains why the Peel Act of July 19, 1844, the foundation of all modern banking systems, prohibited the issuance of unbacked bills yet failed miserably to achieve its objectives of monetary stability and an adequate definition and defense of citizens' property rights with respect to banking. Its failure was due to legislators' inability to comprehend that bank deposits with a fractional reserve have exactly the same nature and economic effects as unbacked banknotes.

As a result, the Act did not outlaw fractional-reserve banking and allowed the age-old practice of "issuing" unbacked (secondary) deposits to continue. In reality secondary deposits predated the fiduciary issue of banknotes, but because the former proved much more complex, only the latter was (very belatedly) prohibited. The monetary bank-deposit contract with a fractional reserve is still legal today, even though it has exactly the same economic nature and produces the same damaging effects as the issuance of unbacked banknotes prohibited in 1844 by the Peel Act.

THE CREDIT TIGHTENING PROCESS

One of the central problems posed by the process of credit expansion and *ex nihilo* deposit creation, and thus by the bank deposit contract involving a fractional reserve, is that just as this process inevitably unleashes forces that *reverse* the effects of credit expansion on the real economy, it also looses forces which lead to a parallel process of *credit tightening or contraction. Ceteris paribus*, any of the following events serve to establish that such a process has been set in motion:

(a) a decrease in original deposits;

(b) an increase in the desire of the public to hold monetary units outside the banking system (i.e., an increase in f);

(c) a rise in banks' "prudence," leading them to boost their reserve ratio, c, in order to be able to comply with the higher average number of possible withdrawal requests;

(d) a sudden rise in loan repayment not offset by an increase in loans granted; and

(e) an escalation in the number of borrowers unable to return their loans, i.e., many more defaulters.

First, it is clear that if a certain sum in original deposits is withdrawn from a bank (for instance, the 1,000,000 m.u. deposited in past illustrations), all created loans and deposits such as we referred to in preceding examples would disappear in a chain reaction, resulting in fewer loans and deposits. If we suppose that $c = 0.1$ and $k = f = 0$, then the decrease in loans and deposits would equal 9,000,000 m.u., implying a significant *drop in the money supply*, which would fall to onetenth of its prior sum. The result is severe *deflation*, or a decline in the amount of money in circulation, leading to a reduction in the prices of goods and services, which, in the short and medium term, further aggravates the recession ultimately caused in the market by all processes of credit expansion.

Second, a desire of the public to keep more money outside the banking system produces the same effects. It provokes an increase in f and a decline in banks' capacity for credit expansion, which in turn brings about a recession and a monetary squeeze.

Third, a decision by banks to be more "prudent" and to increase their reserve ratio leads to a contraction as well.

Fourth, the repayment of loans produces equally deflationary effects (when enough new loans are not granted to at least offset the ones returned). Let us consider this possibility in greater detail. We will begin by imagining a bank with $c = 0.1$, $k = 0$ and $f = 0$, whose borrowers pay back their loans. The accounting entries and balance sheet prepared when the loans are granted are as follows:

Bank A

(64)

Debit		Credit	
1,000,000	Cash	Demand deposits	1,000,000
900,000	Loans	Demand deposits	900,000
900,000	Demand deposits	Cash	900,000

(65)

Bank A
Balance Sheet
$c=0.1$, $k=0$ and $f=0$

Assets		Liabilities	
Cash	100,000	Demand deposits	1,000,000
Loans	900,000		
Total Assets	1,000,000	Total Liabilities	1,000,000

In previous examples we observed the creation through the banking system of new loans and deposits for the sum of 9,000,000 m.u. In this instance, when borrowers return the loans the last two accounting entries are canceled as follows:

Bank A

(66)

Debit		Credit	
900,000	Cash	Demand deposits	900,000
900,000	Demand deposits	Loans	900,000

The balance sheet of Bank A now looks like this:

(67)

Bank A
Balance Sheet
$c=0.1$, $k=0$ and $f=0$

Assets		Liabilities	
Cash	1,000,000	Demand deposits	1,000,000
Total Assets	1,000,000	Total Liabilities	1,000,000

Economically speaking, this means that from the point of view of an individual bank, there has been a 900,000 m.u. decrease in the money supply, which has gone from 1,900,000 m.u. at the time the loans were given (1,000,000 in deposits and 900,000 in money handed over to the borrowers) to 1,000,000 m.u., the only money left once the loans are repaid.

Therefore from the standpoint of an isolated bank the money supply clearly contracts.

Given that all banks expand credit and receive original deposits simultaneously, we already know each bank is able to maintain its cash reserves constant and grant loans for a multiple of its reserves. Hence the balance sheet of any bank, Bank A for instance, would appear as follows:

(68)

Bank A
Balance Sheet
$c=0.1$, $k=0$ and $f=0$

Assets		Liabilities	
Cash	1,000,000	Demand deposits	10,000,000
Loans	9,000,000		
Total Assets	10,000,000	Total Liabilities	10,000,000

If all the bank's borrowers return their loans paying with checks, the bank's balance sheet will look like this:

(69)

Bank A
Balance Sheet
$c=0.1$, $k=0$ and $f=0$

Assets		Liabilities	
Cash	1,000,000	Demand deposits	1,000,000
Total Assets	1,000,000	Total Liabilities	1,000,000

This balance sheet clearly reflects the 9,000,000 m.u. reduction in the money supply or tightening of credit. An identical decline would result from the simultaneous repayment of loans in isolated banks, as in entries (66) and (67).

Fifth, if the loans lose their value due to the failure of the economic activity for which they were employed, the corresponding bank must record this fact as a loss, as shown here:

Bank A

(70)

Debit		Credit	
Losses due to defaulters (expenses)	9,000,000	Loans	9,000,000

The bank's balance sheet would then look like this:

(71)

Bank A
Balance Sheet
$c=0.1$, $k=0$ and $f=0$

Assets		Liabilities	
Cash	1,000,000	Deposits	10,000,000
Losses for the year	9,000,000		
Total Assets	10,000,000	Total Liabilities	10,000,000

If we compare this balance sheet with (69), we see the bank holds the same amount in cash reserves in each instance, yet a very significant difference exists: in (71) the Liabilities column reflects 10,000,000 m.u. in deposits, as opposed to 1,000,000 m.u. in (69). In other words, *the bank has technically failed.* Nevertheless as long as depositors continue to trust it, no decrease in the money supply will take place. In fact, since no one will claim the 9,000,000 m.u. of secondary deposits the bankers created from nothing, they may even consider this amount part of the year's profits, a sum to compensate for the 9,000,000 m.u. lost to defaulters, leaving the balance sheet as it appears in (69). However in terms of deflation this situation is obviously even more dangerous than that following the repayment of a loan: before arriving at this situation, banks will heavily restrict new loans (they will be much more rigorous in their criteria for granting them), accelerating the deflationary process; and if the measures they take do not prove sufficient to avoid defaulters and the risk of failure, they will be one step away from losing the confidence of their depositors, who may force them to suspend payments and/or declare bankruptcy, and in this case even the 1,000,000 m.u. originally deposited in cash would be withdrawn, threatening the existence of the entire banking system.

Under *ordinary conditions* the contraction or deflation we are describing does not occur, because when a customer of one bank returns a loan, the sum is compensated for by another loan granted by another bank; in fact even within the same bank the attempt is always made to replace the repaid loan with a new one. In addition under normal circumstances the bank may consider payment arrears just one more operating cost. The crucial problem posed by credit tightening (as we will examine in the following chapters) consists of the fact that the very process of credit expansion based on a fractional reserve inevitably triggers the granting of loans unsupported by voluntary saving, resulting in a process of intertemporal discoordination, which in turn stems from the distorted information the banking system imparts to businessmen who receive loans generated *ex nihilo* by the system. Hence businessmen rush out to launch investment projects *as if society's real saving had increased, when in fact this has not happened. The result is artificial economic expansion or a "boom," which by processes we will later study in detail, inevitably provokes an adjustment in the form of a crisis and economic recession.* This sums up the negative effects exerted on the real economy by the financial practice of expanding credit through the issuance of fiduciary media (deposits).

The crisis and economic recession reveal that a highly significant number of investment projects financed under new loans created by banks *are not profitable* because they do not correspond to the true desires of consumers. Therefore many investment processes fail, which ultimately has a profound effect on the banking system. The harmful consequences are evidenced by *a widespread repayment of loans* by many demoralized businessmen assessing their losses and liquidating unsound investment projects (thus provoking deflation and the tightening of credit); they are also demonstrated by an alarming and atypical rise in payment arrears on loans (adversely affecting the banks' solvency). Just as the money supply was expanded according to the bank multiplier, artificial economic expansion fostered by the *ex nihilo* creation of loans eventually triggers an endogenous recession, which in the form of a widespread repayment of loans and an increase in arrears, reduces the money supply substantially. Therefore *the fractional-reserve banking system generates an extremely elastic money supply, which "stretches" with ease but then must contract just as effortlessly producing the corresponding effects on economic activity, which is repeatedly buffeted by successive stages of boom and recession.* "Manic-depressive" economic activity, with all of its heavy, painful social costs, is undoubtedly the most severe, damaging effect the current banking system (based on a fractional reserve, in violation of universal legal principles) has on society.

In short, bank customers' economic difficulties, one of the inevitable consequences of all credit expansion, render many loans irrecoverable, accelerating even more the credit tightening process (the inverse of the expansion process). In fact, as in our accounting example, the bank may completely fail as a result, in which case the bills and deposits issued by it (which we know are economically equivalent) *will lose all value*, further aggravating the monetary squeeze (instead of the 9,000,000 m.u. decrease in the money supply caused by the return of a loan, here the money supply would drop by 10,000,000 m.u.; that is, including the 1,000,000 m.u. in primary deposits held by the bank). Furthermore, one bank's solvency problems are enough to sow panic among the customers of all other banks, leading them to suspend payments one by one, with tragic economic and financial consequences. Moreover we must point out that, even if the public continues to trust banks (despite their insolvency), and even if a central bank created *ad hoc* for such situations provides all the liquidity necessary to assure depositors their deposits are fully protected, the inability to recover loans initiates a process of credit tightening that is spontaneously set off when loans are repaid and cannot be replaced by new ones at the same rate. This phenomenon is typical of periods of recession.

When customers default on their loans, banks become more cautious about granting more. Hence the natural reluctance of the demoralized public to request loans is reinforced by banks' greater prudence and rigor when it comes to giving them. In addition, as bankers see their profitability fall along with the value of their assets as a result of irrecoverable loans, they will attempt to be more careful, and other things being equal, to increase their cash on hand by raising their reserve ratio, which will have an even greater tightening effect. Finally business failures and frustration arising from the inability to honor commitments to banks will contribute even more to the *demoralization* of economic agents and to their determination to avoid new investment projects financed with bank loans. In fact many businessmen eventually realize they allowed themselves to be carried away by unjustified optimism in the phases of expansion, *largely due to the excessively generous credit terms bankers initially offered*, and the businessmen correctly attribute their errors in judgment to these easy terms. As a result they resolve not to commit the same errors again. (Whether or not their attempt at rectification is successful and in the future the businessmen remember their unpleasant experiences during the stage of recession is a different issue we will confront later.)

In conclusion, we have seen that the fractional-reserve banking system can contract and drastically reduce the money supply just as easily as it expands credit and increases the money supply. In other words, the system generates an elastic and extremely fragile stock of money which is subject to great convulsions that are very difficult, if not impossible, to mitigate or stop. This monetary and banking system contrasts with inelastic systems (for example, the one that combines the classic gold standard with a 100-percent reserve requirement), which do not permit disproportionate expansion of the money supply (the worldwide production of gold has been growing in recent centuries at the rate of 1 to 2 percent per year). Moreover they offer the following advantage: due to the fact that these systems are inelastic (gold is indestructible and throughout history the world has accumulated a very inflexible stock of it), they do not permit any abrupt decline, nor (logically) any credit or monetary squeezes which exert debilitating effects on the economy, as opposed to the current situation for which the existing banking system is responsible.

10

Bank Credit Expansion and its Effects on the Economic System

In the previous chapter we explained how the monetary bank-deposit contract with a fractional reserve leads to the creation of new money (deposits) and its infusion into the economic system in the form of new loans unbacked by a natural increase in voluntary saving (credit expansion). In this chapter we will focus on the effects of credit expansion on the economic system. We will analyze the distortions the expansion process causes: investment errors, credit squeezes, bank crises and eventually, unemployment and economic recessions.

First, however, we must examine in detail both the theory of capital and the productive structure of a real economy, since a clear grasp of both is essential to understanding the processes triggered in the market by banks' concession of loans not derived from a previous increase in voluntary saving.

Our analysis will reveal that the legal concept which concerns us (the monetary bank-deposit contract with a fractional reserve) does great harm to many economic agents (and to society in general) inasmuch as it is the principal root of recurring economic recessions. Moreover we will show that because credit expansion precipitates economic and bank crises, it renders the "law of large numbers" inapplicable in banking and therefore makes it technically impossible to ensure the completion of banks' fractional-reserve operations.

This fact acquires great significance in light of the inevitable emergence of the central bank as a lender of last resort, which we will explore in depth in a later chapter. We will begin by explaining the processes spontaneously set in motion in an economic system when new loans originate from a voluntary increase in society's real saving; then in contrast and by comparison it will be easier to understand what happens when banks create loans *ex nihilo* through a process of credit expansion.

THE FOUNDATIONS OF CAPITAL THEORY

In this section we will examine the basic tenets of capital theory which are essential to understanding the effects credit expansion exerts on the economic system.1 We will begin by considering the subjectivist conception of human action as a series of productive stages intended to achieve an end.

HUMAN ACTION AS A SERIES OF SUBJECTIVE STAGES

We may begin by defining *human action* as any deliberate behavior or conduct.2 A person acts to attain certain *goals* he/she feels are important. *Value* refers to the degree of subjective appreciation the actor assigns his goal, and the *means* is anything the actor subjectively considers adequate to accomplish it. *Utility* represents the subjective *appraisal* the actor makes of the means, in terms of the value of the goal he believes it will help him to achieve. Means must be *scarce* by definition: if the actor did not regard them as such in light of his objectives, he would not even take them into account before acting. Ends and means are not "given" (i.e., *data*) but instead result from the fundamental entrepreneurial activity of human beings, an activity which consists of creating, discovering or simply realizing which ends and means are relevant for the actor in each set of specific circumstances of time and place he encounters. Once the actor believes he has discovered which ends are worth accomplishing, he forms an idea of the means available to assist him. He then incorporates them, almost always tacitly, into a *plan* of action which he embarks upon through an *act of will.*

Consequently the *plan* is a mental picture, conjured up by the actor, of the different future *stages*, elements and circumstances his action may involve. The *plan* is the actor's personal evaluation of the practical information he possesses and gradually discovers within the context of each action. Moreover each action implies a continuous process of *individual* or *personal* planning through which the actor continually conceives, revises and modifies his plans, as he discovers and creates new subjective information on the goals he sets himself and the means he believes are available to assist him in reaching these goals.

All human action is directed toward the attainment of an *end*, or consumer good, which can be defined as a good that directly and subjectively satisfies the needs of the human actor. The term *first-order economic goods* has traditionally referred to those consumer goods which, in the specific, subjective context of each action, constitute the goal pursued by the actor in performing the action. The achievement of these goals, consumer goods, or first-order economic goods, is necessarily preceded by a series of *intermediate stages* represented by "higher-order economic goods" (second, third, fourth, etc.). The higher the order of each stage, the further the good is from the final consumer good.

Furthermore all human action takes place in *time*, and we are not referring here to the deterministic or Newtonian sense of the word (i.e., merely physical or analogical), but to the subjective sense; that is, the actor's subjective perception of time within the context of his action. According to this subjectivist conception, the actor experiences the passage of time as he acts; in other words, as he realizes new ends and means, designs plans of action and completes the different stages which compose each action.

When human beings act, they inevitably synthesize memories of the past into new expectations and mental images for the future, regarding the different stages in the action process they will follow. This future is never predetermined, but instead the actor imagines, creates and *builds* it step by step. Therefore the future is always uncertain, since it has yet to be built, and the only part of it the actor possesses consists of specific ideas, mental images or expectations he hopes to realize through the completion of the stages he imagines will make up his personal action process. Furthermore the future is *open* to man's every creative possibility, and at any point the actor may modify his objectives or vary, rearrange and revise the stages of the action processes in which he is involved. Hence in economics time is inseparable from human action. It is impossible to conceive of an action which does not take place in time, one that does not take time. Moreover the actor perceives the passage of time as he acts and goes through the different stages in his action process. Human action, which is always directed toward the attainment of a goal or the alleviation of a discomfort, invariably takes time, in the sense that it requires the realization and completion of a series of successive stages. Therefore what separates the actor from the achievement of his goal is the period of time required by the series of successive stages that compose his action process.

The following tendency always exists with respect to the actor's subjective view of the future: as the time period required by an action increases (i.e., as the number and complexity of the successive stages which constitute the action increase), the result or aim of the action becomes more valuable. An action can acquire a greater subjective value—in terms of the number, duration, and complexity of stages involved—in two ways: by enabling the actor to achieve results he subjectively values more and could not achieve via shorter human actions; or by facilitating the attainment of more results than would be possible through shorter action processes.

It is easy to understand the economic principle that human action processes tend to achieve aims of greater value the longer the processes last. Indeed if this were not the case, i.e., if the actor did not attach greater value to the results of longer actions, he would never undertake them and would opt for shorter actions instead. In other words, an actor is separated from his goal precisely by a certain length of time (i.e., by the time necessary to complete the set of stages in his action process). Thus, other things being equal, it is evident that human beings will always try to accomplish their goals as soon as possible, and they will only be willing to postpone the attainment of their ends when they subjectively believe that by doing so they will achieve more valuable objectives. We are now ready to discuss the logical notion of *time preference*, which establishes that, other things being equal, the actor prefers to satisfy his needs or reach his objectives as soon as possible. In other words, when the actor is faced with two goals of equal subjective value to him, he will always prefer the one he can attain in less time. Or to put it even more briefly, other things being equal, "present goods" are always preferable to "future goods." The law of time preference is just another way of expressing the following essential principle: any actor, in the course of his action, tries to achieve the results of the action as soon as possible, and he is separated from his ends by a series of intermediate stages involving a certain time period. Hence the time preference is not a psychological or physiological concept, but necessarily follows from the logical structure of action present in the mind of all human beings. In short, human action is directed toward certain ends and the actor chooses the means to accomplish them. The goal is the actor's purpose in performing any action, and in any action, time is what separates the actor from the goal. Therefore the closer the actor is in time to his goal, the closer he is to achieving the objectives he values. The tendency described above and the time preference we have just explained are simply two different ways of expressing the same reality. According to the former, actors undertake time-consuming actions because they expect to thus achieve more valuable ends; according to the latter, other things being equal, actors always prefer the goods closer to them in time.

Hence it is impossible to imagine a human action to which the principle of time preference does not apply. A world without time preference is inconceivable and would be absurd: it would mean people always preferred the future to the present, and objectives would be postponed, one after the other, just before they were reached, and therefore no end would ever be achieved and human action would be senseless.9

CAPITAL AND CAPITAL GOODS

We may use the term *capital goods* to designate the intermediate stages of each action process, subjectively regarded as such by the actor. Or to put it another way, each of the intermediate stages in an actor's production process is a capital good. Hence this definition of capital goods fits in perfectly with the subjectivist conception of economics presented above. The economic nature of a capital good does not depend on its physical properties, but on the opinion of an actor, who believes the good will enable him to reach or complete a stage in his action process. Therefore capital goods, as we have defined them, are simply the intermediate stages the actor believes he needs to go through before achieving the purpose of his action. Capital goods should always be placed in a *teleological* context, in which the essential defining elements are the aim pursued and the actor's subjective view on the stages necessary to fulfill it.

Hence capital goods are "higher-order economic goods," or factors of production which subjectively materialize at each intermediate stage in a particular action process. Moreover capital goods arise from the union of three essential elements: natural resources, labor and time, all of which are combined in entrepreneurial action conceived and processed by human beings. The *sine qua non* for producing capital goods is *saving*, or the relinquishment or postponement of immediate consumption. Indeed in an action process the actor will only be able to reach successive and increasingly time-consuming intermediate stages if he has first sacrificed the chance to undertake actions which would produce a more immediate result. In other words, he must give up the achievement of immediate ends which would satisfy current human needs (consumption). To illustrate this important concept, we will use the example given by Böhm-Bawerk to explain the process of saving and investment in capital goods carried out by an individual actor in an isolated situation, such as Robinson Crusoe on his island.

Let us suppose that Robinson Crusoe has just arrived on his island and spends his time picking berries by hand, his only means of subsistence. Each day he devotes all of his efforts to gathering berries, and he picks enough to survive and can even eat a few extra daily. After several weeks on this diet, Robinson Crusoe makes the entrepreneurial discovery that with a wooden stick several meters long, he could reach higher and further, strike the bushes with more force and gather the necessary berries much quicker. The only problem is that he estimates it could take him five whole days to find a suitable tree from which to take the stick and then to prepare it by pulling off its branches, leaves, and imperfections. During this time he will be compelled to interrupt his berry picking. If he wants to produce the stick, he will have to reduce his consumption of berries for a time and store the remainder in a basket until he has enough to survive for five days, the predicted duration of the production process of the wooden stick. After planning his action, Robinson Crusoe decides to undertake it, and therefore he must first *save* a portion of the berries he picks by hand each day, reducing his consumption by that amount. This clearly means he must make an inevitable *sacrifice*, which he nevertheless deems well worth his effort in relation to the goal he longs to achieve. So he decides to reduce his consumption (in other words, to save) for several weeks while storing his leftover berries in a basket until he has accumulated an amount he believes will be sufficient to sustain him while he produces the stick.

This example shows that each process of investment in capital goods requires prior saving; that is, a decrease in consumption, which must fall below its potential level. Once Robinson Crusoe has saved enough berries, he spends five days searching for a branch from which to make his wooden stick, separating it from the tree and perfecting it. What does he eat during the five days it takes him to prepare the stick, a production process which forces him to interrupt his daily harvest of berries? He simply consumes the berries he accumulated in the basket over the preceding several week period during which he saved the necessary portion from his handpicked berries and experienced some hunger. In this way, if Robinson Crusoe's calculations were correct, at the end of five days he will have the stick (a capital good), which represents an intermediate stage removed in time (by five days of saving) from the immediate processes of the production of berries (by hand) which up to that point had occupied him. With the finished stick Robinson

Crusoe can reach places inaccessible to him by hand and strike the bushes with force, multiplying his production of berries by ten. As a result, from that point on his stick enables him to gather in one-tenth of a day the berries he needs to survive, and he can spend the rest of his time resting or pursuing subsequent goals that are much more important to him (like building a hut or hunting animals to vary his diet and make clothes).

Robinson Crusoe's production process, like any other, clearly arises from an act of entrepreneurial creativity, the actor's realization that he stands to benefit, i.e., he can accomplish ends more valuable to him, by employing action processes which require a longer period of time (because they include more stages). Thus action or production processes yield capital goods, which are simply intermediate economic goods in an action process whose aim has not yet been reached. The actor is only willing to sacrifice his immediate consumption (i.e., to save) if he thinks that by doing so he will achieve goals he values more (in this case, the production of ten times more berries than he could gather by hand). Furthermore *Robinson Crusoe must attempt to coordinate as well as possible his present behavior with his foreseeable future behavior.*

More specifically, he must avoid initiating action processes that are excessively long in relation to his savings: it would be tragic for him to run out of berries (that is, to consume all he has saved) halfway through the process of producing a capital good and without reaching his goal. He must also refrain from saving too much with respect to his future investment needs, since by doing so he would only unnecessarily sacrifice his immediate consumption. Robinson Crusoe's subjective assessment of his time preference is precisely what enables him to adequately coordinate or adjust his present behavior in relation to his future needs and behavior. On the one hand, the fact that his time preference is not absolute makes it possible for him to forfeit some of his present consumption over a period of several weeks with the hope of thus being able to produce the stick. On the other hand, the fact that he does have a time preference explains why he only devotes his efforts to creating a capital good he can produce in a limited period of time and which requires sacrificing and saving for a *limited* number of days.

If Robinson Crusoe had no time preference, nothing would stop him from dedicating all of his efforts to building a hut right away (which, for example, might take him a month minimum), a plan he would not be able to carry out without first having saved a large quantity of berries. Therefore he would either starve to death or the project, out of all proportion to his potential saving, would soon be interrupted and abandoned. At any rate, it is important to understand that the real saved resources (the berries in the basket) are precisely the ones which enable Robinson Crusoe to survive during the time period he spends producing the capital good and during which he ceases to gather berries directly. Even though Robinson Crusoe is undoubtedly much more productive harvesting berries with his wooden stick than he is with his bare hands, there is also no doubt that the process of berry production using the stick is a more lengthy one in terms of time (it includes more stages) than the production process of berry picking by hand. Production processes tend to increase in length and duration (i.e., to become more complex and include more stages) as a result of the saving and entrepreneurial activity of humans; and the longer and more time-consuming these processes become, the more productive they tend to be.

In a modern economy, in which many economic agents simultaneously perform different functions, we will use the term *capitalist* to denote that economic agent whose function is precisely to save; in other words, to consume less than he creates or produces and to make available to workers the resources they need to live for the duration of the production process in which they participate. (Robinson Crusoe also behaved like a capitalist when he saved berries that later enabled him to survive *while* he produced his wooden stick.) Thus when the capitalist saves, he frees up resources (consumer goods) which can be used to sustain workers who direct their energies to productive stages further removed from final consumption, i.e., the production of capital goods. Unlike in the example of Robinson Crusoe, production processes in a modern economy are extremely complex, and in terms of time, very lengthy. They incorporate a multitude of stages, all of which are interrelated and divide into numerous secondary processes that humans employ in the innumerable action projects they constantly launch.

For instance the process of producing a car consists of hundreds or even thousands of productive stages requiring a very prolonged period of time (even several years) from the moment the car company begins to design the vehicle (the stage furthest from final consumption), orders the corresponding materials from its suppliers, runs these materials through the different assembly lines, orders the different parts for the motor and all accessories, etc., until it arrives at the stages closest to consumption, such as transport and distribution to dealers, the development of advertising campaigns and the presentation and sale of the car to the public. So although when we visit the factory we see a finished vehicle emerge every minute, we must not deceive ourselves by thinking the production process of each car lasts one minute. Instead we should be aware that each car calls for a process of production lasting several years, a process comprised of numerous stages, beginning when the model is conceived and designed and ending when the car is presented to its proud owner as a consumer good.

In addition, in modern societies humans have a tendency to specialize in different stages of the production process. An increasing division of labor (or to be more precise, of knowledge), both horizontal and vertical, causes the stages in the production process to be continuously broken down into other stages as the division of knowledge spreads and deepens. Specific companies and economic agents tend to specialize in each one of these stages. Apart from a stage-by-stage analysis, we can also examine the process by considering the many phases which occur at once. At all times each of the stages coexists with the others and therefore some people spend their time designing vehicles (the cars which will be available to the public in ten years), while others simultaneously order materials from suppliers, others work on assembly lines, and others devote their efforts to the commercial field (very close to final consumption), promoting the sale of vehicles that have already been produced.

Therefore it is clear that, just as the difference between the "rich" Robinson Crusoe with the stick and the "poor" Robinson Crusoe without it lay in the capital good the former had obtained through prior saving, the essential difference between rich societies and poor societies does not stem from any greater effort the former devote to work, nor even from any greater technological knowledge the former hold. Instead it arises mainly from the fact that *rich nations possess a more* extensive network of capital goods wisely invested from an entrepreneurial standpoint. These goods consist of machines, tools, computers, buildings, semi-manufactured goods, software, etc., and they *exist due to prior savings of the nation's citizens.* In other words, comparatively rich societies possess more wealth because they have more *time accumulated* in the form of capital goods, which places them closer in time to the achievement of much more valuable goals. There is no doubt that an American worker earns a much higher wage than an Indian worker, but this is chiefly because the former has at his disposal and uses many more capital goods (tractors, computers, machines, etc.) than the Indian worker, and the goods he uses are of much higher quality. To put it another way, the longer the production process, the more productive it tends to be, as we have seen. The modern tractor plows the earth much more productively than the Roman plow. Nevertheless the tractor is a capital good whose production requires a set of stages much more numerous, complex and lengthy than those necessary to produce a Roman plow.

Capital goods in the extremely complex network which composes the real productive structure of a modern economy *are not perpetual*, but are always temporary in the sense that they are physically used up or consumed during the production process, or they become obsolete. In other words, wear on capital equipment is not only physical, but technological and economic as well (obsolescence). Hence capital goods must be preserved and maintained (in Robinson Crusoe's case, he must take care of his stick and protect it from wear). This means entrepreneurs must repair existing capital goods; and, even more importantly, they must constantly produce new capital goods to replace the old ones they are in the process of consuming. *Depreciation* refers to the wear capital goods undergo during the production process. A certain minimum level of saving is essential in order to compensate for depreciation by producing the capital goods necessary to replace ones that have worn out or depreciated. This is the only way for the actor to maintain his productive capacity intact. Moreover if he wishes to further increase the number of stages, lengthen the processes and make them more productive, he will have to accumulate *even more than the minimum savings required to counteract the strict amortization* rate, the accounting term for the depreciation of capital goods. To save, the actor must reduce consumption in relation to production. If his output is constant, he must curtail his actual consumption; however if his output is growing, he will be able to save (to accumulate capital goods) by keeping his volume of consumption relatively constant. Nevertheless even in this last case saving requires the sacrifice (as always) of the increasing volumes of potential consumption which a growing output would permit.

In every production process (i.e., series of successive stages or capital goods) it is possible to distinguish the stages which are relatively closer in time to the final consumer good from those which are relatively further from it. As a general rule capital goods are difficult to convert, and the closer they are to the final stage of consumption, the more difficult is their convertibility. Nonetheless the fact that capital goods are difficult to adapt does not mean the actor, in his action process, is not often forced to modify the objectives of his action, and consequently, to review and convert the stages he has already completed (i.e., to convert his capital goods as far as is practicable). In any case, when circumstances change or the actor changes his mind and modifies the aim of his action, the capital goods he has produced up to that point may become utterly useless or they may be useful only after a costly conversion. The actor could also find a way to use the goods, yet still feel that had he known in advance they would eventually be needed in a different production process, he would have made them in quite a different way. Finally, it is very rare for a capital good to be so removed from consumption, or for the circumstances to be such, that the good is perfectly useful in any alternative project.

Thus we see the influence of the past on actions carried out today. Action, as we have defined it, is always prospective, never retrospective; and an actor considers a good a capital good based on a planned future action, not on the good's material properties nor on former action projects.15 Nevertheless the past undoubtedly *influences* future action, to the extent that it determines the current starting point. Humans commit countless entrepreneurial errors when conceiving, undertaking, and completing their actions; and consequently, they embark on subsequent actions from a present position they would have attempted to make different had they known about it in advance. However once events have unfolded in a certain way, humans always strive to make the best of their present circumstances with a view to accomplishing their goals for the future. While capital goods are difficult to convert, investors manage to provide them with considerable "mobility" through the juridical institutions of property and contract law, which regulate the different forms of transferring such goods. Thus the (extremely complex and prolonged) productive structure permits the constant mobility of investors, through the exchange and sale of capital goods in the market.

We are now ready to consider the concept of *capital*, which from an economic viewpoint differs from the concept of "capital goods." In fact we will define "capital" *as the market value of capital goods*, a value estimated by the individual actors who buy and sell capital goods in a free market. Thus we see that capital is simply an abstract concept or instrument of economic calculation; in other words, a subjective valuation of or judgment on the market value entrepreneurs attribute to capital goods and on the basis of which they continually buy and sell them, attempting to make a pure entrepreneurial profit with each transaction. Therefore in a socialist economy in which neither free markets nor market prices exist, it is perhaps feasible to speak of capital goods, but not of capital: the latter always requires a market and prices which are freely determined by the economic agents who participate in it. If it were not for market prices and the subjective estimation of the capital value of goods that compose the intermediate stages in production processes, in a modern society it would be impossible to estimate or calculate whether or not the final value of the goods to be produced using capital goods offsets the cost involved in the production processes, neither would it be possible to direct in a coordinated way the efforts of people who contribute to the different action processes.

We have attempted elsewhere to demonstrate that all systematic coercion which impedes the free exercise of entrepreneurship prevents humans from discovering the information they need to carry out their actions.19 It also keeps them from spontaneously transmitting this information and coordinating their behavior with respect to the needs of others. This means that the coercive intervention which is characteristic of socialism, of state interventionism in the economy, and of the granting of privileges to certain groups against traditional legal principles, prevents to a greater or lesser extent the exercise of entrepreneurship, and hence the coordinated action of human beings; it also tends to generate systematic maladjustments in the framework of society. Systematic discoordination can be intratemporal; or, as in the case of human actions related to different stages of production processes or capital goods, *intertemporal*, such that *human beings who cannot act freely tend to adjust* their present behavior poorly to their future behavior and needs.

As we saw from Robinson Crusoe's isolated production process, intertemporal coordination is fundamental to all human action which takes time and especially to those actions related to capital goods; thus the great importance of permitting the free exercise of entrepreneurship in this area. In this way entrepreneurs constantly discover profit opportunities in the market, believing they see new possible combinations of capital goods, and considering these combinations to be undervalued with respect to the market price they estimate they will be able to obtain in the future for the consumer goods they produce. In short we are referring to a process of continual buying and selling, "recombination" and production of new kinds of capital goods, a process which generates a dynamic and very complex productive structure which always tends to expand horizontally and vertically.20 Without free entrepreneurship, nor free markets for capital goods and money, it is impossible to make the necessary economic calculation regarding the horizontal and vertical extension of the different stages in the production process, resulting in widespread discoordinated behavior that throws society off balance and prevents its harmonious development. In entrepreneurial processes of intertemporal coordination, a leading role is played by an important market price: the price of present goods in relation to future goods, more commonly known as the interest rate, which regulates the relationship between consumption, saving and investment in modern societies, and which we will study in detail in the next section.

THE INTEREST RATE

As we have seen, other things being equal, humans always place present goods higher than future goods on their scale of value. However the relative *intensity* of this difference in subjective valuation varies substantially from one person to another; and it can even vary greatly throughout the life of one person based on changes in his circumstances. Some people have a high time preference and value the present greatly in relation to the future; thus they are only willing to sacrifice the immediate achievement of their ends if they expect or believe they will accomplish in the future goals they subjectively value very highly. Other people have a more limited time preference, and although they also value present goods more than future goods, they are more predisposed to relinquish the immediate achievement of their aims in exchange for objectives which they value only a little more and which will be reached tomorrow. This difference in the *psychic intensity* of the subjective valuation of present goods in relation to future goods, a difference reflected on each human actor's scale of value, means that in a market comprising many economic agents, each of which has his own distinct and variable time preference, multiple opportunities arise for mutually beneficial exchanges.

Hence people with a low time preference will be willing to give up present goods in exchange for future goods valued only a bit higher, and they will perform exchanges in which they will hand over their present goods to people with a higher time preference, i.e., people who value the present more intensely than they do. The creativity and alertness inherent in entrepreneurship give rise to a market process that tends to establish a *market price* for present goods with respect to future goods. *We will use the term "interest rate" to denote the market price of present goods in relation to future goods.* Given that in the market many actions are carried out using money as a generally-accepted medium of exchange, the interest rate is the price one must pay to obtain a certain number of m.u. immediately; this price reflects the number of units one must return in exchange at the end of the set term or time period. Generally, for reasons of custom, the price is expressed as a certain yearly percentage. For instance, an interest rate of 9 percent indicates that market transactions are conducted in such a way that it is possible to obtain 100 m.u. immediately (present good) in exchange for a promise to turn over 109 m.u. at the end of one year (future good).

Therefore the interest rate is the price established in a market in which the suppliers or sellers of present goods are precisely the savers; that is, all those relatively more willing to relinquish immediate consumption in exchange for goods of greater value in the future. The buyers of present goods are all those who consume immediate goods and services (be they workers, owners of natural resources or capital goods, or any combination of these). Indeed the market of present and future goods, in which the interest rate is determined, *consists of society's entire structure of productive stages*, in which savers or capitalists give up immediate consumption and offer present goods to owners of the primary or original factors of production (workers and owners of natural resources) and to owners of capital goods, in exchange for the full ownership of consumer (and capital) goods of a supposedly higher value once the production of these goods has been completed in the future. If we eliminate the positive (or negative) effect of pure entrepreneurial profits (or losses), this difference in value tends to coincide with the interest rate.

From a legal standpoint, exchanges of present goods for future goods can take many forms. For instance, in a cooperative the workers themselves simultaneously act as capitalists, waiting until the end of the entire production process to acquire the ownership of the final good and its full value. Nevertheless in most cases workers are not willing to wait until the production process ends nor to take on the risks and uncertainties it entails. Thus instead of forming cooperatives, they prefer to sell the services of their productive effort in exchange for immediate present goods. They agree on a labor contract (an employment contract for another's account) according to which the person who advances them the present goods (the capitalist, saver or supplier of present goods) receives the full ownership of the final good once it has been produced. Combinations of these two different types of contract are also possible. This is not the proper place to analyze the different legal forms which the exchange of present goods for future goods takes in a modern society. Furthermore these forms do not affect the fundamental argument we advance in this book, though they are undoubtedly of great interest from a theoretical and practical standpoint.

It is worth noting that the "loan market," in which one may obtain a loan by agreeing to pay the corresponding interest rate, constitutes a relatively small part of the general market, in which present goods are exchanged for future goods and which encompasses the entire productive structure of society. Here owners of the original means of production (labor and natural resources) and capital goods act as demanders of present goods, and savers act as suppliers of them. Therefore the short-, medium-, and long-term loan market is simply a subset of that much broader market in which present goods are exchanged for future goods and with respect to which it plays a mere secondary and dependent role, despite the fact that the loan market is the most visible and obvious to the general public. It fact it is entirely possible to conceive of a society in which no loan market exists, and all economic agents invest their savings in production *directly* (via internal financing and retained earnings through partnerships, corporations, and cooperatives).

Although in this case no interest rate would be established in a nonexistent loan market, an interest rate would still be determined by the ratio at which present goods are exchanged for future goods in the different intermediate stages in production processes. Under these circumstances the interest rate would be determined by the "*rate of profit*" which would tend to equal the net income at each stage in the production process, per unit of value and time period. Although this interest rate is not directly observable in the market, and even though in each company and in each specific production process it incorporates important external factors (such as the components of pure entrepreneurial profits or losses, and the risk premium), the profit generated in each stage of the entire economic system would tend to correspond to the interest rate, due to the typical entrepreneurial process of equalizing accounting profits over the different stages of the productive structure, assuming no further changes occur and all creative possibilities and opportunities for entrepreneurial profit have already been discovered and exploited.

In the outside world, the only directly-observable figures are what we could call the *gross interest rate* or *market rate of interest* (which coincides with the interest rate in the credit market) and the *gross accounting profits* generated by each production activity (i.e., net income). The first consists of the interest rate as we have defined it (also sometimes called the *originary* or *natural rate of interest*), plus the *risk premium* corresponding to the operation in question, plus or minus a *premium for expected inflation or deflation*; that is, for the expected decrease or increase in the purchasing power of the monetary unit used in exchanges of present goods for future goods and in calculations regarding such transactions. The second figure, which is also directly observable in the market, represents *gross accounting profits* (i.e., net income) derived from the specific productive activity carried out at each stage of the production process. These profits tend to match the gross interest rate (or market rate of interest) as we have defined it in the preceding paragraph, plus or minus pure entrepreneurial profits or losses.24 As in all markets entrepreneurial profits and losses tend to disappear as a result of competition between entrepreneurs; the accounting profits of each productive activity by time period tend to match the gross market interest rate. Indeed the accounting profits reported by each company for a financial year could be considered to include an implicit interest-rate component, with respect to the resources saved and invested by the capitalists who own the company. This implicit component, together with the risk factor and entrepreneurial profits or losses which result from the purely entrepreneurial activity of the business, give rise to accounting profits. From this perspective it is possible for a company to report accounting profits (i.e., net income) when it has actually suffered entrepreneurial losses, if accounting profits fail to reach the amount necessary to exceed the implicit gross-market-interest-rate component that applies to resources capitalists invest in their businesses throughout the financial year.

In any case, regardless of the external form interest takes, the key is to remember that as a market price or social rate of time preference, interest plays a vital role in the coordination of the behavior of consumers, savers, investors, and producers in a modern society. Just as it was crucial for Robinson Crusoe to coordinate his actions and refrain from dedicating to future goals an effort disproportionate to his stock of saved present goods, the same issue, *intertemporal coordination*, arises constantly in society.

In a modern economy, present and future behaviors are reconciled through entrepreneurial activity in the market where present goods are exchanged for future goods and the interest rate, the market price of one type of goods in terms of the other, is established. Thus the more plentiful the savings, i.e., the greater the quantity of present goods sold or offered for sale, other things being equal, the lower their price in terms of future goods; and consequently, the lower the market rate of interest. This indicates to entrepreneurs that more present goods are available, which enables them to increase the length and complexity of the stages in their production processes, making these stages more productive. In contrast, the fewer the savings, i.e., other things being equal, the less economic agents are willing to give up immediate consumption of present goods, the higher the market rate of interest. Thus a high market rate of interest shows that savings are relatively scarce, an unmistakable sign entrepreneurs should heed to avoid unduly lengthening the different stages in the production process and generating as a result discoordination or maladjustments which pose a great danger to the sustained, healthy and harmonious development of society.25 In short the interest rate conveys to entrepreneurs which new productive stages or investment projects they can and should embark on and which they should not, in order to keep coordinated, as much as humanly possible, the behavior of savers, consumers, and investors, and to prevent the different productive stages from remaining unnecessarily short or becoming too long.

Finally we must point out that the market rate of interest tends to be the same throughout the entire time market or productive structure in society, not only *intratemporally*, i.e., in different areas of the market, but also *intertemporally*, i.e., in some productive stages relatively close to consumption as in other productive stages further from it. Indeed if the interest rate one can obtain by advancing present goods in some stages (for example, those closest to consumption) is higher than that one can obtain in other stages (for example, those furthest from consumption), then the entrepreneurial force itself, driven by a desire for profit, will lead people to *disinvest* in stages in which the interest rate or rate of profit is lower, relatively speaking, and to invest in stages in which the expected interest rate or rate of profit is higher.

THE STRUCTURE OF PRODUCTION

Although it is nearly impossible to illustrate with charts the extremely complex structure of productive stages that make up a modern economy, Chart V-1 represents a simplified version of this structure, and we include it with the purpose of clarifying the theoretical arguments we will later develop.

Moreover although this chart is not strictly necessary for explaining the essential theoretical arguments, and in fact, authors of the stature of Ludwig von Mises never used it in their presentation of the theory of capital and of business cycles, traditionally many theorists have considered it helpful to use simplified charts of the stages in real production processes in order to clarify their arguments.

The stages of the productive structure do not represent the production of capital goods and consumer goods in physical terms, but rather their value in m.u. To the left of the chart we assume that the productive structure is composed of five stages whose "order number," in keeping with Menger's classic contribution, increases with the distance from the final stage of consumption. Thus the *first stage* comprises "first-order economic goods" or consumer goods which, in our chart, are exchanged for the value of one hundred m.u. The *second stage* is composed of "second-order economic goods," or the capital goods closest to consumption. The third, fourth, and fifth stages continue this pattern, and the fifth stage is the furthest from consumption. In order to simplify the explanation, we have supposed that each stage requires the time period of one year, and therefore the production process would last five years from its beginning in the fifth stage (the furthest from consumption) to the final consumer goods in the first stage.

There are two ways to consider the stages in our outline: we can regard them as consecutive, as the set of productive stages which must be gone through before arriving at the final consumer good after five years (the diachronic point of view); or can we view them as *simultaneous*, as a "photograph" of the stages taking place at one time in the same financial year (the synchronic point of view). As Böhm-Bawerk indicates, this second interpretation of the chart (as a representation of the production process in the form of a set of *synchronized* stages) bears a strong resemblance to the age pyramids formulated with data from the census. These pyramids represent cross-sections of the real population, which is classified by ages. In them we can also see the change in the number of people of each age who remain alive (mortality table); this second interpretation means viewing the stages as consecutive.

The arrows in our diagram represent the *flows* of monetary income which at each stage in the production process reach the owners of the original means of production (labor and natural resources) in the form of wages and rents, and the owners of capital goods (capitalists or savers) in the form of interest (or accounting profit). Indeed if we begin at the first stage in our example, consumers spend 100 m.u. on consumer goods, and this money becomes the property of the capitalists who own the consumer goods industries. One year earlier, these capitalists had advanced from their savings 80 m.u. corresponding to the services of fixed capital goods and to circulating capital goods produced by other capitalists in the second stage of the production process.

The first capitalists also pay 10 m.u. to the owners of the original means of production (labor and natural resources) which they hire directly in the last stage, corresponding to the production of consumer goods (this payment to the owners of the original means of production is represented on our chart by the *vertical* arrow that begins to the right of last step [100 m.u.] and extends to the upper right-hand box containing 10 m.u.). Since the capitalists of the consumer goods stage advanced eighty m.u. to the owners of the capital goods of the second stage, and ten m.u. to workers and owners of natural resources (a total of 90 m.u.), at the end of one year when these capitalists sell the consumer goods for 100 units, they obtain an accounting profit or interest derived from having advanced 90 m.u. from savings a year earlier. This difference between the total amount they advanced, 90 m.u. (which they could have consumed, yet they saved and invested it), and the amount they receive at the end of a year, 100 m.u., is equal to an interest rate of approximately 11 percent per year (10:90 = 0.11). From an accounting standpoint, this sum appears as profit on the income statement drawn up to reflect the entrepreneurial activity of capitalists of the consumer goods stage.

We can follow the same reasoning with respect to the rest of the stages. Hence for example, the capitalists who own the intermediate goods of the third stage advanced at the beginning of the period 40 m.u. in payment for capital goods produced in the fourth stage, as well as 14 m.u. to owners of the original means of production (labor and natural resources). In exchange for the 54 m.u. they have advanced, the capitalists become owners of the product which, once it is finished, they sell to capitalists of the second stage for 60 m.u., earning a differential of six m.u., which is their accounting profit or interest; it is also close to 11 percent. This pattern repeats itself in each stage.

The upper portion of the chart shows the amounts which the capitalists advance at each stage to the original means of production (workers and owners of natural resources) and which add up to a total of 70 m.u. (18+16+14+12+10=70 m.u.). In a column on the right-hand side, we indicate the monetary sums obtained as accounting profits at each stage. These profits reflect the accounting difference between the m.u. advanced by the capitalists of each stage and those they receive for the sale of their product in the following stage. As we know, this accounting profit tends to coincide with the interest derived from the amount the capitalists of each stage save and advance to capitalists of earlier stages and to the owners of the original means of production. The total of the accounting differences between income and expenses at each stage adds up to 30 m.u., which when added to the 70 m.u. received by the original means of production, equals 100 m.u. of net income, which coincides exactly with the amount spent on final consumer goods during the period.

SOME ADDITIONAL CONSIDERATIONS

We must now discuss some important additional considerations regarding our outline of the stages in the production process:

1. *The arbitrary selection of the time period of each stage.*

First we must state that the decision to make each stage last one year was purely arbitrary, and any other time period could have been chosen. We decided on one year because that is the business and accounting period most commonly used, and therefore it makes the proposed illustrative outline of productive stages easier to understand.

2. *The avoidance of the erroneous concept of "average period of production."*

Second, we should indicate that the five-year duration of the production process in our example is also purely arbitrary. Modern production processes are highly complex, as we know, and they vary greatly from one sector or business to another, with respect to the number and duration of stages. At any rate, it is unnecessary and pointless to refer to an "average period of production," since *a priori* estimates of the length of any particular production process depend on the specific process itself. We know that capital goods are actually the intermediate stages in a production process initiated by an entrepreneur. From a subjective point of view, a production process always has a *beginning*, the specific moment at which the actor first perceives that a particular goal is worthwhile to him, and a certain set of intermediate stages which he conceives in advance and later attempts to carry out as he acts.

Hence our analysis is not based on the idea of an "average period of production" and is therefore immune to criticism of that concept.29 In fact all production periods have a specific origin and cannot be traced back indefinitely in time; instead each stops at the very moment a certain entrepreneur took up the pursuit of an aim which constituted the imagined final stage in his process.30 Thus the first stage of production begins precisely at the moment the entrepreneur conceives of the final stage in the process (a consumer good or a capital good). In identifying the beginning of the first stage, it is totally irrelevant whether or not the production process in question involves the use of capital goods or factors of production completed in advance, yet which no one had ever imagined would eventually be used in such a process. Moreover it is unnecessary to trace back indefinitely in time the conception of a set of stages in a production process because any capital good produced in advance which nevertheless remains unused for a specific purpose for any length of time, ultimately becomes another "original" resource, so to speak, similar in this respect to all other natural resources that generate income, yet are viewed by the actor as just another initial factor in his course of action. In short all production processes are invariably prospective, they have an identifiable beginning and a foreseeable end, and their duration varies according to the process in question yet is never infinite nor undetermined. Therefore the retrospective calculation of supposed, phantasmagoric average periods of production is meaningless.

A third pertinent observation about our portrayal of productive stages is that it includes not only fixed capital goods, but also circulating capital goods and durable consumer goods. From a human actor's prospective point of view, the distinction between fixed and circulating capital goods is irrelevant, since it is largely based on the *physical* characteristics of the goods in question and depends especially upon whether or not these goods are considered to have been "completed." Indeed when fixed capital goods are incorporated into a production process, they are considered "completed," while circulating capital goods are thought to be semi-manufactured or in an "intermediate" process of production. However according to the subjectivist view on production processes aimed at consumption, *both fixed and circulating capital goods constitute* intermediate stages in an action process which only concludes when *the final consumer good satisfies the desires of consumers*; therefore, economically speaking, it is senseless to distinguish between the two.

The same can be said for "inventories" or stocks of intermediate goods held on hand at each of the productive stages. These stocks, which are considered a part of circulating capital, constitute one of the most significant components of the value of each stage in a process of production. Furthermore it has been demonstrated that as the economy evolves and prospers, these stocks become more important because they enable different businesses to minimize the ever-latent risk of unexpected shortages or "bottlenecks" which prolong delivery periods. In this way, inventories make it possible for clients at all levels (not only at the level of consumption, but also at the level of intermediate goods) to have at their disposal a growing variety of products to choose from and acquire immediately. Hence one manifestation of the lengthening of production processes is precisely a continual increase in inventories or stocks of intermediate goods.

4. *The role of durable consumer goods.*

Fourth, durable consumer goods satisfy human needs over a very prolonged period of time. Therefore they simultaneously form a part of several stages at once: the final stage of consumption and various preceding stages, according to their duration. In any case, for our purposes it is irrelevant whether the consumer himself must wait a certain number of years or stages before taking advantage of the latest *services* his durable consumer good can perform. Only when these services are directly received do we reach the last stage, the stage of consumption. The years the owner spends caring for and maintaining his durable consumer good so that it will continue to perform consumer services for him in the future correspond to the stages which appear above and are increasingly distant from consumption: stage two, three, four, etc. Thus one of the manifestations of the lengthening of production processes and of the increase in their number of stages consists precisely of the production of a larger number of durable consumer goods of increasing quality and durability.

5. *The trend toward the equalization of the rate of accounting profit or interest at each stage.*

The fifth fundamental point we must emphasize is the following: In the market there exists a trend (driven by the force of entrepreneurship) toward the equalization of the rate of "profit" in all economic activities. This occurs not only *horizontally*, within each production stage, but also *vertically*, between stages. Indeed when there are disparities in profits, businessmen will devote their effort, creative capacity and investment to those activities which generate relatively higher profits, and they will stop devoting these things to activities which yield lower profits. Significantly, in the example from Chart V-1, the rate of accounting profit, or relative difference between income and expenses, is the same at each stage, i.e., approximately 11 percent per year. If the situation were otherwise; that is, if in one of the stages the rate of accounting profit or interest were higher, then disinvestment would take place, and productive resources would be withdrawn from the stages with a lower rate of profit and directed to those with a higher rate of accounting profit. This redirection of resources takes place until the greater demand for capital goods and original means of production in the receiving stage results in an increase in spending on these components in that stage; and the greater influx of its final goods tends to reduce their prices, until the differential between income and expenses decreases, giving rise to a rate of profit equal to that of other productive stages. *This microeconomic reasoning is key* to understanding modifications made to the number and length of productive stages; we will later examine these changes.

6. *Gross and net investment and saving.*

Sixth, although in the example the total *net income* received by owners of the original means of production and by capitalists in the form of profit or interest (100 m.u.) coincides exactly with the sum spent over the period in consumer goods (and thus *net saving* is equal to zero), there is a significant volume of gross saving and investment. In fact gross saving and investment are reflected in Table V-1, which indicates for each stage, at the left-hand side of the table, the supply of present goods offered by savers in exchange for future goods. At the right-hand side, we find the corresponding demand for present goods experienced by the providers of future goods, mainly owners of the original means of production (labor and natural resources) and the capitalists of earlier stages. We can observe from the table that gross saving, or the total supply of present goods, equals 270 m.u.: overall gross saving which takes place in the economic system and is 2.7 times greater than the amount spent during the year on final consumer goods. This *gross saving* is identical to the *gross investment* of the financial year in the form of spending by the capitalists on natural resources, labor, and capital goods from prior stages in the production process.

7. *Gross and net income for the year.*

Seventh, our outline of the different stages in the production process, as an illustration of the flow of both capital goods and money. Indeed capital goods "flow downward," i.e., from the stages furthest from consumption to the stages closest to it, and money "flows" in the opposite direction. In other words, m.u. are first used to pay for final consumer goods, and from that point they gradually move up the scale of productive stages until they reach those stages furthest from consumption. Therefore to obtain the gross monetary income for the period, we total, from bottom to top, all of the transactions (in terms of m.u.) conducted during the period.

We see from this table that the *gross income* for the period is equal to 370 m.u. Of this amount, 100 m.u. correspond to *net income*, which is spent entirely on final consumer goods; and 270 m.u. correspond to the total supply of present goods or gross saving, which coincides with the total gross demand for present goods during the period.

That is, a relationship exists between the number of m.u. spent on consumer goods and the much larger number spent on capital goods. Hence it is an unquestionable fact that *the amount of money spent on intermediate goods during* any time period is much larger by far than the amount spent during *the same period on consumer goods and services.* It is interesting to note that even minds as brilliant as Adam Smith committed unfortunate errors when it came to recognizing this fundamental economic fact. Indeed, according to Adam Smith, the value of the goods circulated between the different dealers, never can exceed the value of those circulated between the dealers and the consumers; whatever is bought by the dealers, being ultimately destined to be sold to the consumers.

CRITICISM OF THE MEASURES USED IN NATIONAL INCOME ACCOUNTING

The sum of gross income, as we have defined and calculated it, along with its distribution over the different stages in the production process, is crucial for a correct understanding of the economic process which takes place in society. In fact the structure of the stages of capital goods and their value in m.u. are not measures which, once obtained, can be automatically and indefinitely maintained regardless of human decisions made by entrepreneurs who must deliberately and continually choose whether to increase, hold steady or reduce the productive stages undertaken in the past. In other words, whether a certain structure of productive stages remains the same or changes, becoming narrower or broader, depends solely upon whether the entrepreneurs of each stage subjectively decide it is worthwhile to reinvest the same percentage of the monetary income they have received, or instead, they believe it is more beneficial to them to modify this proportion by increasing or decreasing it. In the words of Hayek:

> The money stream which the entrepreneur representing any stage of production receives at any given moment is always composed of net income which he may use for consumption without disturbing the existing method of production, and of parts which he must continuously re-invest. But it depends entirely upon him whether he re-distributes his total money receipts in the same proportions as before. And the main factor influencing his decisions will be the magnitude of the profits he hopes to derive from the production of his particular intermediate product.

Therefore no natural law forces entrepreneurs to reinvest their income in the same proportion in which they have invested in capital goods in the past. Instead, this proportion depends on the specific circumstances present at each moment, and in particular on the entrepreneurs' expectations regarding the profit they hope to obtain at each stage of the production process. This means that, from an analytical standpoint, it is very important to focus on the evolution of the amounts of gross income as reflected in our diagram, and to avoid concentrating exclusively on net values, as is the custom. So we see that even when net saving equals zero, a productive structure is maintained by considerable gross saving and investment, the sum of which is several times larger than even the amount spent on consumer goods and services during each productive period. Therefore the key is to study gross saving and investment, i.e., the aggregated value, in monetary terms, of the stages of intermediate goods prior to final consumption, an amount which remains hidden if we focus exclusively on the evolution of accounting figures in net terms. This is precisely why we should be especially critical of traditional national income accounting measures. For example, the traditional definition of "gross national product" (GNP) contains the word "gross," yet in no way reflects the true gross income spent during the year on the entire productive structure.

On the one hand, GNP figures hide the existence of different stages in the production process. On the other hand, what is even more serious and consequential is that the gross national product, despite the "gross" in its name, *does not reflect the total gross monetary spending which takes place in all productive stages and sectors of the economy.* This is because it is based solely on the production of goods and services delivered to *final* users. In fact it rests on a narrow accounting criterion of added value which is foreign to the fundamental truths of the economy; it only adds the value of consumer goods and services and of the *final* capital goods completed during the year. *It does not incorporate the other* intermediate products which make up the stages in the production process and which pass from one stage to another during the financial *year.* Hence gross national product figures only include a small percentage of the total of capital goods. Indeed GNP incorporates the value of the sales of fixed or durable capital goods, such as real estate, industrial vehicles, machinery, tools, computers, etc., which are finished and sold to their final users during the year, and thus are considered *final* goods. However it in no way includes the value of circulating capital goods, intermediate non-durable products, nor of capital goods which are not yet finished or if so, pass from one stage to another during the process of production.

In short the Gross National Product is an aggregate figure representing added values, and it excludes intermediate goods. The only reason national accounting theorists offer for using this figure is that with this criterion they avoid the problem of "double counting." Yet from the standpoint of macroeconomic theory, this argument rests on a narrow accounting concept applicable to individual companies and is very dangerous, as it excludes from the computation the enormous volume of entrepreneurial effort which each year is dedicated to the production of intermediate capital goods, the bulk of economic activity but not at all worth evaluating, according to GNP figures. To get an idea of the amounts involved, it suffices to consider that the gross output (calculated according to our criterion) of an advanced country like the United States is equal to more than twice the country's official GNP.

Therefore traditional national income accounting figures tend to eliminate at a stroke the central role intermediate stages play in the process of production; specifically, these measures ignore the undeniable fact that the continuance of intermediate stages is not guaranteed, but results from a constant, uncertain series of concrete entrepreneurial decisions which depend on expected accounting profits and on the social rate of time preference or interest rate. The use of GNP in national income accounting almost inevitably implies that production is instantaneous and requires no time, i.e., that there are no intermediate stages in the production process and that time preference is irrelevant with respect to determining the interest rate. In short the standard measures of national income completely do away with the largest, most significant part of the production process, and moreover they do so in a disguised manner, since, paradoxically and despite the label "gross," they cause non-experts (and even most experts) in the field to overlook the most significant part of each country's productive structure.

If national income accounting measures were modified and made truly "gross," they would include all intermediate products, and it would be possible to follow the proportion of the amount spent each year on consumer goods and services to the amount spent at all intermediate stages. This ratio is ultimately determined by the social rate of time preference, which establishes the proportion of gross saving and investment to consumption. Clearly the weaker the time preference, and therefore the more savings generated in society, the larger the proportion of gross saving and investment to final consumption. At the same time, a strong time preference means interest rates will be high, and the ratio of gross saving and investment to consumption will decrease. Adequate intertemporal coordination of the decisions of economic agents in a modern society requires that the productive structure adapt to different social rates of time preference quickly and efficiently, something the entrepreneurial spirit itself, driven by the search for profit, tends to guarantee, as entrepreneurs try to equalize profit over all stages. If we wish to find a statistical measure which, instead of concealing, sheds as much light as possible on this important intertemporal coordination process, we must replace the current gross national product estimate with another such as gross national output, as defined here.

THE EFFECT ON THE PRODUCTIVE STRUCTURE OF AN INCREASE IN CREDIT FINANCED UNDER A PRIOR INCREASE IN VOLUNTARY SAVING THE THREE DIFFERENT MANIFESTATIONS OF THE PROCESS OF VOLUNTARY SAVING

In this section we will examine what happens within the structure of production when, for whatever reason, economic agents reduce their rate of time preference; that is, when they decide to increase their saving or supply of present goods. This can take place in any of the following ways:

First, capitalists of the different stages in the productive structure may decide, beginning at a certain point, to modify the proportion in which they had been *reinvesting* the gross income derived from their productive activity. In other words, nothing guarantees the continuity, from one period to the next, of the ratio in which the capitalists of one productive stage spend the income they receive from that stage on the purchase of capital goods from earlier stages and on labor and natural resources. Capitalists may very possibly decide to increase their supply of present goods. That is, they may decide to reinvest a greater percentage of the income they receive per period, acquiring capital goods and services as well as original means of production (labor and natural resources). In that case, in the short run, their accounting profit margin will decrease, which is equivalent to a downward trend in the market interest rate. The profit margin falls as a result of an increase in monetary costs in relation to income. The capitalists are willing to *temporarily* accept this drop in accounting profits, since they expect to generate in this way, in a more or less distant future, total profits larger than those they would have earned had they not modified their behavior. Given that the market in which present goods are exchanged for future goods encompasses society's entire structure of productive stages, such increases in saving and their manifestation in new investments are often the most important in society.

Second, owners of the original means of production (workers and owners of natural resources) may decide not to consume, as in the past, the entire sum of their social net income. They may instead decide to reduce their consumption beginning at a certain point and to invest the m.u. they no longer spend on final consumer goods and services, in the productive stages they decide to launch *directly* as capitalists (a category which includes members of cooperatives). Though this procedure takes place in the market, the resulting savings are not normally very substantial in real life.

Third, it could occur that both the owners of the original means of production (workers and the owners of natural resources) as well as capitalists (to the extent they receive net income in the form of accounting profits or market interest) decide beginning at a certain point not to consume their entire net income, but to *loan* a portion of it to capitalists of the different stages in the production process, enabling them to broaden their activities by purchasing more capital goods from prior stages and more natural resources, and by hiring more labor.

This third procedure is carried out through the *credit market*, which, despite being the most visible and conspicuous in real economic life, is of *secondary* importance and plays a *subsidiary* role in relation to the more general market in which present goods are exchanged for future goods through self-financing or capitalists' direct reinvestment of present goods in their productive stages (the first and second procedures of saving-investment mentioned above). Though this system of saving is important, it is usually secondary to the first two procedures for increasing saving we described above. Nevertheless a very strong connection exists between the flows of saving and investment of both procedures, and in fact both sectors of the "time market"—the general sector of the productive structure and the particular sector of the credit market—behave as if they were communicating vessels.

ACCOUNT RECORDS OF SAVINGS CHANNELLED INTO LOANS

From an economic standpoint, all three of these procedures for increasing saving invariably entail the following: an increase in the supply of present goods held by savers, who transfer these present goods to the owners of original resources and material means of production (capital goods) from previous productive stages. For instance, if we follow the accounting example, which involves the third procedure described above, the following journal entries result:

The saver who loans his resources in the form of present goods records this entry in his journal:

(72)	Debit	Credit	
1,000,000	Loan granted	Cash	1,000,000

This entry is clearly the accounting record of the fact that the saver offers 1,000,000 m.u. of present goods, which he relinquishes. In doing so he loses the complete availability of the goods and transfers it to a third person; for instance, the entrepreneur of a certain productive stage. The entrepreneur receives the m.u. as a loan, which he records in his journal via the following entry:

(73)	Debit	Credit	
1,000,000	Cash	Loan received	1,000,000

The entrepreneur who receives these present goods uses them to acquire:

(1) capital goods from prior productive stages;

(2) labor services;

(3) natural resources.

Through this third procedure, savers who do not wish to involve themselves directly in the activity of any of the productive stages can save and invest through the credit market by entering into a loan contract. Although this method is indirect, it ultimately produces a result identical to that of the first two procedures for voluntarily increasing saving.

THE ISSUE OF CONSUMER LOANS

It could be argued that sometimes loans are not granted to entrepreneurs of productive stages, to enable them to lengthen their production processes through investment, but are instead granted to *consumers who purchase final goods.* First, we must note that the very nature of the initial two saving procedures described above precludes the use of the saved resources for consumption. It is only possible to conceive of a consumer loan in the credit market, which as we know plays a subsidiary role and is secondary to the total market where present goods are offered and purchased in exchange for future goods. Second, in most cases consumer loans are granted to finance the purchase of *durable consumer goods,* which as we saw in previous sections, *are ultimately comparable* to capital goods maintained over a number of consecutive stages of production, while the durable consumer good's capacity to provide *services to its owner lasts.*

Under these circumstances, by far the most common, the economic effects of consumer loans, with respect to encouraging investment and lengthening productive stages, are *identical to and indistinguishable from* the effects of any increase in savings directly invested in the capital goods of any stage in the productive structure. Therefore only a hypothetical consumer loan allocated for financing a household's *current expenditure* on non-durable consumer goods would have the effect of immediately and directly increasing final current consumption. Nonetheless despite the fact that relatively little credit is allotted to final current consumption, the existence of such consumer loans in the market indicates a certain latent consumer demand for them. Given the connection between all sectors of the market of present and future goods, once this residual demand for loans for *current* consumption is satisfied, most real resources saved are freed to be invested in the productive stages furthest from consumption.

THE EFFECTS OF VOLUNTARY SAVING ON THE PRODUCTIVE STRUCTURE

We will now explain how the price system and the coordinating role of entrepreneurs in a free market spontaneously channel decreases in the social rate of time preference and the resulting increases in saving into modifications of society's structure of productive stages, making this structure more complex and lasting, and in the long run, appreciably more productive. In short we will explain one of the most significant coordinating processes which exist in all economies. Unfortunately, as a result of monetarist and Keynesian economic theories, for at least two generations of economists the majority of economics textbooks and study programs have almost completely ignored this process. Consequently most of today's economists are unfamiliar with the functioning of one of the most important processes of coordination present in all market economies.

For analytical purposes we will begin by considering an extreme situation which nevertheless will be of great assistance in graphically illustrating and better understanding the processes involved. We will suppose that economic agents *suddenly* decide to save 25 percent of their net income. Our starting point will be the clear, numerical example of the last section, in which we assumed net income was equal to 100 m.u., which corresponded to the original means of production and the interest capitalists received, and which was spent entirely on consumer goods. We will now suppose that, as a result of a fall in time preference, economic agents decide to *relinquish* 25 percent (i.e., one-fourth) of their consumption and to save the corresponding resources, offering this excess of present goods to potential demanders of them. Three effects simultaneously follow from this increase in voluntary saving. Given their great importance, we will now consider them separately.

FIRST: THE EFFECT PRODUCED BY THE NEW DISPARITY IN PROFITS BETWEEN THE DIFFERENT PRODUCTIVE STAGES

If there is an increase in social saving of one-fourth of net income, clearly the total monetary demand for consumer goods will decrease by the same proportion.

Before the increase in saving, 100 m.u. of net income were spent on final consumer goods produced by companies which first incurred expenses totaling 90 m.u. Of this amount, 80 m.u. corresponded to the purchase of capital goods from the stage immediately preceding, and 10 m.u. were paid for original means of production hired or purchased in the last stage (labor and natural resources). This determined an accounting profit of 10 m.u., roughly equal to an interest rate of 11 percent, which as we saw in the last section, was the *market rate of interest which accounting profits of all productive* stages, both those closest to and those furthest from final *consumption, tended to match.*

If we suppose there is an increase in saving equal to 25 percent of net income, the situation in the final stage (consumption) at point t+1. Immediately following the rise in saving, we see that the monetary demand for final consumer goods decreases from 100 to 75 m.u. in each time period. Nevertheless a reduction in expenditures does not immediately accompany this fall in cash income which businesses devoted to the final stage of production experience. On the contrary, in their account books these companies record *unchanged* expenditures of 90 m.u. Just as in the previous case, 80 m.u. of this amount is spent on capital goods from the preceding stage (machinery, suppliers, intermediate products, etc.) and 10 m.u. are paid to the owners of the original means of production (workers and the owners of natural resources). As a result of this increase in saving, companies devoted to the final stage (consumption) suffer an accounting loss of 15 m.u. This sum becomes 25 m.u. when we consider the *opportunity cost* derived from the fact that the entrepreneurs not only experience the above accounting loss, but also *fail to earn* the 10 m.u. which capital invested in other productive stages generates as interest. Therefore we could conclude that all *increases in saving cause considerable relative losses to or* decreases in the accounting profits of the companies which operate closest to final consumption.

However let us now remember that the sector of consumption constitutes only a relatively small part of society's total productive structure and that the sum of the m.u. spent on final consumption makes up only a fraction of the value of the gross national output, which encompasses all stages of the production process. Therefore the fact that accounting losses occur in the final stage does not immediately affect the stages prior to consumption, in which a positive difference continues to exist between income and expenditures, a difference similar to the one which preceded the increase in saving. Only after a prolonged period of time will the depressive effect which the rise in saving exerts upon the final stage (that of consumer goods) begin to be felt in the stages closest to it, and this negative influence will increasingly weaken as we "climb" to productive stages relatively more distant from final consumption. At any rate the accounting profits of the stages furthest from consumption will tend to remain constant, stage five, point in time t. Here we observe that activity in this stage continues to yield an accounting profit of 11 percent, the result of a total income of 20 m.u. and total expenses of 18 m.u.

Hence the increase in saving clearly gives rise to a great disparity between the accounting profits received by companies devoted to the first stage, that of consumer goods, and those earned by companies operating in the stages furthest from final consumption (in our example, the fifth stage in the productive structure). In the consumer goods sector an accounting loss follows from the upsurge in saving, while the industries of the fifth stage, which are further from consumption, continue to enjoy profits roughly equal to 11 percent of the capital invested.

This disparity in profits acts as a warning sign and an incentive for entrepreneurs to restrict their investments in the stages close to consumption and to channel these resources into other stages which still offer relatively higher profits and which are, given the circumstances, the stages furthest from final consumption. Therefore entrepreneurs will tend to transfer a portion of their demand for productive resources, in the form of capital goods and primary factors of production, from the final stage (consumption) and those closest to it, to the stages furthest from consumption, where they discover they can still obtain comparatively much higher profits. The increased investment or demand for more productive resources in the stages furthest from consumption produces the effect, point in time t+1. Indeed entrepreneurs from the fifth stage increase their investment in original factors and productive resources from 18 m.u. to 31.71 m.u., a figure nearly double their initial outlay. (Of this amount 21.5 m.u. are spent on the productive services of capital goods and 10.21 m.u. are spent on labor services and natural resources). This leads to a rise in the production of goods in the fifth stage, which in monetary terms, increases from 20 m.u. to 32.35 m.u., resulting in an accounting profit of 0.54 m.u. Although in terms of percentage this amount is lower than former profits (1.70 percent as opposed to the 11 percent earned previously), it is comparatively a much higher profit than that which the industries producing final consumer goods obtain (industries which, as we saw, are sustaining absolute losses of 15 m.u.).

Consequently growth in saving gives rise to a disparity between the rates of profit in the different stages of the productive structure. This leads entrepreneurs to reduce immediate production of consumer goods and to increase production in the stages furthest from consumption. A *temporary lengthening* of production processes tends to ensue, lasting until the new social rate of time preference or interest rate, in the form of differentials between accounting income and expenditures in each stage, now appreciably lower as a result of the substantial increase in saving, spreads uniformly, throughout the entire productive structure.

The entrepreneurs of the fifth stage have been able to increase their supply of present goods from 18 m.u. at point t to 31.71 m.u. at point t+1. This has been possible due to greater social saving, or a greater supply of present goods in society. The entrepreneurs finance this larger investment in part through the increase in their own saving, i.e., by investing a portion of the money which in the past they earned as interest and spent on consumption, and in part through new saving they receive from the credit market in the form of loans *fully backed by a prior rise in voluntary saving*. In other words, the increase in investment in the fifth stage materializes by any of the three procedures described in the last section.

Moreover the increase one might expect to observe in the prices of the factors of production (capital goods, labor and natural resources) as a result of the greater demand for them in the fifth stage does not necessarily occur (with the possible exception of very specific means of production). In fact each increase in the demand for productive resources in the stages furthest from consumption is mostly or even completely neutralized or offset by a parallel increase in the supply of these inputs which takes place as they are gradually freed from the stages closest to consumption, where entrepreneurs are incurring considerable accounting losses and are consequently obliged to restrict their investment expenditure on these factors. Thus for entrepreneurial coordination to exist between the stages in the productive structure of a society which is immersed in a process of increased saving and economic growth, it is particularly important that the corresponding factor markets, especially the markets for original means of production (labor and natural resources), be very flexible and permit at a minimum economic and social cost the gradual transfer of these factors from certain stages of production to others.

Finally the drop in investment in the consumer goods sector, which tends to stem from accounting losses generated by the increase in voluntary saving, normally accounts for a certain *slowdown* in the arrival of new consumer goods to the market (regardless of the increase in the stock of them). This slowdown lasts until the rise in the complexity and number of stages in the production process unquestionably improves productivity, which in turn brings a significantly larger quantity of consumer goods to the market. One might expect the *temporary* reduction in the supply of consumer goods to push up their price, other things being equal. However this rise in prices does not materialize, precisely because from the outset the decrease in supply is more than compensated for by the parallel fall in the demand for consumer goods, a result of the prior increase in voluntary saving.

To sum up, the increase in voluntary saving is invested in the productive structure, either through direct investments or through loans granted to the entrepreneurs of the productive stages relatively distant from consumption. These loans are backed by real voluntary saving and lead to an increase in the monetary demand for original means of production and capital goods used in such stages. As we saw at the beginning of this chapter, production processes tend to be more productive the more stages distant from consumption they contain, and the more complex these stages are. Therefore this more capitalintensive structure will eventually bring about a considerable increase in the final production of consumer goods, once the newly-initiated processes come to an end. Hence growth in saving and the free exercise of entrepreneurship are the necessary conditions for and the motor which drives all processes of economic growth and development.

SECOND: THE EFFECT OF THE DECREASE IN THE INTEREST RATE ON THE MARKET PRICE OF CAPITAL GOODS

The increase in voluntary saving, i.e., in the supply of present goods, gives rise, other things being equal, to a decrease in the market rate of interest. As we know, this interest rate tends to manifest itself as the accounting difference between income and expenses in the different productive stages and is also visible in the interest rate at which loans are granted in the credit market. It is important to note that the fall in the interest rate caused by all rises in voluntary saving greatly affects the value of capital goods, especially all of those used in the stages furthest from final consumption, goods which, relatively speaking, have a long life and make a large contribution to the production process. Let us consider a capital good with a long life, such as a building owned by a company, an industrial plant, a ship or airplane used for transport, a blast furnace, a computer or high-tech communications device, etc., which has been produced and performs its services in different stages of the productive structure, all of which are relatively distant from consumption.

The *market value* of this capital good tends to equal the value of its expected future flow of rents, discounted by the interest rate. An inverse relationship exists between the present (discounted) value and the interest rate. By way of illustration, a decrease in the interest rate from 11 to 5 percent, brought about by an increase in saving, causes the present value of a capital good with a very long life to more than double (the present value of a perpetual unitary rent at 11 percent interest is equal to 1/0.11 = 9.09; and the present value of a perpetual rent at 5 percent interest is equal to 1/0.05 = 20). If the capital good lasts, for example, twenty years, a drop in the interest rate from 11 to 5 percent produces an increase of 56 percent in the market or capitalized value of the good.46 Therefore if people begin to value present goods less in relative terms, then the market price of capital goods and durable consumer goods will tend to increase.

Moreover it will tend to increase in proportion to the duration of a good; i.e., to the number of productive stages in which it is used and to the distance of these stages from consumption. Capital goods already in use will undergo a significant rise in price as a result of the drop in the interest rate and will be produced in greater quantities, bringing about a horizontal *widening* of the capital goods structure (that is, an increase in the production of *pre-existing* capital goods). At the same time, the fall in the interest rate will reveal that many production processes or capital goods which until then were not considered profitable begin to be so, and consequently entrepreneurs will start to introduce them. In fact in the past entrepreneurs refrained from adopting many technological innovations and new projects because they expected the cost involved to be higher than the resulting market value (which tends to equal the value of the estimated future rent of each capital good, discounted by the interest rate). However when the interest rate falls, the market value of projects for lengthening the productive structure through new, more modern stages further from consumption begins to rise and may even come to exceed the cost of production, rendering these projects worthwhile. Hence the second effect of a decrease in the interest rate caused by an increase in voluntary saving is the deepening of the investment goods structure, in the form of a vertical lengthening involving *new* stages of capital goods increasingly distant from consumption. Both the widening and deepening of the capital goods structure follow from the role of entrepreneurs and their collective capacity for creativity and coordination. They are able to recognize an opportunity and a potential profit margin when a difference arises between the market price of capital goods (determined by the present value of their expected future rent, which increases appreciably when the interest rate falls) and the cost necessary to produce them (a cost which remains constant or may even decrease, given the greater market supply of original means of production coming from the stage of final consumption, which initially shrank when saving increased).

Thus this *second effect* also entails a lengthening of the capital goods structure, just as we saw with the first effect. Fluctuations in the value of capital goods, which arise from variations in saving and the interest rate, also tend to spread to the *securities* which represent these goods, and thus to the stock markets where they are traded. Hence an increase in voluntary saving, which leads to a drop in the interest rate, will further boost the price of stocks of companies which operate in the capital goods stages furthest from consumption, and in general, the price of all securities representing capital goods. Only securities which represent the property of the companies closest to consumption will undergo a temporary, relative decline in price, as a result of the immediate, negative impact of the decrease in the demand for consumer goods that is generated by the upsurge in saving. Therefore it is clear that, contrary to popular opinion, and in the absence of other monetary distortions we have not yet touched on, the stock market does not necessarily reflect mainly companies' profits. In fact, in relative terms with the capital invested, the accounting profits earned by the companies of the different stages tend to match the interest rate.

Thus an environment of high saving and low relative profits (i.e., with a low interest rate) constitutes the setting for the greatest growth in the market value of securities representing capital goods. Moreover the further the capital goods are from final consumption, the higher the market price of the corresponding securities.48 In contrast, growth in relative accounting profits throughout the productive structure, and thus in the market rate of interest, other things being equal, will manifest itself in a drop in the value of securities and a consequent fall in their market value. This theoretical explanation sheds light on many general stock-market reactions which ordinary people and many "experts" in finance and economics fail to understand, since they simply apply the naive theory that the stock market must merely reflect, automatically and faithfully, the level of accounting profits earned by all companies participating in the production process, without considering the stages in which the profits are earned nor the evolution of the social time preference (interest rates).

THIRD: THE RICARDO EFFECT

All increases in voluntary saving exert a particularly important, immediate effect on the level of *real* wages. Hence it is easy to understand why increases in saving are generally followed by decreases in the prices of final consumer goods.49 If, as generally occurs, the wages or rents of the original factor labor are initially held constant in nominal terms, a decline in the prices of final consumer goods will be followed by a rise in the *real* wages of workers employed in all stages of the productive structure. With the same money income in nominal terms, workers will be able to acquire a greater quantity and quality of final consumer goods and services at consumer goods' new, more reduced prices. This increase in real wages, which arises from the growth in voluntary saving, means that, relatively speaking, it is in the interest of entrepreneurs of all stages in the production process to replace labor with capital goods. To put it another way, via an increase in real wages, the rise in voluntary saving sets a trend throughout the economic system toward longer and more capital-intensive productive stages. In other words, entrepreneurs now find it more attractive to use, relatively speaking, more capital goods than labor. This constitutes a third powerful, additional effect tending toward the lengthening of the stages in the productive structure. It adds to and overlaps the other two effects mentioned previously.

The first to explicitly refer to this third effect was David Ricardo. He did so in his book, *On the Principles of Political Economy and Taxation*, the first edition of which was published in 1817. Here Ricardo concludes that [e]very rise of wages, therefore, or, which is the same thing, every fall of profits, would lower the relative value of those commodities which were produced with a capital of a durable nature, and would proportionally elevate those which were produced with capital more perishable. Afall of wages would have precisely the contrary effect.50 In the well-known appendix "On Machinery," which was added in the third edition, published in 1821, Ricardo concludes that "[m]achinery and labour are in constant competition, and the former can frequently not be employed until labour rises."

The same idea was later recovered by F.A. Hayek, who, beginning in 1939, applied it extensively in his writings on business cycles. Here we will for the first time use it, integrated with the prior two effects, to explain the consequences an upsurge in voluntary saving has on the productive structure and to detract from theories on the so-called "paradox of thrift" and the supposedly negative influence of saving on effective demand. Hayek offers a very concise explanation of the "Ricardo Effect" when he states that [w]ith high real wages and a low rate of profit investment will take highly capitalistic forms: entrepreneurs will try to meet the high costs of labour by introducing very labour-saving machinery—the kind of machinery which it will be profitable to use only at a very low rate of profit and interest.

Hence the "Ricardo Effect" is a third microeconomic explanation for the behavior of entrepreneurs, who react to an upsurge in voluntary saving by boosting their demand for capital goods and by investing in new stages further from final consumption.

It is important to remember that all increases in voluntary saving and investment initially bring about a decline in the production of new consumer goods and services *with respect to the short-term maximum which could be achieved* if inputs were not diverted from the stages closest to final consumption. This decline performs the function of freeing productive factors necessary to lengthen the stages of capital goods furthest from consumption. Furthermore the consumer goods and services left unsold as a result of the rise in voluntary saving play a role remarkably similar to that of the accumulated berries in our Robinson Crusoe example.

The berries permitted Crusoe to sustain himself for the number of days required to produce his capital equipment (the wooden stick); during this time period he was not able to devote himself to picking berries "by hand." In a modern economy, consumer goods and services which remain unsold when saving increases fulfill the important function of making it possible for the different economic agents (workers, owners of natural resources and capitalists) to sustain themselves during the time periods that follow. During these periods the recently-initiated lengthening of the productive structure causes an inevitable slowdown in the arrival of new consumer goods and services to the market. This "slowdown" lasts until the completion of all of the new, more capital-intensive processes that have been started. If it were not for the consumer goods and services that remain unsold due to saving, the temporary drop in the supply of new consumer goods would trigger a substantial rise in the relative price of these goods and considerable difficulties in the provision of them.

CONCLUSION: THE EMERGENCE OF A NEW, MORE CAPITAL-INTENSIVE PRODUCTIVE STRUCTURE

The three effects we have just examined are provoked by the entrepreneurial process of seeking profit, and the combination of the three tends to result in a new, narrower and more elongated structure of capital goods stages. Moreover the differential between income and costs at each stage, i.e., the accounting profit or interest rate, tends to even out *at a lower level* over all stages of the new productive structure (as naturally corresponds to a larger volume of saving and a lower social rate of time preference).

However beginning in the fourth stage (and upward, each stage further from consumption than the one before it), the demand in monetary terms grows. The increase is gradual at first. In the fourth stage, the figures rise from 40 m.u. to 42.75 m.u. It then becomes proportionally much more substantial in the fifth stage, where the value of the product grows from 20 m.u. to 32.25 m.u. Furthermore two *new stages*, stages six and seven, appear in the area furthest from consumption. These stages *did not exist before.*

After all necessary adjustments have been made, the rate of profit for the different stages tends to even out at a significantly lower level than that reflected in Chart V-1. This phenomenon derives from the fact that the upsurge in voluntary saving generates a much lower market rate of interest, and the rate of accounting profit for each stage (in our example, approximately 1.70 percent annually) approaches this figure. The *net income* received by the owners of the original means of production (workers and owners of natural resources) and by the capitalists of each stage, according to the net interest rate or differential, amounts to 75 m.u., which coincides with the monetary income spent on consumer goods and services. It is important to point out that even if only 75 m.u. are spent on consumer goods and services, i.e., 25 units less than in Chart V- 1, once all new production processes are completed, the production of new final consumer goods and services will increase substantially in real terms. This is because production processes tend to become more productive as they become more roundabout and capital-intensive. Moreover a larger quantity, in real terms, of produced consumer goods and services can only be sold for a lower total number of m.u. (in our example, 75).

Therefore there is a dramatic decline in the unit price of new consumer goods and services reaching the market, and correspondingly the income received by owners of the original means of production (specifically, workers' wages and hence, their living standard) undergoes a sharp increase in real terms. Tables V-3 and V-4 reflect both the supply of and the demand for present goods, as well as the composition of the gross national output for the year, after all adjustments provoked by the increase in voluntary saving. We see that the supply of and demand for present goods rests at 295 m.u., i.e., 25 m.u. more. This is because gross saving and investment have grown by precisely the 25 m.u. of additional net saving voluntarily carried out. However , the gross national output for the year remains unaltered at 370 m.u., of which 75 m.u. correspond to the demand for final consumer goods, and 295 m.u. to the total supply of present goods. In other words, even though the gross national output is identical in monetary terms to its value in the last example, *it is now distributed in a radically different manner:* over a narrower and more elongated productive structure (that is, a more capital-intensive one with more stages).

Hence we see that the voluntary increase in saving provokes the following effects:

- *First*: a *deepening* of the capital goods structure. This outcome manifests itself as a *vertical* "lengthening" of the productive structure via the addition of new stages (in our example, stages six and seven, which did not exist before).
- *Second*: a *widening* of the capital goods structure, embodied in a broadening of the existing stages (as in stages four and five).
- *Third*: a *relative narrowing* of the capital goods stages closest to consumption.
- *Fourth*: In the final stage, the stage of consumer goods and services, the jump in voluntary saving invariably generates an initial drop in consumption (in monetary terms). However the lengthening of the productive structure is followed by a substantial real increase (in terms of quantity and quality) in the production of consumer goods and services. Given that the monetary demand for these goods is invariably reduced, and given that these two effects (the drop in consumption and the upsurge in the production of consumer goods) exert similar influences, the increase in production gives rise to a *sharp drop in the market prices of consumer goods*. Ultimately this drop in prices makes it possible for a significant real rise in wages to occur, along with a general increase in all real income received by owners of the original means of production.

In short, in our example there has been no drop in the money supply (and therefore no external deflation, strictlyspeaking), nor has the demand for money risen. So if we assume both of these factors remain constant, then the general fall in the price of consumer goods and services arises exclusively from the upsurge in saving and the increase in productivity, itself a consequence of the more capital-intensive productive structure. Moreover this brings about marked growth in wages (in real terms), which, though their nominal value remains the same or even diminishes somewhat, permit the earner to acquire an increasing quantity of consumer goods and services of higher and higher quality: the decline in the price of these goods is proportionally much sharper than the possible decline in wages. In brief this is the healthiest, most sustained process of economic growth and development imaginable. In other words, it involves the fewest economic and social maladjustments, tensions, and conflicts and historically has taken place on various occasions, as the most reliable studies have shown.

THE THEORETICAL SOLUTION TO THE "PARADOX OF THRIFT"

Our analysis also allows us to solve the problems posed by the supposed dilemma of the paradox of thrift or saving. This "paradox" rests on the concept that, though saving by individuals is positive in the sense that it allows them to augment their income, socially speaking, when the aggregate demand for consumer goods diminishes, the decrease eventually exerts a negative effect on investment and production.58 In contrast we have presented the theoretical arguments which demonstrate that this interpretation, based on the old myth of underconsumption, is faulty. Indeed, even assuming that gross national output in monetary terms remains constant, we have shown how society grows and develops through an increase in real wages, even when the monetary demand for consumer goods declines. We have also demonstrated how, in the absence of state intervention and increases in the money supply, an immensely powerful market force, driven by entrepreneurs' search for profit, leads to the lengthening of and growing complexity in the productive structure. In short, despite the *initial* relative decrease in the demand for consumer goods which stems from growth in saving, the productivity of the economic system is boosted, as is the final production of consumer goods and services, and real wages.

THE CASE OF AN ECONOMY IN REGRESSION

Our reasoning up to this point can be reversed, with appropriate changes, to explain the effects of a hypothetical *decrease* in society's voluntary saving. If society as a whole decides to save less, the result will be an increase, of for instance 25 m.u., in the monetary demand for consumer goods and services. Therefore the monetary demand will rise from 75 m.u. to 100 m.u., and the industries and companies of the stages closest to consumption will tend to grow dramatically, which will drive up their accounting profits. Though these events may appear to provoke the effects of a consumer boom, in the long run they will lead to a "flattening" of the productive structure, since productive resources will be withdrawn from the stages furthest from consumption and transferred to those closest to it. In fact the increased accounting profits of the stages close to final consumption will, relatively speaking, discourage production in the most distant stages, which will tend to bring about a reduction in investment in these stages. Moreover the drop in saving will push up the market rate of interest and diminish the corresponding present value of durable capital goods, deterring investment in them. Finally a reverse "Ricardo Effect" will exert its influence: growth in the prices of consumer goods and services will be accompanied by an immediate decline in real wages and in the rents of the other original factors, which will encourage capitalists to replace capital equipment with labor, now relatively cheaper.

The combined result of all these influences is a flattening of the productive structure, which, although it reflects a greater demand for consumer goods and services in monetary terms, shows *there has been a generalized impoverishment of society in real terms.* In fact the less capital-intensive productive structure will result in the arrival of fewer consumer goods and services to the final stage, which nevertheless undergoes a considerable rise in monetary demand. Hence there is a decrease in the production of consumer goods and services, along with a substantial increase in their price, a consequence of the two previous effects combined. The result is the generalized impoverishment of society, especially of workers, whose wages shrink in real terms, since, while in monetary terms they may remain constant or even increase, such a rise never reaches the level of growth undergone by monetary prices of consumer goods and services.

According to John Hicks, Giovanni Boccaccio, in an interesting passage in the Introduction to *Decameron*, written around the year 1360, was the first to describe, in rather precise terms, a process very similar to the one we have just analyzed when he related the impact the Great Plague of the fourteenth century had on the people of Florence. In fact the epidemic caused people to anticipate a drastic reduction in life expectancy, and thus entrepreneurs and workers, instead of saving and "lengthening" the stages in their production process by working their lands and tending their livestock, devoted themselves to increasing their present consumption.60 After Boccaccio, the first economist to seriously consider the effects of a decline in saving and the resulting economic setback was Böhm-Bawerk in his book, *Capital and Interest*,61 where he explains in detail that a general decision by individuals to consume more and save less triggers a phenomenon of capital consumption, which ultimately lowers productive capacity and the production of consumer goods and services, giving rise to the generalized impoverishment of society.

THE EFFECTS OF BANK CREDIT EXPANSION UNBACKED BY AN INCREASE IN SAVING: THE AUSTRIAN THEORY OR CIRCULATION CREDIT THEORY OF THE BUSINESS CYCLE

In this section we will examine the effects banks exert on the productive structure when they create loans unbacked by a prior increase in voluntary saving. These circumstances differ radically from those we studied in the last section, where loans were fully backed by a corresponding rise in voluntary saving. In accordance with the credit expansion process triggered by fractional-reserve banking (a process we examined in detail in chapter 4), a bank's creation of credit would result in an accounting entry which, in its simplest form, would resemble this one:

(73)	Debit	Credit	
1,000,000	Cash	Demand deposits	1,000,000
(74)			
900,000	Loans granted	Demand deposits	900,000

These book entries, which are identical to numbers (17) and (18), record in a simplified and concise fashion the unquestionable fact that the bank is able to generate from nothing new m.u. in the form of deposits or fiduciary media which are granted to the public as loans or credit even when the public has not first decided to increase saving.63 We will now consider the effects this important event has on social processes of coordination and economic interaction.

THE EFFECTS OF CREDIT EXPANSION ON THE PRODUCTIVE STRUCTURE

The creation of money by the banking system in the form of loans has some real effects on the economy's productive structure, and it is necessary to clearly distinguish between these effects and those we studied in the last section with respect to loans backed by saving. More specifically, the generation of loans *ex nihilo* (i.e., in the absence of an increase in saving) raises the supply of credit to the economy, especially to the different capital goods stages in the productive structure. From this standpoint, the increased supply of loans which results from bank credit expansion will initially exert an effect very similar to that produced by the flow of new loans from saving which we analyzed in detail in the last section: it will tend to cause a widening and lengthening of the stages in the productive structure. The "widening" of the different stages is easy to understand, since basically the loans are granted for the production processes which constitute each of the stages. Credit extended to finance durable consumer goods also leads to a widening and lengthening of the productive structure, because (as we have seen) durable consumer goods are economically comparable to capital goods throughout the period during which they are fit to render their services. Therefore even in the case of consumer loans (to finance durable consumer goods), the greater influx of loans will tend to increase both the quantity and quality of such goods.

The "lengthening" of the productive structure derives from the fact that the only way banks can introduce into the economy the new money they create from nothing and grant as loans is by temporarily and artificially reducing the interest rate in the credit market and by easing the rest of the economic and contractual conditions they insist on when granting loans to their customers. This lowering of the interest rate in the credit market does no. necessarily manifest itself as a decrease in absolute terms. Instead a decrease in relative terms, i.e., in relation to the interest rate which would have predominated in the market *in the absence of credit expansion*, is sufficient.64 Hence the reduction is even compatible with an increase in the interest rate in nominal terms, if the rate climbs less than it would have in an environment without credit expansion (for instance, if credit expansion coincides with a generalized drop in the purchasing power of money). Likewise such a reduction is compatible with a decline in the interest rate, if the rate falls even more than it would have had there been no credit expansion (for example, in a process in which, in contrast, the purchasing power of money is growing). Therefore this lowering of the interest rate is a fact accounted for by theory, and one it will be necessary to interpret historically while considering the circumstances particular to each case.

The relative reduction credit expansion causes in the interest rate boosts the present value of capital goods, since the flow of rents they are expected to produce increases in value when discounted using a lower market rate of interest. In addition, the lowering of the interest rate gives the appearance of profitability to investment projects which until that point were not profitable, giving rise to new stages further from consumption, i.e., stages which are more capital-intensive. The process through which these stages come into existence closely resembles the one involved when society's voluntary saving actually increases. Nevertheless we must emphasize that although the *initial* effects may be very similar to those which, as we saw, follow an upsurge in voluntary saving, *in this case the productive stages are lengthened and widened*65 *only as* a consequence of the easier credit terms banks offer at relatively lower interest rates yet without any previous growth in voluntary *saving*. As we know, a sustainable lengthening of the productive structure is only possible if the necessary prior saving has taken place in the form of a drop in the final demand for consumer goods. This drop permits the different productive agents to sustain themselves using the unsold consumer goods and services while the new processes introduced reach completion and their more productive result begins to reach the market in the form of consumer goods.

In short, entrepreneurs decide to launch new investment projects, widening and lengthening the capital goods stages in the productive structure; that is, they act *as if* society's saving had increased, when in fact such an event has not occurred. In the case of an upsurge in voluntary saving, which we examined in the last section, the individual behavior of the different economic agents tended to become compatible, and thus the real resources that were saved and not consumed made the preservation and lengthening of the productive structure possible. Now the fact that entrepreneurs respond to credit expansion by behaving as if saving had increased *triggers a* process of maladjustment or discoordination in the behavior of the *different economic agents*. Indeed entrepreneurs rush to invest and to widen and lengthen the real productive structure even though economic agents have not decided to augment their saving by the volume necessary to finance the new investments. In a nutshell, this is a typical example of an inducement to mass entrepreneurial error in economic calculation or estimation regarding the outcome of the different courses of action entrepreneurs adopt. This error in economic calculation stems from the fact that one of the basic indicators entrepreneurs refer to before acting, the interest rate (along with the attractiveness of terms offered in the credit market), is temporarily manipulated and artificially lowered by banks through a process of credit expansion.

At first the discoordination expresses itself in the emergence of a period of exaggerated and disproportionate optimism, which stems from the fact that economic agents feel able to expand the productive structure without at the same time having to make the sacrifice of reducing their consumption to generate savings. In the last section the lengthening of the productive structure was shown to be made possible precisely by the prior sacrifice required by all increases in saving. Now we see that entrepreneurs hasten to widen and lengthen the stages in production processes when no such prior saving has taken place. The discoordination could not be more obvious nor the initial excess of optimism more justified, since it seems possible to introduce longer production processes without any sacrifice or previous accumulation of capital. In short a mass error is committed by entrepreneurs, who adopt production processes they consider profitable, but which are not. This error feeds a generalized optimism founded on the belief that it is possible to widen and lengthen the stages in production processes without anyone's having to save. *Intertemporal discoordination* increasingly mounts: entrepreneurs invest *as if* social saving were constantly growing; consumers continue to consume at a steady (or even increased) pace and do not worry about stepping up their saving.

To illustrate the initial effect credit expansion exerts on the real productive structure, we will follow the system used in the last section to present several graphs and tables which reflect the impact of credit expansion on the productive structure. A word of caution is necessary, however: it is practically impossible to represent in this way the complex effects produced in the market when credit expansion triggers the generalized process of discoordination we are describing. Therefore it is important to exercise great care in interpreting the following tables and charts, which should only be valued insofar as they illustrate and facilitate understanding of the fundamental economic argument. It is nearly impossible to reflect with charts anything other than strictly static situations, since charts invariably conceal the dynamic processes which take place between situations. Nonetheless the tables and graphs we propose to represent the stages in the productive structure may well help illustrate the essential theoretical argument and greatly facilitate an understanding of it.

However new money is created (deposits or fiduciary media) and enters the system through credit expansion and the relative reduction in the interest rate (along with the typical easing of the contractual conditions and the requirements for obtaining a loan) necessary to persuade economic agents to take out the newly-created loans. Therefore the rate of profit in the different productive stages, which as we know tends to coincide with the interest rate obtained at each stage by advancing present goods in exchange for future goods, now drops from the 11 percent to slightly over 4 percent yearly. Moreover the new loans allow the entrepreneurs of each productive stage to pay more for the corresponding original means of production, as well as for the capital goods from earlier stages which they obtain for their own productive processes.

Thus credit expansion has the effect of artificially raising the supply of present goods, which are demanded at lower interest rates by owners of the original means of production and by capitalists of the earlier stages further from consumption.

In our example, this effect expresses itself in the lengthening of the productive structure via the appearance of two new stages, six and seven. Prior to the expansion of credit these stages did not exist, and they are the furthest from final consumption. In addition the preexisting productive stages (two through five) are widened. The sum of the m.u. which represent the monetary demand embodied in each new widening or lengthening of productive stages, and which on the chart is reflected by the shaded areas, amounts to 113.75 m.u., the exact rise in gross monetary income for the year, an increase which stems exclusively from the creation of new money through credit expansion brought about by banks.

Let us not be deceived the new structure of productive stages it illustrates rests on generalized intertemporal discoordination, in turn the result of the mass entrepreneurial error provoked by the introduction of a large volume of new loans which are granted at artificially reduced interest rates, without the backing of real prior saving. This anomalous state of discoordination cannot be maintained, and the next section will include a detailed explanation of the reaction credit expansion inevitably sets off in the market. *In other* words, from the standpoint of pure microeconomic theory, we will examine the factors that will cause the reversal of the "macroeconomic" discoordination we have revealed.

Hence we will study the reasons the intertemporal discoordination process, initially set in motion by credit expansion, will completely reverse. Any attack on the social process, be it intervention, systematic coercion, manipulation of essential indicators (such as the price of present goods in terms of future goods, or the market rate of interest), or the granting of privileges against traditional legal principles, spontaneously triggers certain processes of social interaction which, as they are driven precisely by entrepreneurship and its capacity to coordinate, tend to halt and rectify errors and discoordination. Great credit goes to Ludwig von Mises for being the first to reveal, in 1912, that credit expansion gives rise to booms and optimism which sooner or later invariably subside. In his own words:

The increased productive activity that sets in when the banks start the policy of granting loans at less than the natural rate of interest at first causes the prices of production goods to rise while the prices of consumption goods, although they rise also, do so only in a moderate degree, namely, only insofar as they are raised by the rise in wages. Thus the tendency toward a fall in the rate of interest on loans that originates in the policy of the banks is at first strengthened. *But soon a countermovement sets in: the prices of* consumption goods rise, those of production goods fall. That is, the rate of interest on loans rises again, it again approaches the *natural rate.*

As we will have the opportunity to study later, prior to Mises various scholars of the School of Salamanca (Saravia de la Calle for instance) and others of the nineteenth century, mainly intellectuals of the Currency School (Henry Thornton, Condy Raguet, Geyer, etc.), sensed that booms provoked by credit expansion ultimately and spontaneously reversed, causing economic crises. Nonetheless Mises was the first to correctly formulate and explain, from the standpoint of economic theory, the reasons this is necessarily so. Despite Mises's momentous initial contribution, a completely formulated analysis of the different economic effects which comprise the market's reaction to credit expansion first became available with the writings of Mises's most brilliant student, F.A. Hayek. In the next section we will examine these effects in detail.

THE MARKET'S SPONTANEOUS REACTION TO CREDIT EXPANSION

We will now consider the *microeconomic* factors which will halt the process of exaggerated optimism and unsustainable phenomena (economic crises, depression, and unemployment) back to their fundamental microeconomic roots. We will now study, one by one, the six microeconomic causes of the reversal of the boom that credit expansion invariably triggers:

1. *The rise in the price of the original means of production.*

The first temporary effect of credit expansion is an increase in the relative price of the original means of production (labor and natural resources). This rise in price stems from two separate causes which reinforce each other. On the one hand, capitalists from the different stages in the production process show a greater monetary demand for original resources, and this growth in demand is made possible by the new loans the banking system grants. On the other hand, with respect to supply, we must keep in mind that when credit expansion takes place without the backing of a prior increase in saving, no original means of production are freed from the stages closest to consumption, as occurred in the process we studied earlier, which was initiated by a real upsurge in voluntary saving. Therefore the rise in the demand for original means of production in the stages furthest from consumption and the absence of an accompanying boost in supply inevitably result in a gradual increase in the market price of the factors of production. Ultimately this increase tends to accelerate due to competition among the entrepreneurs of the different stages in the production process.

The desire of these entrepreneurs to attract original resources to their projects makes them willing to pay higher and higher prices for these resources, prices they are able to offer because they have just received new liquidity from the banks in the form of loans the banks have created from nothing. This rise in the relative price of the original factors of production begins to push the cost of the newly launched investment projects above the amount originally budgeted. Nevertheless this effect alone is still not sufficient to end the wave of optimism, and entrepreneurs, who continue to feel safe and supported by the banks, usually go ahead with their investment projects without a second thought.74

2. *The subsequent rise in the price of consumer goods.*

Sooner or later the price of consumer goods begins to gradually climb, while the price of services offered by the original factors of production starts to mount at a slower pace (in other words, it begins to fall in relative terms). The combination of the following three factors accounts for this phenomenon:

(a) First, *growth in the monetary income of the owners of the original factors of production.* Indeed if, as we are supposing, economic agents' rate of time preference remains stable, and therefore they continue to save the same proportion of their income, the monetary demand for consumer goods increases as a result of the increase in monetary income received by the owners of the original factors of production. Nonetheless this effect would only explain a similar rise in the price of consumer goods if it were not for the fact that it combines with effects (b) and (c).

(b) Second, a *slowdown* in the production of new consumer goods and services in the short- and mediumterm, a consequence of the lengthening of production processes and the greater demand for original means of production in the stages furthest from final consumption.

This decline in the speed at which new consumer goods arrive at the final stage in the production process derives from the fact that original factors of production are withdrawn from the stages closest to consumption, causing a relative shortage of these factors in those stages. This shortage affects the *immediate* production and delivery of final consumer goods and services. Furthermore as the capital theory outlined at the beginning of the chapter explains, the generalized lengthening of production processes and the incorporation into them of a greater number of stages further from consumption invariably leads to a short-term decrease in the rate at which new consumer goods are produced. This slowdown lasts the length of time necessary for newly initiated investment processes *to reach completion.* It is clear that the longer production processes are, i.e.,. the more stages they contain, the more productive they tend to be.

However it is also clear that until new investment processes conclude, they will not allow a larger quantity of consumer goods to reach the final stage. Hence the growth in income experienced by the owners of the original factors of production, and thus the increase in monetary demand for consumer goods, combined with the short-term slowdown in the arrival of new consumer goods to the market, accounts for the fact that the price of consumer goods and services eventually climbs more than proportionally; that is, faster than the increase in monetary income experienced by the owners of the original means of production.

(c) Third, the rise in monetary demand for consumer goods which is triggered by *artificial* entrepreneurial profits that result from the credit expansion process. Banks' creation of loans ultimately entails an increase in the money supply and a rise in the price of the factors of production and of consumer goods. These increases eventually distort entrepreneurs' estimates of their profits and losses. In fact entrepreneurs tend to calculate their costs in terms of the historical cost and purchasing power of m.u. prior to the inflationary process. However they compute their earnings based on income comprised of m.u. with less purchasing power. All of this leads to considerable and purely fictitious profits, the appearance of which creates an *illusion of entrepreneurial prosperity* and explains why businessmen begin to spend profits that have not actually been produced, which further increases the pressure of the monetary demand for final consumer goods.

It is important to underline the effect of the more-than proportional rise in the price of consumer goods with respect to the rise in the price of original factors of production. Theoretically this is the phenomenon which has most escaped the notice of many scholars. As they have not fully comprehended capital theory, the analyses of these theorists have not accounted for the fact that when more productive resources are devoted to processes further from consumption, processes which begin to yield results only after a prolonged period of time, there is a reduction in the speed at which new consumer goods arrive at the last stage in the production process. Moreover this is one of the most significant distinguishing features of the case we are now considering (in which the lengthening of production processes is financed with loans the banks create *ex nihilo*) with respect to the process initiated by an upsurge in voluntary saving (which by definition produced an increase in the stock of consumer goods that remained unsold and which sustained the owners of the original factors of production while new processes of production could be completed). When there is no prior growth in saving, and therefore consumer goods and services are not freed to support society during the lengthening of the productive stages and the transfer of original factors from the stages closest to consumption to those furthest from it, the relative price of consumer goods inevitably tends to rise.

3. *The substantial relative increase in the accounting profits of the companies from the stages closest to final consumption.*

The price of consumer goods escalates faster than the price of original factors of production, and this results in relative growth in the accounting profits of the companies from the stages closest to consumption with respect to the accounting profits of companies who operate in the stages furthest from consumption. Indeed the relative price of the goods and services sold in the stages closest to consumption increases very rapidly, while costs, though they also rise, do not rise as fast. Consequently accounting profits, or the differential between income and costs, mount in the final stages. In contrast, in the stages furthest from consumption the price of the intermediate goods produced at each stage does not show a major change, while the cost of the original factors of production employed at each stage climbs continuously, due to the greater monetary demand for these factors, which in turn originates directly from credit expansion. Hence companies operating in the stages furthest from consumption tend to bring in less profit, an accounting result of a rise in costs more rapid than the corresponding increase in income. These two factors produce the following combined effect: it gradually becomes evident throughout the productive structure that *the* accounting profits generated in the stages closest to consumption are higher in relative terms than the accounting profits earned in the *stages furthest from it.* This prompts entrepreneurs to rethink their investments and even to doubt their soundness. It compels them to again consider the need to reverse their initial investment of resources by withdrawing them from more capital- intensive projects which have barely gotten off the ground and returning them to the stages closest to consumption.

4. The *"Ricardo Effect."*

In addition, the more-than-proportional rise in the price of consumer goods with respect to the increase in original-factor income begins to drive down (in relative terms) the real income of these factors, particularly wages. This real reduction in wages provokes the "Ricardo Effect," which we have covered in detail, but which now exerts an impact contrary to the one it exerted in our last example, where real growth took place in voluntary saving. In the case of voluntary saving, the temporary decrease in the demand for consumer goods brought about a real increase in wages, which tended to give rise to the substitution of machines for labor and therefore to lengthen the productive stages, distancing them from consumption and making them more capital-intensive. However *now the effect is just the opposite*: the more-than-proportional growth in the price of consumer goods with respect to the rise in factor income drives this income, particularly wages, down in real terms, providing entrepreneurs with a powerful financial incentive to substitute labor for machinery or capital equipment, in keeping with the "Ricardo Effect."

This results in a relative drop in the demand for the capital goods and intermediate products of the stages furthest from consumption, which in turn further aggravates the underlying problem of the fall in accounting profits (even losses) which begins to be perceived in the stages furthest from consumption. In short, here the "Ricardo Effect" exerts an impact contrary to the one it exerted when there was an upsurge in voluntary saving.

Then we saw that an increase in saving brought about a short-term decrease in the demand for consumer goods and in their price, and thus a boost in real wages which encouraged the substitution of machinery for workers, growth in the demand for capital goods and a lengthening of productive stages. Now we see that the relative rise in the price of consumer goods causes a drop in real wages, motivating entrepreneurs to substitute labor for machinery, which lessens the demand for capital goods and further reduces the profits of companies operating in the stages furthest from consumption.

The last temporary effect consists of an escalation in interest rates in the credit market. This rise occurs sooner or later, when the pace of credit expansion unbacked by real saving stops accelerating. When this happens the interest rate will tend to return to the relatively higher levels which prevailed prior to the beginning of credit expansion. In fact if, for instance, the interest rate is around 10 percent before credit expansion begins and the new loans the banking system creates *ex nihilo* are placed in the productive sectors via a reduction in the interest rate (for example, to 4 percent) and an easing of the rest of the "peripheral" requirements for the granting of loans (contractual guarantees, etc.), it is clear than when credit expansion comes to a halt, if, as we are supposing, no increase in voluntary saving takes place, *interest rates will climb to their previous level* (in our example, they will rise from 4 to 10 percent).

They will even exceed their pre-credit-expansion level (i.e., they will rise above the originary rate of 10 percent) as a result of the combined effect of the following two phenomena:

(a) Other things being equal, credit expansion and the increase in the money supply which it involves will tend to drive up the price of consumer goods, i.e., to reduce the purchasing power of the monetary unit. Consequently if lenders wish to charge the same interest rates in real terms, they will have to add (to the interest rate which prevails prior to the beginning of the credit expansion process) a component for "inflation," or in other words, for the expected drop in the purchasing power of the monetary unit.

(b) There is another powerful reason interest rates climb to and even exceed their prior level: entrepreneurs who have embarked upon the lengthening of production processes despite the rise in interest rates will, to the extent that they have already committed substantial resources to new investment projects, *be willing to* pay very high interest rates, provided they are supplied with the funds necessary to complete the projects they have *mistakenly launched.*

This is an important aspect which went completely unnoticed until Hayek studied it in detail in 1937. Hayek demonstrated that the process of investment in capital goods generates an autonomous demand for subsequent capital goods, precisely ones which are *complementary* to those already produced. Furthermore this phenomenon will last as long as the belief that the production processes can be completed. Thus entrepreneurs will rush to demand new loans regardless of their cost, before being forced to admit their failure and altogether abandon investment projects in which they have allocated very important resources and with respect to which they have jeopardized their prestige. As a result, the growth in the interest rate which takes place in the credit market at the end of the boom is not only due to monetary phenomena, as Hayek had previously thought, but also to *real factors* that affect the demand for new loans.83 In short, entrepreneurs, determined to complete the new more capital-intensive stages Thus they start a "fight to the death" to obtain additional financing.

The entrepreneurs cannot procure the funds they need for the further conduct of their ventures. The gross market rate of interest rises because the increased demand for loans is not counterpoised by a corresponding increase in the quantity of money available for lending. (Mises, *Human Action*, p. 554) 84 Entrepreneurs determined to complete their endangered long-term capital projects turn to the banks for more bank credit, and a tug-of-war begins. Producers seek new bank loans, the banking system accommodates the new loan demand by creating new money, product prices rise ahead of wage costs. In each market period the process repeats itself, with product prices always rising ahead of wages. (Moss and Vaughn, "Hayek's Ricardo Effect: A Second Look," p. 554) In *Human Action* Mises explains the process in this way:

This tendency toward a rise in the rate of originary interest and the emergence of a positive price premium explain some characteristics of the boom. The banks are faced with an increased demand for loans and advances on the part of business. The entrepreneurs are prepared to borrow money at higher gross rates of interest. They go on borrowing in spite of the fact that banks charge more interest. Arithmetically, the gross rates of interest are rising above their height on the eve of the expansion. Nonetheless, they lag catalactically behind the height at which they would cover originary interest plus entrepreneurial component and price premium. The banks believe that they have done all that is needed to stop "unsound" speculation when they lend on more onerous terms. They think that those critics who blame them for fanning the flames of the boom-frenzy of the market are wrong. They fail to see that in injecting more and more fiduciary media into the market they are in fact kindling the boom. It is the continuous increase in the supply of the fiduciary media that produces, feeds, and accelerates the boom. The state of the gross market rates of interest is only an outgrowth of this increase. If one wants to know whether or not there is credit expansion, one must look at the state of the supply of fiduciary media, not at the arithmetical state of the interest rates. (Mises, *Human Action,* pp. 558–59)

6. *The appearance of accounting losses in companies operating* in the stages relatively more distant from consumption: the inevitable advent of the crisis.

The above five factors provoke the following combined effect: sooner or later companies which operate in the stages relatively more distant from consumption begin to incur heavy accounting losses. These accounting losses, when compared with the relative profits generated in the stages closest to consumption, finally reveal beyond all doubt the serious entrepreneurial errors committed and the urgent need to correct them by paralyzing and then liquidating the investment projects mistakenly launched, withdrawing productive resources from the stages furthest from consumption and transferring them back to those closest to it. In a nutshell, entrepreneurs begin to realize a massive readjustment in the productive structure is necessary.

Through this "restructuring" in which they withdraw from the projects they began in the stages of capital goods industries and which they were unable to successfully complete, they transfer what is left of their resources to the industries closest to consumption.

It has now become obvious that certain investment projects are unprofitable, and entrepreneurs must liquidate these and make a massive transfer of the corresponding productive resources, particularly labor, to the stages closest to consumption. Crisis and economic recession have hit, essentially due to a lack of real saved resources with which to complete investment projects *which, as has become apparent, were too ambitious.* The crisis is brought to a head by *excessive investment* ("overinvestment") in the stages furthest from consumption, i.e., in capital goods industries (computer software and hardware, high-tech communications devices, blast furnaces, shipyards, construction, etc.), and in all other stages with a widened capital goods structure. It also erupts due to a parallel *relative shortage in investment* in the industries closest to consumption. The combined effect of the two errors is generalized *malinvestment* of productive resources; that is, investment of a style, quality, quantity, and geographic and entrepreneurial distribution typical of a situation in which much more voluntary saving has taken place. In short, entrepreneurs have invested an inappropriate amount in an inadequate manner in the wrong places in the productive structure because they were under the impression, *deceived as they were by bank credit expansion*, that social saving would be much greater. Economic agents have devoted themselves to lengthening the most capital intensive stages in the hope that once the new investment processes have, with time, reached completion, the final flow of consumer goods and services will increase significantly.

However the process by which the productive structure is lengthened requires a very prolonged period of time. Until this time has passed, society cannot profit from the corresponding rise in the production of consumer goods and services. Yet economic agents are not willing to wait until the end of that more prolonged period of time. Instead they express their preferences through their actions and demand the consumer goods and services *now*, i.e., much sooner than would be possible were the lengthening of the productive structure to be completed.

Society's savings can be either wisely or foolishly invested. Credit expansion brought about by the banking system *ex nihilo* encourages entrepreneurs to act *as if* social saving had increased substantially, precisely by the amount the bank has created in the form of new loans or fiduciary media. The microeconomic processes examined above invariably and spontaneously bring to light the error committed. This error derives from the fact that for a prolonged period of time economic agents believed available savings to be much more considerable than they actually were. This situation is very similar to the one in which our Robinson Crusoe from section 1 would find himself if, having saved a basket of berries large enough to permit him to spend a maximum of five days producing a capital good without having to devote himself to the collection of more berries, *through an error in calculation*86 were to believe that this amount of savings would allow him to undertake the construction of his cabin. After five days spent just digging the foundations and gathering materials, he would have consumed all of his berries and would therefore be unable to complete his illusory investment project. Mises likens the general error committed to the one a builder would make if he were to misjudge the amount of materials available to him and use them all up laying the foundations of a building, which he would then be forced to leave unfinished.

As Hayek puts it, we are thus dealing with a crisis of *overconsumption*, or in other words, *insufficient saving*. It has become obvious that saving is inadequate to permit the completion of the more capital-intensive investments made by mistake. The situation would resemble that of the imaginary inhabitants of an island who, having undertaken the construction of an enormous machine capable of completely satisfying their needs, had exhausted all of their savings and capital before finishing it and had been left with no other choice but to temporarily abandon the project and return all of their energy to the daily search for food at a mere subsistence level, i.e., without the assistance of any capital equipment.88 In our society such a shortage of savings leads to the following: many factories are closed, particularly in the stages furthest from consumption, numerous investment projects launched in error are paralyzed, and many workers are laid off. Furthermore pessimism spreads throughout society, and the notion that an *inexplicable* economic crisis has erupted, shortly after people had begun to believe that the boom and optimism, far from reaching their peak, would last indefinitely, demoralizes even the most persistently high-spirited.

Though the nominal value of the monetary income received by their owners has mounted substantially, the even more rapid increase in the price of consumer goods places the owners of these factors at a considerable disadvantage in real terms. Moreover the interest rate, or rate of accounting profit approached at each stage, has risen above 13.5 percent, i.e., to a level which even exceeds that of the interest in the credit market *prior to* credit expansion (11 percent per year). This higher rate reflects a premium to compensate for the drop in the purchasing power of money; the keener competition among the different entrepreneurs, who desperately wish to obtain new loans; and the increase in the components of risk and entrepreneurial uncertainty which influences the interest rate whenever pessimism and economic distrust are rampant.

We must emphasize that the productive structure which remains following the necessary readjustment, cannot continue to match the structure that existed *prior to* credit expansion. This is due to the fact that *circumstances have changed significantly*. Heavy inevitable losses of specific capital goods have been incurred to the extent that society's scarce resources have been channeled into investments that cannot be restructured and therefore are devoid of economic value. This gives rise to general impoverishment of society, a state which manifests itself as a decline in capital equipment per capita, resulting in a decrease in the productivity of labor, and consequently, a further reduction in real wages. Furthermore there has been a shift in the distribution of income among the different factors of production, as well as a realignment of all the investment processes which, though initiated in error, are still of some use and economic value. All of these new circumstances make the productive structure qualitatively very different from and quantitatively much flatter and poorer than the one that existed before banks brought about credit expansion.

In summary, we have described the microeconomic basis for the spontaneous market reaction which consistently tends to follow credit expansion. This reaction gives rise to the consecutive cycles of boom and recession which have regularly affected western economies for nearly two centuries (and even much longer). We have also demonstrated that *there is no theoretical possibility that banks'* increase in loans, if not backed by a corresponding prior rise in voluntary saving, will permit society to reduce the necessary sacrifices all processes of economic growth require, and foster and accelerate sustainable growth in the absence of a voluntary decision *made by citizens to sacrifice and save.* Given that these are highly significant conclusions, in the next section we will analyze their implications for the banking sector, particularly, the manner in which they explain that this sector cannot operate independently (i.e., without a central bank) while maintaining a fractional reserve. Thus we will conclude the theoretical analysis we set out to produce to demonstrate on the basis of economic theory that it is impossible for the banking system to insure itself against suspensions of payments and bankruptcy via a fractional-reserve requirement, since the supposed insurance (the fractional-reserve requirement) is precisely what triggers a process of credit expansion, boom, crisis and economic recession which invariably has a detrimental effect on banks' solvency and ability to pay.

Bibliography

Ariel Buira: *Challenges to the World Bank and IMF: Developing Country Perspectives*, London, Anthem Press, 2003.

Auerbach, Alan J.: *Fiscal Policy, Lessons from Economic Research*, The MIT Press, Cambridge Massachusetts, London, 1997.

Bhagwati, J.: *Trade, Balance of Payments and Growth: Essays in Honor of C. P. Kindleberger*, Amsterdam, North-Holland Publishing Company, 1971.

Borio, C.: *'The Implementation of Monetary Policy in Industrial Countries: A Survey"*, BIS Economic Papers, BIS, Basel, 1997.

Bouman, F.J.A.: *Small, Short and Unsecured: Informal Rural Finance in India*, Delhi, Oxford University Press, 1989.

Cooley, Thomas F.: *Frontiers of Business Cycle Research*, Princeton University Press, 1995.

Cooper, S. Kerry and Donald, R. Fraser: *Banking Deregulation and the New Competition in Financial Services*, Ballinger Publishing Company, Cambridge 1984.

Edwards, S.: *Capital Controls, Exchange Rate and Monetary Policy in the World Economy*, Cambridge, Cambridge University Press, 1995.

Goodhart, Charles: *The Evolution of Central Banks*, The MIT Press, Cambridge, 1988.

Greer, Douglas F.: *Industrial Organization and Public Policy*, MacMillan Publishing Company, 1992.

Guhan, S.: *The World Bank's Lending in South Asia*, Washington, Brookings Institution, 1995.

Hinshaw, R.: *Global Economic Priorities: The Hamburg Dialogue*, Hamburg, Verlag Weltarchiv, 1983.

Le Prestre, Philippe: *The World Bank and the Environmental Challenge*, London, Associated University Presses, 1989.

Magliveras, Konstantinos D. *Banks, Fraud and Crime*, Lloyd's of London Press, London, 2000.

Musalem, Errico, Luca & Alberto: *Offshore Banking: An Analysis of Micro-and Macro-Prudential Issues*, IMF, Washington, D.C., 1999.

Posterba, James N.: *'Public Policies and Household Savings"*, A National Bureau of Economic Research Project Report, The University of Chicago Press, 1994.

Raj, K.N.: *New Economic Policy*, Delhi, Oxford University Press, 1986.

Index

G

H

I

L

M

N

O

P

R

S

T

□□□